FRIENDLY FIRE in the CIVIL WAR

FRIENDLY FIRE in the CIVIL WAR

MORE THAN 100 TRUE STORIES OF COMRADE KILLING COMRADE

Webb Garrison

RUTLEDGE HILL PRESS®
Nashville, Tennessee

Published by Rutledge Hill Press, Inc., 211 Seventh Avenue North, Nashville, Tennessee 37219-1823.
Distributed in Canada by H. B. Fenn & Company, Ltd., 34 Nixon Road, Bolton, Ontario L7E 1W2.
Distributed in Australia by The Five Mile Press Pty., Ltd., 22 Summit Road, Noble Park, Victoria 3174.
Distributed in New Zealand by Southern Publishers Group, 22 Burleigh Street, Grafton, Auckland.
Distributed in the United Kingdom by Verulam Publishing, Ltd., 152a Park Street Lane, Park Street,
St. Albans, Hertfordshire AL2 2AU.

Jacket and cover design by Bateman Design
Typography by Roger A. DeLiso, Rutledge Hill Press®

Library of Congress Cataloging-in-Publication Data:
Garrison, Webb B.
    Friendly fire in the Civil War / Webb Garrison.
        p.   cm.
    Includes bibliographical references (p. 213) and index.
    ISBN 1-55853-714-7 (hardcover). — ISBN 1-55853-736-8 (pbk.)
    1. United States—History—Civil War, 1861-1865 Anecdotes. 2. Friendly fire (Military
    science)—United States—History—19th century Anecdotes. 3. Soldiers—United States
    Biography Anecdotes.
    I. Title.
E468.9.G374   1999
973.7—dc21   99-21414
                                                      CIP

Printed in the United States of America
1 2 3 4 5 6 7 8 9—02 01 00 99

Contents

Introduction . . . . *vii*

PART I: FIRE FROM THE REAR

1 A Volley in the Dark—
   Fairfax Court House, Virginia, June 1–2, 1816 3

2 Watchwords and Armbands—
   Two Virginia Churches Called Bethel, June 10, 1861 9

3 "Greener than Grass"—
   Blackburn's Ford, Virginia, July 18, 1861 17

4 "Utter Madness"—
   Bull Run, aka First Manassas, July 21, 1861 21

5 Incommunicado—
   Fort Clark, North Carolina, August 28, 1861 27

6 Friendly Fire from Two Directions—
   Glasgow, Missouri, September 18, 1861 32

7 At Least Thirty-Four Casualties—
   Munson's Hill, September 29–30, 1861 36

8 Melee in the Dark—
   Santa Rosa Island, Florida, October 9, 1861 41

9 "A Most Murderous Fire"—
   Hampton Roads, Virginia, March 8, 1862 46

10 Nodine Retired in Haste—
   Pea Ridge, Arkansas, March 6–8, 1862 53

11 Eternal Peace . . . for 3,500—
   Shiloh, Tennessee, April 6–7, 1862 59

12 Lincoln under Fire—
   Sewell's Point, Virginia, May 8, 1862 66

13 Death from the River—
   Secessionville, South Carolina, June 16, 1862 71

14 "For God's Sake, Stop!"—
   Malvern Hill, Virginia, July 1, 1862 76

15 Six Times in One Day—
   Baton Rouge, Louisiana, August 5, 1862 83

16 Cover-Up—
    South Mountain, Maryland, September 14, 1862 88

17 Record Maker—
    Antietam, aka Sharpsburg, Maryland, September 17, 1862 93

PART II: BRIEF BITES

18 Twenty-Five Misadventures—*1861–1862* 101

19 Friends Keep Killing Friends—*1863*. 119

20 Will It Ever Stop?—*1864–1865* 134

PART III: WEIGHTY MISSILES

21 Deadly Mortars—
    Port Hudson, Louisiana, March 14, 1863 149

22 Mighty Stonewall—
    Chancellorsville, Virginia, May 2, 1863 154

23 Hotchkiss Shells—
    Vicksburg, Mississippi, May 22, 1863 161

24 Warhorse Down—
    The Wilderness, May 5–7, 1864. 166

25 "Fire Gun Number One!"—
    The Wilderness, May 6, 1864 172

26 Fifty Officers, Fifty Days—
    Charleston, South Carolina, June 12–August 3, 1864 177

27 Two Acres of Hell—
    The Crater, Petersburg, Virginia, July 30, 1864 185

28 "The Immortal 600"—
    Morris Island, South Carolina, September 7–October 20, 1864 193

Conclusion, "Victory Is the Name of the Game" 201

Notes 203

Bibliography. 213

Index 219

Introduction

A long time ago it was a tragedy without a name. During America's Civil War, soldiers were hard pressed to describe this type of battlefield accident in just a few words. It would take almost 100 years and the involvement of U.S. forces in the awkward Vietnam War for American troops to come up with a phrase that described it with some irony and honesty. It is a phrase now familiar to every viewer of TV news. It is the combat incident every fighting man fears: friendly fire.

Military historians know that "friendly fire" and accidents in battle are as old as warfare. But they have discovered, for a want of a name, that it is impossible to mount a conventional search for records of instances in which American Civil War troops came under fire from their comrades. Logic suggests that computers at the U.S. Army Military History Institute in Carlisle, Pennsylvania, would provide clues to such occurrences. But this immense data bank, largest of its kind in the world, does not include a single reference to "friendly fire" from 1861 through 1865. And if the CD-ROM produced by the Writers' Guild of Indiana is accurate, the 130,000 or so pages of the federal government's *Official Records* of the war do not include one mention of the term that is now familiar to everyone.

But just because the term "friendly fire" does not crop up in research, it does not mean historians cannot find many reports of it happening. It only points out that researchers can find no firsthand accounts of it by using indices. Rifles, light artillery, howitzers, mortars, siege guns, and virtually all other instruments that could be loaded and fired were accidently turned on comrades during the Civil War. These incidents began before the July 1861 First Battle of Bull Run and did not end until after the Confederacy's fugitive president, Jefferson Davis, was captured in the spring of 1865. And while no soldier gave it a universally recognized name, and the majority of battlefield leaders seemed to have preferred to go about their business as though such accidents never happened, scores of men in uniform wrote about these tragedies.

In Virginia at the July 1862 Battle of Malvern Hill, Union General Fitz-John Porter saw the lethal effects of what he called "fire in the rear." Porter's phrase for this mishap, however, was not widely popular. A similar instance of Union troops inadvertently coming under fire from other Union soldiers happened during fighting for Baton Rouge, Louisiana, in 1862. On that occasion it was described as a "misadventure." In South Carolina during a seven-week siege of Charleston in the summer of 1863, both Union and Confederate troops intentionally set up prisoner-of-war pens in spots where the captives occasionally came under fire from their own armies. Both sides described this as "brutality" or "barbarity," or they used terms that likened the prisoners to human shields or the men who put them in harm's way to criminals.

This book looks into "friendly fire" incidents in the Civil War. But I cannot claim that it covers the entire gamut. Scores or even hundreds of instances of friendly fire may not be included here. It is, however, the first work to look at this aspect of the war between the North and South and even to reveal a few instances where officers ordered their men to fire on known comrades.

Readers of this volume will notice the preponderance of events described here involve fighting men in blue. This does not suggest that Union troops were more careless or reckless than their foes. It does, however, underscore the familiar fact that more Federal reports, diaries, letters, and newspaper accounts were written and survived the war years, and many of them were more comprehensive than Confederate documents. Other pertinent facts about this book: Regardless of grade, every general officer here is usually identified as "Gen."; some commanders are so universally known that they are often referred to only by their surnames; though strategy and troop movements seldom warrant more than brief treatment here, this volume deals with more than two dozen battles in some broad detail; contrarily, some stories of "friendly fire" are treated only as vignettes, as interesting sidelights in major events.

I came upon most of these stories about friendly fire in secondary sources. But the majority have been confirmed and amplified by such standard sources as the army's and the navy's *Official Records*, *The Rebellion Record*, the *Confederate Military History*, and the voluminous publications of the Military Order of the Loyal Legion of the United States.

FRIENDLY FIRE in the
CIVIL WAR

Part I
Fire from the Rear

1

A Volley in the Dark

Fairfax Court House, Virginia—June 1–2, 1861

Three weeks after his inauguration, President Abraham Lincoln saw the nation's secession crisis move toward war more rapidly than he or anyone else had anticipated. On Monday April 1, 1861, after lengthy consultation with Secretary of State William H. Seward, he signed a secret order: Naval personnel were to fit out the warship USS *Powhatan*. It appeared the vessel would be sent to the relief of Maj. Robert Anderson's small U.S. Army garrison, a group that had been holding Fort Sumter in South Carolina's Charleston Harbor since late December 1860.

Charleston secessionists, insisting that Fort Sumter was state, not U.S., property, had ringed the city's harbor with cannon. Most of the guns were aimed directly at Anderson's post. When South Carolinians got word of plans to outfit the *Powhatan,* they speculated that it would be sent to relieve the fort. This kicked off an exchange of communciations between officials in Washington, D.C., and the new Confederate capital, Montgomery, Alabama, and between Washington negotiators and firebrands in Charleston.

Last-minute peace talks came to nothing, and early on the morning of April 12 Confederate Gen. P. G. T. Beauregard, commanding Charleston forces, opened up an artillery duel with Anderson. Unsupported by the *Powhatan* or any other U.S. vessel, the Sumter garrison took a terrific drubbing. The fort formally surrendered on April 14.

Magnanimous in victory, Beauregard did not treat the defeated Federal troops as prisoners of war; he put them aboard a New York–bound steamer. When they arrived off Manhattan, they and their commander were given heroes' welcomes. Meanwhile, on Monday, April 15, Lincoln

Maj. Robert Anderson, the Federal commander at Fort Sumter, refused to surrender the installation and thereby provoked the attack considered to have started the war.—
LESLIE'S ILLUSTRATED WEEKLY

issued a proclamation declaring that a state of insurrection existed, and that 75,000 men were needed to serve as soldiers in Federal service for 90 days. This call to arms persuaded Virginia to secede and other wavering Cotton Belt states followed her lead.

Secessionists seized the big U.S. arsenal at Harpers Ferry, Virginia, and the vital U.S. Navy yard at Norfolk. Virginia's geographical location persuaded leaders on both sides that this state was likely to be the scene of a major military conflict before the terms of service of Lincoln's April volunteers expired in midsummer. As units of these 90-day men trickled into Washington, Confederates voted to move the site of their national capital. Richmond, Virginia, replaced Montgomery as the home of the Confederate president and his legislature. Virginia Gov. Henry A. Wise calculated that this event made it ever more likely his state would be the scene of the war's first big battle and that it would likely take place just west of Washington, D.C. Southern officials concurred in this opinion and gave Beauregard command of the "Alexandria Line," territory outside the Union capital where it was deemed likely the Northern and Southern armies would clash. The community of Manassas Junction sat at the center of this "line," and secessionists quickly took firm control of it and the surrounding area.

Capt. Benjamin S. Ewell, having just resigned his U.S. Cavalry commission to serve with the Southern forces, was made a lieutenant colonel in Gen. Robert E. Lee's command and given charge of an inexperienced "corps of observation" serving along the Alexandria Line. At the end of May 1861, Ewell and his men rode into the important road junction hamlet of Fairfax Court House, a county seat. Sitting 14 miles west of Alexandria on what is now U.S. Highway 50, Fairfax Court House boasted 300 residents, a hotel, the county courthouse, and a Methodist church. Lee personally inspected the settlement two days before Ewell arrived and determined it was a spot worth seizing and holding.[1]

Ewell used the hotel as his headquarters, billeted 60 horse soldiers in the courthouse, then made the church quarters for Capt. William W. Thornton and his 60 cavalrymen and for Lt. Col. John Quincy Marr of the Warrenton Rifles and 90 infantrymen. Future Confederate general and state governor William "Extra Billy" Smith also showed up in Fairfax Court House about 5 P.M. on May 31. A "volunteer colonel" and man of importance in state affairs, Smith had had no defined role in the events of recent days. But his recollection of what later transpired would prove interesting to historians.

By the evening of May 31, Ewell had selected his defensive positions. Stretching his force of infantry and cavalry very thin, he extended the

*Gen. P. G. T. Beauregard, whose artillery duel in Charleston was the signal for Federal and Rebel forces to begin clashing wherever they met.—*NATIONAL ARCHIVES

right of his line toward the Occaquan River and the left more than mile along the Leesburg Road. By at least one account, this line of defenders did not amount to much. Visiting "Colonel" Smith later vividly remembered that the troops he found at Fairfax Court House "had seen no service, and were entirely undisciplined." According to him, the two cavalry units, known as the Rappahannock and the Prince William companies, "had very few fire arms and no ammunition."[2]

Some hours after Ewell's troops were assigned quarters, Lt. Charles H. Tompkins of the 2nd U.S. Cavalry's Co. B led 75 men out of Washington, D.C.'s Fort Stevens "on a scout" to the west. He and his men pulled out about 10:30 P.M., and after riding for more than four hours, they were on the Falls Church Road not far from Fairfax Court House. Tompkins planned only "to reconnoiter the country," but his troops—all professional soldiers—captured a secessionist picket guard and rode into the tiny community of Fairfax Court House. To their surprise, they were "fired upon by the Rebel troops from the windows and house-tops." The U.S. Army professionals returned fire briskly, but almost at random. Meanwhile, Tompkins realized he was outnumbered and "deemed it advisable to retreat."[3]

All the action took place in pitch-black night. Well after dawn the dead body of John Quincy Marr—commander of 90 of the men at the church—was found between the hotel and the church. He went into the historical record as one of the first Confederates killed in combat. His body was in "very rank and tall clover that completely enveloped his person"; it was not found until a search for him was mounted. Smith, noting that Marr died without a struggle, concluded the Virginian was "struck by a random shot to the left, fired by the enemy as he passed the court house."[4]

About the time Marr went down unnoticed in the dark, the men of the Prince William County cavalry retreated up the turnpike with the Federals close behind them. Men of the Rappahannock cavalry effected a formation of sorts when the shooting started, then moved into the street; near the Stevenson road they turned sharply to avoid the enemy. But in the confusing dark of night, infantry heard the noise of riders. They assumed that the riders were U.S. cavalry and released a volley on them. In utter confusion the Confederate horsemen and infantry "dispersed and sought safety in darkness" as intense as Smith had ever seen.[5]

The Fairfax Court House fight saw the start of a bureaucratic habit that continued throughout the war; each leader minimized his own casualties and exaggerated enemy losses. Smith, the future governor, who put together perhaps the only Virginia account of the melee, dismissed the clash between two of his state's units as resulting only in "severely wounding one of the cavalry." Soon after, however, a different summary appeared in the *New York Evening Post* under a July date line. Presumably written by an unknown member of Tompkins's cavalry, it said: "This morning the rebel troops stationed at Fairfax Court-

The courthouse, later held by Federal forces, named the village in which it sat and dominated the surrounding countryside.—NATIONAL ARCHIVES

Though brief, the conflict at Fairfax Court House involved fierce hand-to-hand fighting.—Pictorial Battles of the Civil War

House, Va. were advancing upon the Federal lines, when a regiment of their infantry fired by mistake upon a company of their cavalry, killing seven or eight men, and wounding several others."[6]

Few details are known about the Civil War's first recorded instance of friendly fire; untrained officers had not begun to file formal reports, and had it not been for the unexpected presence of Smith in the hamlet, it is unlikely a secessionist account of the action would have survived.

2

Watchwords and Armbands

Two Virginia Churches Called Bethel—June 10, 1861

Lt. Charles H. Thompkins's professionals must have heard Confederates firing at each other at Fairfax Court House. But if one of them sent a dispatch about the incident to the New York papers, the casualty count he gave was only a wild guess. Nonetheless, a report recording the Civil War's first instance of friendly fire must have made its way up the Union chain of command to Gen. Benjamin F. Butler at Fort Monroe, Virginia. It had to interest him.

Butler and other minor Union commanders were maneuvering around southern and eastern Virginia, waiting to launch movements that would lead to a significant battle. Small parties of men on both sides scoured the countryside near their bases. Given the clumsy Confederate performance at Fairfax Court House, the Northern troops roamed confidently. Inevitably they collided with Southerners in the first encounter of sufficient magnitude to go into the records as an "action." It took place June 10, 1861, near two rural Virginia churches, both named Bethel, not far off the Alexandria Line.

This fight, at the time called the Battle of Big Bethel, turned out badly for the Union and gave Northern commanders a taste of what Confederate leaders experienced after the Fairfax Court House affair. Years later, noted historian Benson Lossing characterized the collision as a disaster that "surprised and mortified" the North. From Vicksburg, Mississippi, a correspondent for the London *Times* reported: "Soldiers of the South have gained a mighty victory." The Raleigh, North Carolina, *Standard* gloated that Tarheels bore "a prominent part in achieving the first decisive triumph on Virginia soil defending the grave of Washington." Long afterward, the *Richmond Dispatch* called the June 10 clash "an affair of

Little Bethel lay a short distance southeast of Big Bethel and was only a few miles from Hampton Roads.—PICTORIAL FIELD BOOK OF THE CIVIL WAR

considerable importance, inasmuch as it sent the first gleam of sunlight through the dark cloud of war that overspread this section."[7]

The North's depression and the South's exhuberence over the outcome at Big Bethel would later seem greatly exaggerated. Contemporary historian Thomas W. Higginson, sizing up Big Bethel next to the battles of Antietam and Gettysburg, dismissed the action as no more than "an aimless contest" fought by a handful of inexperienced men. But, though casualty figures were low, five Union and six Confederate officers filed 35 pages of formal reports on the fight. Among other things, they revealed that Northern troops were also vulnerable to friendly fire.[8]

According to an unsigned Confederate account, "a party of 300 Yankees came up from Hampton and occupied Bethel Church" late in May. Idle soldiers spent time putting graffiti on the church walls that proclaimed "Down with the Rebels" and "Death to Traitors." Rebel Col. John B. Magruder learned about the scrawl and, offended by the sacrilegious vandalism, decided to end the effrontery by "carrying the war into the enemy's country."[9]

George Scott, a black man who regularly informed Federal officers about Rebel movements, said Confederates held a defended position near the larger of the two Bethel churches. Each church was situated about eight miles from both Newport News and Hampton. Scott's information about these positions was scanty, but correct. Close to the larger of the churches Confederates dug entrenchments and set up a battery believed to hold "twenty guns, some of them of rifled construction."[10]

Butler at Fort Monroe, a Democrat, an ardent abolitionist, and the first of Lincoln's "political generals," sensed an opportunity to score a significant victory. On the evening of June 9 he personally drew up plans to seize enemy installations close to his own camps. Judging that it would be necessary to take both Little Bethel and Big Bethel, he instructed Gen. Ebenezer Pierce to start his troops from two points and march at midnight in order to be at his objective early on June 10.

Pierce had no combat experience, but he was undeterred by obstacles some of his men thought forbidding. One of their toughest challenges would be to begin their march and maneuver themselves to a place in front of the enemy during the blackest hours of the night. On leaving camp, Pierce, expecting the fight to start at dawn, issued a terse, explicit directive to his volunteers: "If we find the enemy and surprise them, we will fire a volley if desirable, *not reload*, and go ahead with the bayonet."

Scouts reported the Rebels held strong positions. Hugh J. Kilpatrick, a recent West Point graduate and future cavalry general, was a captain in the 5th New York and led a reconnaissance that revealed Southerners dug in around the larger church numbered 1,800 and were under the personal command of Col. D. H. Hill and Col. John Magruder. Their earthworks sat by the Back River; attackers would have to cross the stream to reach them. Pierce advanced cautiously. About 9 A.M. he and his aides looked over the area in front of Big Bethel and decided—despite the Southerners' cannon—that the position could be taken. Pierce told Col. Abram Duryeé to lead the attack.

Duryeé, a wealthy New York merchant, had organized a colorfuly uniformed Zouave regiment designated the 5th New York. Southerners mocked these men in bright crimson pants, calling them "red legs." At this early point in the war no standard uniforms were required of the volunteer regiments. As this small campaign progressed, this detail would prove calamitous. But on the day of the battle, each of Duryeé's 200 showily dressed men carried 20 cartridges and were ready to fight.[11] They were backed up by the 3rd New York, troops described on this day as moving forward "in line of battle as if on parade." Close behind the regiments came Lt. John T. Greble, a West Point–trained U.S. Army officer, with a three-gun section of field artillery.

It was long past dawn. The light was strong and the Rebels saw Duryeé's men coming on. The men of the 5th shouted "Zou! Zou!" and raced forward. The defenders shot at the advancing volunteers, and their fire "was answered by cheers from the Union troops," who steadily advanced in the face of heavy fire, intending to "dash across the stream and storm the works." Manning one of his own guns, Lt. Greble was hit by a Rebel shell fragment and died almost instantly.[12]

Confederate cannon fire grew even more accurate. Union skirmishers, the Zouaves, and the units behind them withdrew into the shelter of some trees. Confederate Col. Hill boasted that his marksmen "were all in high glee, and seemed to enjoy it as much as boys do rabbit-hunting."

But the late Lt. Greble's gunners moved steadily forward until they were about 200 yards from the enemy. They held that position for more than two hours.

This turned out to be the high point of the Federal assault. During the course of the fight, a charge by the bulk of the Federal force failed, partly because many of its 90-day militia volunteers wore gray uniforms. Their comrades mistakenly believed them to be Magruder's Confederate troops engaged in a flanking movement. In the melee that ensued, Maj. Theodore Winthrop took a bullet in the forehead—reputedly fired by "a drummer boy from North Carolina."[13] An estimated 50 cadets from the North Carolina Military Institute took part in the action. Some were just 16 years old.

"Their tail feathers drooping like a gamecack that has taken a beating," wrote one Confederate, "the enemy gave up and retreated from the field." One analyst described the ground they left behind as "the War's first scene of post-battle horror." Wounded soldiers lay all over it, in numbers estimated between 60 and 175.[14] On the road back to their camps the Federals felt humiliated; they had been thrashed in their first deliberate meeting with the enemy. Later, their commanders were even more chagrined when people learned about what went on before the fight.

Butler remembered what had happened to the Confederates at Fairfax Court House. He realized "green troops" could easily fire on one another. To prevent trouble, he ordered two columns to start from different camps and converge on Big Bethel. He also instructed Pierce to have soldiers from Camp Hamilton shout the watchword "Boston!"

Despite the wooded and hilly terrain, Federal units attempted to maintain precise formations.—AUTHOR'S PRIVATE COLLECTION

when approaching another body of troops. Men of the 7th New York Infantry, based near Newport News, were selected for the Big Bethel maneuver and told to shout "Saratoga!" to identify themselves if they came across troops in the field. Given that everyone would start out marching in the dark, Butler said it would also help for each Federal soldier "to wear something white on the arm." But Col. John E. Bendix of the 7th New York, who conveyed orders to one body of troops, later swore he was told nothing about the use of watchwords and identifying armbands.[15]

On the morning of the fight, Pierce and a few of his aides rode at the head of their column as it neared Big Bethel. Slightly before daylight these mounted men emerged from a dense thicket and, seen through the gloom by the 7th's Col. Bendix at a distance of about 100 yards, were mistaken for Rebel cavalrymen. Apparently, no man in either body remembered to shout a watchword. Then the gray-uniformed Union volunteers of the 3rd New York marched into view. If anyone on Bendix's side of the field noticed the troops of the 3rd were wearing white armbands, he said nothing about it.

Within seconds of spotting another force, the two Union units started firing at one another. Some later swore Bendix and the men of the 7th started the shooting. Other survivors said the men of the 3rd fired into one of their own companies when it was seen across a wooded ravine . . . and that this fire was returned with a vengeance. Then one of the artillery pieces—dragged onto the field by as many as 100 men—started barking at Union troops.[16]

The men marching with Pierce believed they were following instructions. Earlier, Pierce carefully told his officers, "If we capture the Little Bethel men, push on to Big Bethel and similarly capture it. Burn up both Bethels. Blow up, if brick." Townsend and his men, who later said it seemed evident that they had stumbled into an ambush by Rebels who held Little Bethel, began taking out their comrades as rapidly as they could get their muskets into action.

These were fatal mistakes, and blood flowed freely. Members of the 3rd New York were such poor marksmen that all their shots went high or wild; Bendix and his men did not suffer a single scratch. But among the men of the 3rd, it was a different story. In one version of his official report, the 3rd's Townsend said: "The result of the fire upon us was, two mortally wounded (one since dead), three dangerously, and four officers and twelve privates slightly, making a total of twenty-one [casualties]." A different version of Townsend's summary prepared for Pierce boosted his unit's casualty count to 29.[17]

Lt. John Trout Greble posed for a formal photograph a few weeks before his death.—
LIBRARY OF CONGRESS

If Townsend's reports of the action are accurate, Little Bethel was the first, but far from the last, action in which a general officer came under fire from his own men. With Capt. A. P. Chamberlain at his side, Pierce was "about two hundred and fifty paces in advance of the regiment." When his small party emerged from the woods, "the fire was opened upon them by a discharge of small-arms." Seconds later, Townsend's 3rd responded. The colonel wrote, "my men then generally discharged their pieces and jumped from the right to the left of the road, and recommenced loading and firing. In a few minutes the regiment was reformed in the midst of this heavy fire, and by the General's directions, retired in a thoroughly military manner, and in order to withdraw his supposed enemy from his position. On ascertaining that the enemy were our friends, and on providing for the wounded, we joined Col. Duryea [sic] and Col. Bendix [in order to proceed to the primary objective of Big Bethel]. Some seven or more miles on, we found the enemy in force, well fortified."[18]

On the night of June 10 it was unlikely that Confederates knew the Federals had started their day by shooting each other up. But Magruder was jubilant. Not only had he bested the enemy in a fight, but he reported a ridiculously low number of Rebel casualties. Only one of his men—Henry L. Wyatt of North Carolina—died on the field and just seven other Confederates were wounded. This contrasted brightly with the 2 Federal officers and 16 privates he believed his men killed. And when the Yankees did their own count, they numbered 53 wounded; when the rolls were called, the number missing boosted that casualty count by 5. For Magruder, the only puzzle was the white armbands seen on enemy troops. The colonel and a few of his officers had noticed them on some Federals, but in the end they decided it was some kind of awkward ruse; they acknowledged that secessionists sometimes pinned scraps of white cloth to their headgear.[19]

Pierce, a senior officer in the Massachusetts militia, was in field command when almost 4,400 Union troops suffered a humiliating defeat. Blame for the loss was placed at his feet and he was disgraced. So many hurled criticism at him that the War Department refused to confirm his rank in the newly created Union army.

Disgusted and howling mad, Pierce dumped his militia position and enlisted in the U.S. Volunteers as a private. Meanwhile, Col. Townsend of the 3rd demanded a court of inquiry be convened in order to determine exactly what happened near Little Bethel. But such a body never convened. For his part, Butler branded the clash between his troops as an "almost criminal blunder." He downplayed its consequences by reporting to the supreme commander of all Union troops, Gen. Winfield Scott, that only two men were killed "and eight (more or less) wounded." He concluded by indulging in some undeserved self-congratulation: "I think, in the unfortunate combination of circumstances and the result which we experienced, we have gained more than we have lost. Our troops have learned to have confidence in themselves under fire. The enemy have shown that they will not meet us in the open field. Our officers have learned wherein their organization and drill are inefficient."

Butler did himself no harm. In Washington, by a slim two-vote edge, the U.S. Senate affirmed Abraham Lincoln's nomination of Butler for a

After taking a fatal wound, Lt. John T. Greble toppled backward from his piece.— ATWATER KENT MUSEUM

Gen. Ebenezer Pierce, who had no combat experience, was one of the oldest general officers then in the field.—PICTORIAL FIELD BOOK OF THE CIVIL WAR

major-generalship. Horace Greeley's powerful *New York Tribune* urged the chief executive to show his wisdom by making peace with the South at once if he was not willing to send into Virginia generals who were "up to their work."[20]

When the dust over this incident settled, not only did Butler have a larger command, but Rebel commanders Hill and Magruder were set up to receive their own commissions as generals. But if anybody in Washington or Richmond raised his voice warning that more and deadlier "friendly fire" incidents loomed in the future, no one paid much attention. Wary officers looked back on what happened at Fairfax Court House and the battle of the Bethels and tried to take precautions, but too often their safeguards proved useless in the heat of combat.

3

"Greener than Grass"

Blackburn's Ford, Virginia—July 18, 1861

F ive U.S. Army officers who resigned their commissions in order to put their influence behind the secessionist cause quickly became Confederate generals. Of this quintet, P. G. T. Beauregard, a West Point classmate of the Union's main field army commander, Gen. Irvin McDowell, was selected by Confederate President Jefferson Davis to command the Confederate force that was judged sure to fight before the middle of August. A network of spies in Washington immediately began feeding information to the Confederate commander. With McDowell's forces about to march, it appeared increasingly likely that Federal forces would strike at eastern Virginia's vital Orange & Alexandria Railroad.[21]

Another member of the quintet, James Longstreet, took command of a Rebel brigade in Virginia on July 6. He usually drilled his men three times a day, despite their constant grumbling. As clearly as any general officer on either side, this man, who was wounded at Chapultepec in the Mexican War, realized that a battle would require units to fight as a whole. This meant recruits needed to master the elaborate processes by which a regiment or a brigade could maneuver smoothly. His men had been drilling for just ten days when Beauregard learned Federal forces were moving west on the Warrenton Turnpike toward Centreville.[22]

Beauregard's demands for more men, initially disregarded in Richmond, now brought him substantial reinforcements. Having decided to make a stand along a stream called Bull Run, he set out to cover each of six fords at which the stream was habitually crossed near Manassas Junction. For this purpose, Longstreet led his three Virginia regiments to Blackburn's Ford, about three miles from both Centreville and Manassas.

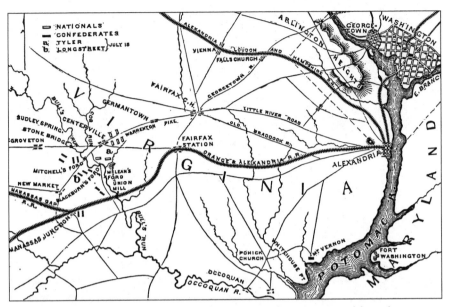

The all-important Orange and Alexandria Railroad meandered westward from the Potomac River. Troop positions are shown as of July 18.—PICTORIAL FIELD BOOK OF THE CIVIL WAR

Longstreet's commission as a brigadier general had been issued almost exactly one month earlier.[23]

A Union division under the command of Gen. Daniel Tyler reached the hamlet of Centreville about 9 A.M. on July 18. Without McDowell's permission, the Federal commander immediately dispatched Col. Israel B. Richardson's brigade on a scouting expedition. Around 10 A.M. these men spotted Rebels massed on the banks of Bull Run. Located at a spot where the stream turned north, locals knew the place as Blackburn's Ford.[24]

Following Beauregard's orders, Longstreet put men to work as soon as they reached the ford. Using driftwood, rails, and a few logs, they managed to throw up a short line of low defensive works. Then Beauregard halted construction because it was going so slowly. When Federal forces arrived at Centreville on July 18, only one company of Confederate skirmishers was deployed on the north bank at Blackburn's Ford. About the time the Federals saw them, Longstreet spotted Richardson through a borrowed opera glass and correctly judged that an attack was imminent.[25]

Two Federal shells fired shortly before noon signaled the beginning of an attempt to dislodge Rebels from the ford. Half an hour after artillery began "the softening up process," Gen. Daniel Tyler, a Connecticut volunteer, decided it was time for infantry units to move. Some of his colleagues and aides opposed this action, but the 62-year-old West Point graduate waved their objections aside. At Tyler's signal, three companies of the 1st Massachusetts, led by Lt. George D. Wells, marched directly toward Confederate positions along the creek.[26]

At the outer limit of musket range, Bay State volunteers began firing at inexperienced Confederate troops. "The first pouring-down volleys were most startling to the new troops," Longstreet later reported. At least a score of these Rebels, who were described as being "greener than grass," broke and ran. Their comrades who saw them flee to safety seemed almost paralyzed by the sound of "bullets that screamed overhead like a swarm of hornets." Waving his saber and clenching a cigar in his teeth, Longstreet dashed up on his big bay horse. He rallied his men so quickly that the Union attack was repelled.

Only a handful of Richardson's men were hit, and not one was killed. As soon as they were beyond the range of Rebel muskets, their leader ordered them to hunker down while he planned another assault. Tyler arrived on the scene as two cannon were placed at strategic spots. After Union gunners used all of the canister on hand, Tyler authorized a second advance—this time by an entire brigade. It seemed briefly to promise Union victory. But the assault stalled and was repulsed after repeated surges took men close to the ford.

Convinced the enemy would launch still another attack, Longstreet sent for reinforcements. Beauregard ordered seven cannon of the famous Washington Artillery to the ford in company with one regiment from Louisiana and two from Virginia under the command of Col. Jubal Early. Approaching the ford, Early's 24th Virginia Regiment wheeled to the right, while men of his 7th Virginia veered to the left. This movement put the newly arrived 7th Virginia squarely behind men of Longstreet's 1st Virginia, who were facing the enemy.[27]

Gestures of officers in the 7th regiment convinced Longstreet they were about to order "raw men to fire on the line in front of them." He dashed forward to prevent it, but muskets began to speak seconds after he appeared between the two units. The veteran soldier dove from the saddle and huddled against the ground as Rebel bullets whistled over him. For the first time, a Confederate general officer had been subjected to friendly fire—shots that he described as "tremendous" in volume. Confederates on the field briefly thought their commander had been killed. Longstreet did not mention this incident in his official report. Later, he wrote, "soldiers and officers became mixed and a little confused."[28]

Gen. Daniel Tyler of the Connecticut Volunteers ordered his men to march against Blackburn's Ford despite opposition by his colleagues and subordinates.—PICTORIAL FIELD BOOK OF THE CIVIL WAR

In the aftermath of this dramatic quarter hour, James Franklin Jr. penned one of the few surviving eyewitness accounts of the incident. He wrote that sergeants and corporals "chunked up" their men about daybreak, told them there would be no drills that day, and then gave strict orders for them to remain quiet. Later, after sporadic fighting, the reinforcements under Early arrived, and the near-tragic events got under way: "Just as Early's line approached the edge of the bushes they mistook our men for the yanks, and some of them fired. Gen. Longstreet, being between his brigade and Gen. Early's line, jumped off his horse to keep from being shot. His horse ran out and we thought the General had been killed."[29] And Rebels who succeeded in crossing Bull Run briefly found themselves between the enemy in front and "fire from our friends in the rear."

After about an hour of combat on McDowell's order, Federals withdrew for the last time. Longstreet's men rejoiced. They initially called this "the great victory of Bull Run"—a label soon attached to a far bigger struggle that took place three days later.[30]

If minié balls from the muskets of Early's men resulted in Confederate casualties, they were not reported. Partly because "the affair at Blackburn's Ford" so closely preceded First Bull Run, partly because it involved relatively few combatants, and because only about 150 casualties resulted, this action received little attention then and later. Logic suggests, however, that Longstreet's memories of the first day he nearly died from Confederate bullets must have flashed through his mind years later when he was actually hit by friendly fire in the Battle of the Wilderness.[31]

4

"Utter Madness"

Bull Run, aka First Manassas—July 21, 1861

Years later, reflecting on the first full-scale battle of the Civil War, Confederate Gen. P. G. T. Beauregard explained the Union debacle in a single phrase: "A new army is very liable to panic." One nineteenth-century analyst started out overstating the fight's importance, calling Bull Run "the greatest battle ever fought in the western hemisphere." Later, he qualified his remark, admitting that the battle, which is also called Manassas, "was certainly one of the most confusing of battles."

Panic, confusion, and an almost ridiculous level of disorganization are this fight's hallmarks in American history. So is its distinction as being a bloody affair set off and fought almost completely by rank military amateurs. No more than a few officers and men on either side had ever faced armed and highly trained soldiers intent on taking their lives. One of the few was the Union Army's supreme field commander, Irvin McDowell, a former West Point tactics instructor and Mexican War general staff officer.

Trying to pull off a critical military operation with 90-day volunteers angered and saddened McDowell, a 16-year army veteran. He later wrote: "On the eve of the battle, the Fourth Pennsylvania Regiment of Volunteers and the battery of Volunteer Artillery of the Eighth New York Militia, whose term of service expired, insisted on their discharge. I wrote the regiment as pressing a request as I could pen, and the honorable Secretary of War, who was at the time on the ground, tried to induce the battery to remain at least five days, but in vain. They insisted on their discharge that night. It was granted: and the next morning, when the army moved into battle, these troops moved to the rear to the sound of the enemy's cannon. . . . In the next few days, day by day, I should have lost ten thousand [men whose terms expired]."

Though Beauregard was not leading a corps of professionals either, he was not faced with discharging large numbers of men at the last minute. But both he and McDowell found their forces ungainly. Each had about 30,000 men he could send to the field, and each was only able to put 18,000 troops into action.

Beauregard and McDowell each expected to fight with Napoleonic battlefield tactics, having their troops make precise moves near the Manassas railroad junction, about 29 miles southwest of Washington. Both knew the field of battle consisted of rolling hills drained by Bull Run and dotted with a few farmhouses. Neither general anticipated that an anonymous observer from England would characterize the day's action as "utter madness."

Col. Samuel Heintzelman of the 17th U.S. Infantry, acting as a division commander that day, sent Col. William B. Franklin's brigade against Rebels who were partly concealed in a clump of small pines. "At the first fire [from the enemy] they broke, and the greater portion fled to the rear, keeping up a desultory firing [that they hoped would be] over the heads of their comrades in front," Heintzelman's report read. Col. N. L. Farnham and some of his officers, members of the brigade, were described as having behaved gallantly, "but the regiment, as a regiment, did not appear again on the field."

Nearby, an unidentified Minnesota regiment fell apart soon afterward. Once Rebels began to fire, Heintzelman wrote, "the regiment broke and ran. I considered it useless to attempt to rally them. The want of discipline in these regiments was so great, that most of the men would run from

At Bull Run, at least two regiments of Federal volunteers refused to fight because enlistments had expired; in the aftermath of the battle, Union leaders resorted to conscription and payment of bounties.—AUTHOR'S PRIVATE COLLECTION

fifty to several hundred yards to the rear and continue to fire—fortunately for the braver ones, very high in the air—compelling those in front to retreat."[32]

Col. Franklin's report echoed the verdict of his commander. Men of his brigade knew so little about maneuvers that they "fired without command" and more than once when formed in columns they "closed in mass." Members of the 5th and 11th Massachusetts Regiments were especially reckless, "the rear files sometimes firing into and killing the front ones," and thereby making "the rear ranks almost as deadly to friend as to enemy."[33]

James Tinkham, a volunteer

Gen. Irvin McDowell had just been elevated to command of the Army of the Potomac.— LIBRARY OF CONGRESS

in an unidentified Massachusetts unit, described the action as seen through the eyes of a man with no experience and little training. "We aimed at the puffs of smoke we saw rising in front and on the left of us," he said. "The men were all a good deal excited. Our rear rank had singed the hair of the front rank, who were more afraid of them than of the Rebels."

A line formed by men commanded by Union Col. O. O. Howard was made up of the 3rd Maine plus "a remnant of the 5th Maine." The latter regiment, only a skeleton of the body that marched from Washington to decimate the Rebels, "had been discomfited by our own cavalry," so part of its men had abandoned the field.[34]

These were just a few of the disasters that typified this day of defeat for the Union Army. About 5:45 P.M., having retreated to Centreville, McDowell summarized his defeat in a telegram to Gen. Winfield Scott. In it, he cited confusion caused by members of his units "firing into each other" as a major cause of the Federal debacle. A bit later he telegraphed from Fairfax Court House admitting, "The larger part of the men are a confused mob, entirely demoralized."[35]

Confederates, displaying slightly more discipline that day, also lost men to their comrades' fire. A rare report, relatively detailed, described some of the actions of the First Special Battalion, Louisiana Volunteers. Confederate Maj. C. R. Wheat wrote that after having formed his command to the left of the Stone Bridge, his men followed orders and moved farther to the left into an open field near a wooded area. From what Wheat called "this covet," to his surprise the battalion "received a volley of musketry which unfortunately came from our own troops, mistaking us for the enemy, killing three and wounding several of my men. Apprehending instantly the real cause of the accident, I called out to my men not to return the fire. Those near enough to hear, obeyed; the more distant, did not."[36]

South Carolina volunteers caused this battlefield accident. What effect the return fire of Wheat's men had on their comrades remains a mystery.[37]

At Big Bethel, the men of the 3rd New York who drew the fire of the 7th New York wore gray uniforms. At Blackburn's Ford, three companies of Massachusetts men were fortunately close enough to other Federal units to be identified as friends despite their gray uniforms.[38] But at Bull Run, the early lessons about uniforms meant little.

Records fail to reveal how many Federals wore gray at Bull Run; only occasional references to uniforms appear in reports. But Col. William T. Sherman of the 13th U.S. Infantry, the famous future general, observed what this color did to men of the 2nd Wisconsin. "This regiment is uni-

Confederate victory at Bull Run stemmed partly from the fact that outdoorsmen from the South were better "green soldiers" than were city dwellers from the North.—LESLIE'S ILLUS-TRATED WEEKLY

formed in gray cloth," he reported, "almost identical with that of the great bulk of the secession army, and when the regiment fell into confusion and retreated toward the road there was an universal cry that they were being fired on by our own men."[39]

Men on both sides recognized the blue and scarlet uniforms and white turbans of the Union Zouaves, but in these early days of the war, gray Federal uniforms and blue Confederate uniforms kept soldiers guessing what they saw. At Bull Run about 1:30 P.M., according to one of Virginia Col. Thomas J. Jackson's subordinates, forces that clashed at one point wore very similar uniforms, "and from the direction of their approach it was difficult at first for the officers in charge of the Federal batteries to make sure that the advancing troops were not their own."[40] Col. Jackson himself, a Mexican War veteran, wore blue items from his old U.S. uniform to this first great fight.

Allan C. Redwood, a Confederate who fought with the 55th Virginia Regiment at Bull Run, pondered the significance of colors and in retrospect found the matter to be frightening. "So variegated were the costumes on both sides at the first battle of Bull Run," he wrote afterward, "that both Confederates and Federals frequently fired upon their own men. There are instances where the colonel of a regiment notified his supporters to which side he belonged before daring to advance in front of them."[41]

In postwar years, Charles King pondered the color question and became more troubled about it than Redwood had been. This veteran pointed out that "at the outset of the war there was no regular or prescribed uniform, and in many regiments each company varied from the others. One company might even be clad in red, another in gray, another in blue, and still another in white. Since many of the men of the North were clad in gray, at the first battle of Bull Run some fatal mistakes occurred, and soldiers fired upon their own friends. Thereafter all the soldiers of the Union army were dressed practically alike in blue, with slight variations in the color of insignia to designate cavalry, artillery, and infantry."[42]

King probably did not know that though it may have been at its height on July 21, 1861, "the color question" was never fully resolved during the war. Late in 1864 the governor of North Carolina had new uniforms shipped to numerous regiments from the state. Each garment was almost exactly the color of the standard Federal uniform, since factories of the Tarheel State had exhausted their supplies of gray dyestuffs and could produce no uniforms that silently shouted "Confederate!" at a glance.

Varicolored Federal uniforms made it difficult or impossible for men in some units to know whether or not they were firing on their comrades; left to right, Garibaldi Guards, 14th New York, and 11th New York regiments.—AUTHOR'S PRIVATE COLLECTION

No one, whether on the field at First Bull Run or attempting to analyze the action later, has the faintest idea of how many men were shot at, killed, or wounded there by their comrades. This much is certain, however: A substantial fraction of the approximately 5,000 casualties suffered that torrid day in July 1861 resulted from friendly fire on both sides.

5

Incommunicado

Fort Clark, North Carolina—August 28, 1861

In 1861 Union leaders were desperately in need of two things. First on their wish list was a military victory, large or small. Second was a foothold on the Confederate-held stretch of the Atlantic Coast. Ambitious Gen. Benjamin Butler hoped both goals could be achieved by means of a single operation. Several times after Bull Run he eagerly proposed leading an expedition to seize Hatteras Inlet, North Carolina.

Earlier, Gen. Winfield Scott had made public his personal plan for victory. Unlike Lincoln, whose eagerness for quick restoration of the Union led him to ignore military advisors and take steps that made Manassas Junction known everywhere, the general in chief of the U.S. Army was patient. He urged a series of slow movements whose effect would be to "choke the Confederacy to death" over a period of time. Seizure of Hatteras Inlet would be an important first step toward implementing the 75-year-old general's "Anaconda Plan."

At Fort Monroe, 35 days after Bull Run, acting assistant adjutant general C. C. Churchill issued "Special Orders No. 13," directing Butler to prepare "860 troops for an expedition to Hatteras Inlet" to capture batteries there. Plans for this joint army-navy expedition in which Commodore Silas H. Stringham was ordered to take a leading role gave the two leaders just 24 hours in which to get under way.[43]

With the USS *Minnesota* as flagship, the flotilla consisted of the USS *Cumberland,* USS *Susquehanna,* USS *Monticello,* USS *Pawnee,* the steamer *Harriet Lane,* and transport steamers *Adelaide, George Peabody,* and *Fanny.* In addition to their usual complements of naval personnel, these ships carried the 9th and 20th regiments of New York Volunteers plus 60 men from the 2nd U.S. Artillery. The vessels got

Benjamin F. Butler, a Democrat and a "political general," commanded Federal forces.— LIBRARY OF CONGRESS

under way promptly at 1 P.M. on Monday, August 26, and by 4 P.M. on Tuesday had reached the waters off Hatteras Inlet.[44]

About 10 A.M. on Wednesday, despite heavy surf breaking on the beach, Butler landed his men. As they rowed ashore, guns of the *Monticello* and the *Harriet Lane* fired on Confederate Forts Clark and Hatteras. But by the time 315 soldiers, 55 U.S. marines, and two 12-inch guns were ashore, all four of their boats were useless. That meant Butler's men were "wet up to the shoulders, cut off entirely from the fleet, with wet ammunition, and without any provisions."[45]

Most of the men stranded on the beach were German-speaking volunteers from New York with reputations for plundering and destroying enemy civilian property. William H. Wiegel, a civilian aide to Butler, led a party three miles toward Fort Clark, the smaller of the two enemy installations, to find that its flag had been lowered. The Union invaders reached Fort Clark and rejoiced at finding it empty. The square redoubt, whose earthen walls were 18 feet thick at some points, was armed with five large naval guns of undesignated size plus two 6-pounders. On the heels of clumsily spiking their guns, members of the garrison had moved about 700 yards to larger and stronger Fort Hatteras.[46]

But aboard the armed vessels, standing as close as possible to shore, some gunners ran into trouble. They had been firing at an unidentified enemy blockade runner. Their shots, however, fell far short of their mark; they were told to cut longer fuses that would not cause detonations before 15 seconds. No modification of procedures was ordered with respect to firing on the Confederate installations; many shots hit both of them as soon as the big Union guns began covering the landing.[47]

In his report of the action, Col. Weber noted that "the secession flag" was taken down and the American flag hoisted by an officer as soon as

Fort Clark was entered. His description of the eventful morning continues: "Myself followed with the rest of the troops, when the Navy commenced firing upon us, shells bursting right over us and in our midst, so that a further advance was impossible. Two shells burst in the fort."[48]

Most U.S. Navy gunners were career fighting men thoroughly familiar with their weapons and ammunition. Unlike volunteer soldiers, they needed no drills and no additional training before being ready for action. Why on earth, then, did these fellows pour shot after shot into a little fort over which the American flag was already flying?[49]

Distance made it difficult to identify the flag with certainty, and officers may have considered its use to be a ruse by the enemy. The U.S. Navy had a time-hallowed and reasonably efficient system by which flags and lanterns were used to transmit terse messages from one ship to another. Federal ground forces also had a system of signals, not then given the high priority in Washington that this matter received in Richmond, but slow and workable. The heart of the matter on the morning of August 28 lay in the fact that soldiers did not understand naval signals, and sailors could not read the signals transmitted by ground forces.[50]

This dilemma was reported by an unidentified correspondent of the *New York Herald,* who took it very seriously. Friendly fire at Hatteras Inlet stemmed directly from the fact that Federal soldiers were incommunicado once they hit the North Carolina beach. Vessels of the joint expedition might as well have been in the China Sea, so far as transmission to them of the fact that their own forces occupied Fort Clark was concerned![51] Weber said his men suffered only one casualty, but he did

The USS Pawnee *was one of the few steam-powered vessels of the U.S. Navy.—*
OFFICIAL RECORDS OF THE UNION AND CONFEDERATE NAVIES

The USS Harriet Lane *was equipped with sails plus a steam engine that drove her side wheels.*—U.S. NAVAL HISTORY INSTITUTE

not comment that the toll would have been a great deal higher if men manning the 163 naval guns had been more accurate. The *Herald* correspondent reported that not one but "two of our flags were raised and floating from the ramparts" when attackers came under the fire of U.S. naval guns. According to him, "the fire [from big navy guns] was kept up on our forces, until they were compelled to retreat" about 5 P.M.[52]

Howell Cobb, president of the Confederate Congress, transmitted to Jefferson Davis a formal request for information about the affair at Hatteras. The interest of secessionist lawmakers was not, however, focused on the way in which Federal forces handled themselves. They wanted to know what steps could be taken "to put the coast in a state of defense."[53]

Not an officer among those in the fleet so much as mentioned in a report this instance of friendly fire. So far as Commander John P. Gillis of the U.S. Navy was concerned, a minute list of damages to the *Monticello* was significant enough to take up the bulk of his report. Butler alluded only briefly to the fact that men who planted the American flag at Fort Clark were under "great danger from the fire of their own friends." Yet in reporting to Gen. John E. Wool, Butler gloated at length that when Hatteras Inlet fell, his forces took "715 prisoners, 1,000 stand of arms, 30 pieces of cannon, one 10-inch columbiad, a prize brig loaded with cotton, a sloop loaded with provisions and stores, two light-boats, a schooner in ballast, 5 stand of colors, and 150 bags of coffee."[54]

Men of the 20th Indiana camped on Hatteras Island after Fort Clark was taken.— LIBRARY OF CONGRESS

Both Butler and Stringham, whose report went to U.S. Secretary of the Navy Gideon Welles, were elated at having played a leading role in the first Union victory over Confederates. They had established a beach-head within Confederate territory, and little else mattered. Neither of these leaders nor any other high-ranking U.S. military or naval officer got busy trying to prevent a repetition of the communication problem their forces experienced in North Carolina. Failure to take it seriously meant that many more casualties from friendly fire would occur among men in blue before the unconditional surrender of the Confederates.

6

Friendly Fire from Two Directions

Glasgow, Missouri—September 18, 1861

People who managed to keep abreast of events happening west of the Mississippi River expected action to pick up during the week of September 15, 1861. On Sunday, the first day of that week, Gen. Albert S. Johnston superseded Gen. Leonidas Polk as commander of Confederate Department No. 1, which included the divided state of Missouri.

During the next three days three men became Union generals: William "Bull" Nelson, Horatio G. Wright, and William T. Ward. Their Confederate opponents elevated only one man, Leroy P. Walker, into the ranks of general officers during this period.

Meanwhile, Missouri's Hannibal & St. Joseph Railroad was being threatened by Confederates. Union Gen. Benjamin M. Prentiss was assigned to command a long strip of land that included the entire railroad. Rival forces clashed at two points in Missouri on September 17—Blue Mills Landing and Morristown.[55]

A few days earlier, a "significant action" took place at the edge of the state. Union Col. Jefferson C. Davis of the 22nd Indiana Infantry learned from Col. James D. Eads that an estimated 3,000 Rebels under Confederate Gen. Sterling Price were advancing toward Booneville. The bulk of Price's command was busy besieging the nearby town of Lexington. According to a Rebel diary, some of the 10,000 men under Price were concentrated at Camp Cowskin, where they were armed with "shotguns, old flintlock rifles, smoothbore muskets, pitchforks, scythe blades, bludgeons, etc." It was this motley body that clashed with Federals at Booneville. No report of Federal casualties was filed, but Union Col. Davis estimated that Rebels lost about 57 men there. Some of them probably belonged to the state's Callaway Guard, earlier armed with "some sixty rifles, ranging from squirrel to big game" by secessionist Gov. Claiborne Jackson.[56]

Jubilant at having scored a victory at Booneville—however small—Federal leaders herded some of their men into four small steamers. The community of Glasgow was rumored to be an arms depot that might hold more than 5,000 stand of weapons. A quick strike could add Rebel muskets and rifles to the list of captures, so the boats were soon chugging up the Missouri River. Aboard them, observers noticed that the towns of Arrow Rock and Saline seemed to be deserted. In

Because Gen. William Nelson roared his orders, many subordinates called him "Bull."
—Harper's History of the Great Rebellion

Saline, not a single person could be seen and all stores and houses were closed. Because darkness fell unexpectedly early on August 19, the *War Eagle, Intan, White Cloud,* and *Des Moines* tied up for the night at a point about five miles from Glasgow.

A Lt. Col. Hendricks decided that it would be wise to learn something about the countryside, so he sent out a party to scout the vicinity. Soon after these men left, six other companies from the 18th and 26th Indiana Regiments were directed "to proceed by land through a cornfield and the 'woods' to the town and take it by surprise." Led by Maj. George Tanner on horseback and accompanied by an unidentified Indiana soldier who doubled as a correspondent for the *Brown County Union,* these six companies moved forward under a brilliant moon. Tanner and a party of perhaps a dozen men stopped briefly on a knoll that was clearly visible from a considerable distance.

Suddenly "a volley of musketry, judging from the volume of sound, amounting to, at least, a platoon, opened upon us," one newspaper correspondent reported. Shot through the hips, Tanner toppled from his horse. "The first volley was immediately followed by another," and soldier W. A. Coffin was mortally wounded. Hats were knocked off, gun stocks were

Leroy Pope Walker became a Confederate general in mid-September 1861.—
PICTORIAL FIELD BOOK OF THE CIVIL WAR

split, and the pocket of a William H. Taggert's jacket was cut.

Members of Tanner's command began firing from the hillside above the spot where their major lay "and the pickets from the 26th Indiana, previously thrown out above our boats without our knowledge, were returning the fire. We were thus between two fires," a letter from an unidentified participant explained. Escaping bullets because he was knocked down, the writer was one of only a handful of Federals who were simultaneously subjected to friendly fire from two directions at once.[57]

These events created intense excitement and confusion on the boats, and firing upon comrades should have ended, but it did not. About mid-

*Soon after Col. Jefferson C. Davis was elevated in rank, he murdered Gen. William Nelson in a Louisville hotel, but escaped punishment because Federal forces had their hands more than full trying to defeat Rebels.—*LESLIE'S ILLUSTRATED WEEKLY

night "the picket guard which had been stationed near the edge of the wood hailed some party, and getting no answer, fired a gun. Immediately troops under a Col. Wheatley, stationed around the *White Cloud* and the *Desmoines*, opened fire in the direction of the supposed enemy." Without waiting to learn what had happened, masters of two boats backed them out so hurriedly that lines were not untied. They then dropped downriver and lay at the deserted town of Saline until morning. Soon the other two boats joined them there, and all aboard the tiny flotilla rejoiced that at last they were safe from their own men.[58]

Gen. Benjamin M. Prentiss.—USAMHI

So many shots had been exchanged between Federals that the letter writer from Indiana failed to report how many men were wounded. But he was glad to note that only four men were killed. The events of one of the most unusual evenings early in the war were alluded to by only one officer. Writing from Jefferson City, Missouri, more than a month later, Col. Davis, not yet aware that Tanner's wound would ultimately be mortal, sent a very brief report to Gen. John C. Frémont. Indiana regiments, Davis said, had "taken possession of all points as far as Glasgow, but unfortunately for their reputation as soldiers their scouts fired into each other, severely wounding Major Tanner and several others, and killing three."[59]

Had it not been for men who wanted folks back home in Brown County and St. Louis to know what happened on a crazy night in September 1861, the story of these Hoosiers who killed and wounded one another might never have been known.

CHAPTER

7

At Least Thirty-Four Casualties

Munson's Hill, Virginia—September 29–30, 1861

F ew spots where the only fighting between hostile forces was a minor skirmish rate so many mentions in Civil War literature as does Munson's Hill, Virginia. Its location within sight of the unfinished dome of the Capitol in Washington was the key to the importance of the little eminence. As soon as numerous volunteers arrived in the city, Federal leaders established Camp Dupont as a training center near the small, but prominent hill. Federal units retreating toward the capital after the First Battle of Bull Run reported, "We did not halt at Fairfax Court House, but kept right on to the Long Bridge at Washington, by way of Munson's Hill and Arlington." Confederates followed their defeated foes without really pursuing them, then occupied Munson's Hill. "The inhabitants of Washington could see [Rebel] flags waving" there.[60]

While troops marched toward Munson's Hill, U.S. Secretary of War Simon Cameron took steps designed to prevent the Maryland Legislature from assembling.—AUTHOR'S PRIVATE COLLECTION

With Munson's Hill as the approximate center of their position, Confederate pickets under Col. J. E. B. Stuart fanned out over the surrounding area and stayed there for most of the summer. To some men of the 1st Maryland Regiment, Confederate Army of the Potomac, picket duty was grand during a period when no significant battle was fought. Describing this near-idyllic period, one officer wrote, "We became attached to this life. The constant excitement of skirmishing was such an agreeable variety to the monotony of camp, that we were loath to give it up, and frequently asked and obtained permission to double our tours of picket duty there."[61]

Monotony vanished during the second week of September. Many Maryland secessionists had not become soldiers, but nevertheless Washington feared

The unfinished dome of the U.S. Capitol was clearly visible from Munson's Hill.—LIBRARY OF CONGRESS

the state would leave the Union. To prevent this from happening, U.S. Secretary of War Simon Cameron, through Gen. George B. McClellan, instructed Gen. Nathaniel P. Banks on September 11 to stop the state legislature from assembling, thus preventing a vote on the question of secession.

Lawmakers began arriving at Frederick on September 17, and both houses were called to order. Neither house had a quorum, so the bodies adjourned until the next day. By that time, Banks's aide, R. Morris Copeland, had reached the town with a body of troops. He surrounded Frederick with pickets, preventing anyone from leaving. On September 18 he arrested at least 19 lawmakers, thereby "saving Maryland for the Union."[62]

News of swift-moving events in Maryland caused such rejoicing in the area's Federal camps that, following the coup, officers did not attempt to maintain discipline. Ten days after Copeland's swift action in Frederick, several Pennsylvania regiments were ordered to march on Poolesville, Virginia, from their camp. Two days' cooked provisions were hurriedly prepared, and soldiers planned to strike their tents at 8 A.M. on Sunday, September 29. According to Lt. Col. Dennis O'Kane of

Gen. George B. McClellan, "the Young Napoleon," succeeded McDowell as commander of the Army of the Potomac.— NATIONAL ARCHIVES

the 69th Pennsylvania Regiment, "Tattoo was beat at the usual hour on the evening of the 28th, and the regiment had retired to rest, when at 11:15 o'clock General [William F.] Smith rode up." He demanded to know why the regiment was not in line.

Explanations were waved aside by Smith; orders or no orders, he wanted action at once, not the following morning. O'Kane later reported that Smith demanded the regiment form in line at once. "Ammunition was issued, and the regiment marched along the road through camp and over the hill by Fort Baker." Only Smith knew the nature and location of their objective. "The officers were in entire ignorance of the purpose or direction of the movement."

Officers and men were told that pickets would precede them and would point out directions when their posts were reached. "These were all the instructions received," the Pennsylvania officer wrote, "no orders in writing having been issued." The line was promptly formed, and men began marching before midnight. O'Kane wrote, "After about an hour, firing was heard in front of the column, which has been attributed to the pickets firing upon the line, and by which several lives were lost. The regiment moved steadily on, and in about thirty minutes was brought to a halt and was resting in line, when three dragoons rode rapidly along, and when about the center of the regiment one of them fired his revolver, exclaiming, 'Take care, boys; here they come.' Simultaneously, a number of skirmishers suddenly appeared from the adjoining woods on the road, when some of our men, supposing the secessionists were on them, discharged their pieces, which led to a general alarm and firing along the line, which unfortunately resulted in the death of a Sergeant Gillan of Company B, and the wounding of 2 more of this regiment."

When order was restored, the line was re-formed, and the men marched a short distance. Without having heard the whine of a bullet from a Confederate musket, about 11 A.M. on Monday they were ordered to march back to camp.[63]

Many other Pennsylvanians, led by Lt. Col. Isaac J. Wistar, followed the route taken by O'Kane and his regiment. Sixteen companies of infantry plus a battery of four guns constituted this segment of the force, ordered to an unknown target for an unexplained mission. This large column encountered the New York regiment's pickets close to their camp, then "began to come in collision with picket guards who said they belonged to the Fourth Michigan."

Col. Edward D. Baker refused a promotion because it would have required him to give up his seat in the U.S. Senate.—LESLIE'S ILLUSTRATED WEEKLY

By this time, Pennsylvanians were on a road that was lined with thick woods on both sides. Two more pickets, made up of about 36 men, were passed before all hell broke loose. Wistar reported, "A regular volley was fired into the second and third companies of my line from immediately behind the fence which lined the woods on my left. The head of the column having now passed the woods on our right, the latter was replaced by open fields, exposing us to the light of the rising moon, while the woods on our left, whence an invisible enemy continued to pour his fire, was in deep shade."

Despite his attempts to restrain them, Wistar's own men began to fire and kept it up for an estimated two minutes until "parties in the woods retired." His horse having been shot, the Pennsylvanian started sending his dead and wounded to the rear and was dressing his line when unseen men in the woods "threw in another volley" from a distance of about six yards. By the time the melee ended, Wistar said that 4 of his men were dead and 14 wounded.[64]

Col. Edward D. Baker, commander of the brigade that included the units under O'Kane and Wistar, was absent during the period in which friendly fire erupted repeatedly "near Vanderburgh's house, Munson's Hill, Virginia." Reporting to the adjutant general of the Federal Army of the Potomac, he did not mention Smith's enigmatic and never-explained orders. Instead, he simply transmitted the reports of his two subordinates (from which brief segments were quoted here); without giving a casualty count, he commented: "It is only necessary for the commanding general to peruse them to be satisfied that the casualties which occurred on the night of the 28th ultimo were inevitable results of causes over which the troops themselves had no control. The circumstances were peculiarly trying, and the confusion, though great, did not impair the courage or steadiness of most of the officers and men."[65]

A brief account of the night's events soon appeared in a Washington newspaper. Readers were told nine men, of whom three were officers, were killed and "about twenty-five wounded."[66]

In spite of the fact that Munson's Hill had been stained red with Federal blood, several units camped there for much or all of the following winter. Common sense suggests that men who were sprawled around campfires there spent many a night talking and wondering. In this place of death the 1st Rhode Island Light Artillery or the 4th Artillery of the U.S. Army or the 4th Michigan Regiment might suddenly come under deadly fire from unseen fellow fighting men in blue. Though that did not happen, the never-to-be-forgotten night filled with flashes of light from unseen muskets has no exact counterpart in annals of the Civil War.

Federal troops crossed Washington's Long Bridge as they started toward Munson's Hill.—
HARPER'S HISTORY OF THE GREAT REBELLION

8

Melee in the Dark

Santa Rosa Island, Florida—October 9, 1861

C onfederates rejoiced at the fall of Fort Sumter in April 1861. But
some were dejected that Fort Pickens, sitting on Santa Rosa
Island in Florida's Pensacola Harbor, a Union bastion that had
been more or less besieged since Florida seceded in January 1861, had
failed to surrender.

Braxton Bragg, commanding the Pensacola district, believed his
promotion to the rank of major general was jeopardized because he
could not show results in this contest of wills between himself and
island Federals. The situation there closely resembled the one that
had played out at Charleston. But in this instance the small group of
Union troops that first held Pickens withstood isolation, harassment,
and occasional shelling, and were eventually reinforced by U.S. Army
regulars and volunteers sent in by sea. Meanwhile, both the Union
and Confederate press gave this stalemate on the Rebel frontier comparatively little coverage. By autumn, the standoff at Pensacola had
achieved an uneasy status quo, a tense, unresolved state that 100
years later would seem familiar to Americans and Russians of the
cold war era.

Bragg delegated resolution of the problem to subordinate commanders and approved a risky night attack on Fort Pickens in early October.[67]
On October 8, members of the 1st Florida Infantry were informed they
had been chosen to strike Federal facilities on the island—Fort Pickens
included, despite its known strength. After evening drill, men were
assembled by companies and sergeants called out, "All who want to go,
step out two paces!" Pensacola standoff veteran W. H. Treinner's
detailed report of preparations for the attack noted only 18 men from

Col. Richard Anderson led Confederate troops in their "wildly confused" assault.— <small>LIBRARY OF CONGRESS</small>

each company could be included in the mission; married men were ordered back into the ranks.[68]

Twenty-four hours later, qualified volunteers assembled on Knapps's Wharf in Pensacola and set out for Santa Rosa on lumber flats towed by the steamers *Ewing* and *Neafie*. Col. Richard H. Anderson, a future Confederate general, led the landing party that hit the island's beach between 1:30 and 2 A.M. on October 9. He stepped ashore about four miles from Pickens, where the island is about three-fourths of a mile wide. Though Confederates hoped to strike at the massive Federal fortress, the camp of the famous 6th New York Regiment—a Zouave unit commanded by Col. William Wilson—was a second major objective. According to Wilson, he was so hated by his foes that they had offered a "dead or alive" reward for him of $5,000.[69]

Rebel forces ran into trouble as soon as the units moved. Sand on the island was so deep and loose that walking was difficult and marching impossible. Some of the attackers managed to reach the Zouave camp, where they fired many of its tents. Awakened by volleys of musketry, Col. Harvey Brown of the U.S. Army, commanding the Federal forces, had drummers beat the long roll and sent Maj. Israel Vodges with two companies to meet the invaders. Simultaneously, Maj. Lewis G. Arnold was ordered to man the big guns of Fort Pickens.[70]

Musket fire soon became heavy, and at his headquarters Brown clearly saw "the light of the burning camp." Arnold was pulled from the fort in order to lead two companies to the support of Vodges, and Wilson was told "to advance and attack the enemy." By the time Vodges was a mile from Pickens, leading both infantry and artillery units, "from the obscurity of the night, he found himself and his command completely intermingled with the enemy." During the ensuing free-for-all, the major was captured by jubilant Rebels.[71] Then the attackers, with four or five times as many troops as the 250 or so men sent to meet them, soon realized they were accomplishing little and decided to retire from the field.

Reports of casualties from this affair vary widely; as usual, both sides claimed excessive numbers of enemy dead and wounded, and both sides minimized their own losses. One report suggested the ranks of the attackers were thinned by at least 350 men, while Federal losses were only about 60.[72] But everyone who commented about the affair agreed that opposing forces met in darkness so great it was impossible "to discover a man ten feet off." Inevitably, this led to confusion plus an intermingling of forces on a scale that was massive for the number of combatants involved. A Rebel who sent an account to the *Atlanta Intelligencer* wrote that soon after his unit landed, "we found ourselves among a squad of picket guard, who gave our close ranks a most destructive fire, throwing the company into great disorder."

No one ever knew positively whether it was the 5th Georgia or the 10th Mississippi Regiment that set fire to the tents of their Zouave enemies.

"Amid this excitement and conflagration, the wildest disorder reigned. Companies were disorganized and no such thing as a regiment was known. Our men retired in great confusion, and the line was a confused

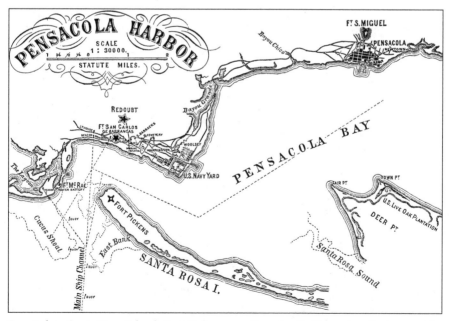

Located on Santa Rosa Island, Fort Pickens was the only significant installation outside Charleston Harbor to be in Federal hands when the war began.—THE REBELLION RECORD

Colorful Zouaves were among the Federal forces who took part in the action at Santa Rosa Island.—AUTHOR'S PRIVATE COLLECTION

mass, moving without orders, and almost without object," newspaper readers were told. Close to the spot at which Anderson—soon to become a general—was wounded, the Rebel account said, "Several times we met hostile squads and mistook them for friends, occasioning us heavy loss."[73]

Official reports, filling 26 pages, were sprinkled with comments about the chaos in which the struggle swirled. Reporting to Gen. Joseph G. Totten in Washington, Union Maj. Z. B. Tower excused what he considered to be a low casualty count among Rebel forces by pointing out that "in the confusion of a night attack matters do not always get on well." Wilson described a few hand-to-hand incidents in his report to Harvey Brown: "Sentinels stood their ground manfully, firing while retreating. Corp. William Parsonage of Company H (since dead), while supporting a sentinel and fighting manfully, was shot through the body in three places and bayoneted, but killed his opponent. Private William Scott of Company C, on the approach of the enemy from the Gulf beach, waited until they approached to within 10 feet, and deliberately shot Captain Richard Bradford, who was leading them on."

Capt. James M. Robertson of the 2nd Artillery, U.S. Army, described actions of Pvt. Michael M. O'Doud, who shielded himself behind a pine tree and got off 16 rounds. After O'Doud was killed, the officer examined the tree and found "seven musket balls buried in it in front of where his body was." Lt. Alexander N. Shipley of the 3rd Infantry, U.S. Army, believed the firing of his men threw attackers "into great confusion."[74]

Both sides claimed a great victory. Reporting to Rebel Gen. Samuel Cooper in Richmond, Bragg wrote, "We chastised the enemy, drove him from his camps, burned his tents and many stores, spiked some of his guns, and retired in good order."

He was especially elated that Vodges was taken prisoner. In a joint session of its two houses, with the encouragement of Gov. John Milton, the Florida legislature passed a resolution of thanks for "the daring and brilliant achievements of our troops on Santa Rosa Island."[75]

Among defenders of the island, Brown was most emphatic in saying that the only significant damage done to his force was "the burning of one-half of the tents of the Sixth Regiment." Rebels, he reported to Washington, "did not reach within 500 yards of either of the batteries the guns of which he was to spike." According to this officer, he was in possession of "nine spikes, taken from bodies of the dead, designed for our guns." Maj. Z. B. Tower of the U.S. Corps of Engineers confirmed Brown's summary, but noted that the Zouaves who were so despised by their foes "proved of little account" because of Wilson's poor leadership.[76]

Pvt. W. J. Milner of a Georgia unit known as the Clinch Rifles apparently knew nothing of the chaos caused earlier in the war by uniform colors. He used the word *splendid* to characterize his dark green uniform trimmed with gold lace and brass buttons. Alone among participants in the struggle, he noted many attackers wore a "strip of white cloth upon their left arms which was to be our mark to distinguish friend from foe." If his account is accurate, these "badges" were no more helpful in Florida than they had been to Yankees at the Bethels in Virginia.

Admitting that disbanded attackers retired "in great disorder," Milner wrote, "We had gone only a few steps when we saw glistening in the light of the burning [Zouave] camp a line of bayonets just across our way and only a few yards distant. Someone said, 'They are our men.' A volley from them, which killed and wounded some of our men, caused the cry, 'They are Yankees!' and the fire was returned by us. Col. Jackson, coming up about this time, gave the order to cease firing, saying, 'They are our men.' Most of the men seemed not to hear or understand the Colonel's order. At any rate it was not obeyed, and the firing was kept up by some of our men, while others were saying: 'Don't shoot! They are our men!'"[77]

During the wild confusion of that dark October night, only Confederates are reported to have shot into the ranks of their comrades. How many Federals killed and wounded on Santa Rosa Island were hit by bullets of guns wielded by their friends is impossible to determine.

CHAPTER

9

"A Most Murderous Fire"

Hampton Roads, Virginia—March 8, 1862

Stephen R. Mallory of Florida knew a great deal about ships and the sea, despite never having served in the U.S. Navy. His long experience as chairman of the Committee on Naval Affairs of the U.S. Senate meant that few other Confederates had a comparable background. That's why on February 21, 1861, Jefferson Davis named him to head the nonexistent naval department of the Confederate States of America. Since the military-minded president—who habitually gave his generals specific directions—knew little or nothing about warships, he paid little attention and gave no instructions to Mallory.

A reluctant secessionist, the Confederate secretary of the navy faced what seemed to be an impossible task. He took office at a time when the fledgling nation lacked a single vessel afloat as well as the money and resources to match the massive program of shipbuilding being launched by the Union. Having no other choice if he expected former U.S. naval officers to fight against old comrades, Mallory decided to risk everything on bold innovations. Less than 60 days after the fall of Fort Sumter, he spent many hours with a joint committee of the C.S. Congress. Already, he told them, he knew the key to victory on the seas. Secessionists must boldly take the route indicated by a few experiments overseas and begin building warships of iron instead of wood.[78] Mallory did not divulge all of his plans to senators, for he wanted nothing but blanket approval—plus money—from them. In secret, though, he was already at work on an ironclad.

On April 20, 1861, when Federal forces learned Virginia troops were approaching, they evacuated Norfolk's Gosport Navy Yard. Squads of men raced about the installation and tried to follow orders to burn any-

46

U.S. frigate Merrimac *before her conversion into a Confederate ironclad.*—CAMPFIRES AND BATTLEFIELDS

thing and everything secessionists could use. When they attempted to fire the USS *Merrimack* (or *Merrimac*), they bungled the job. Though it burned to the waterline, its engines and hull suffered little damage. Raised by Rebels after just ten days and renamed the CSS *Virginia*, it was soon being converted into "a floating armored casemate." Before work was completed, it was designated the flagship of the James River Squadron and assigned to Capt. Franklin Buchanan.

Since secessionists had numerous spies in Washington and Federal agents swarmed over Richmond, news of the Confederate experiment reached each side long before the *Virginia* was ready for a trial run. Moving with reckless speed, U.S. Secretary of the Navy Gideon Welles, assistant navy secretary Gustavus V. Fox, and their subordinates drafted and issued a contract to Swedish-born inventor John Ericsson. Turning his back on conventional warship designs, Ericsson on October 25 laid the keel of a novel "armored raft with revolving gun turret." With Lt. John L. Worden as its commander, the USS *Monitor* was commissioned on February 25, 1862, and fitted out for blockade duty off the North Carolina coast.

Mallory received regular reports about the vessel that Federals hoped would be superior to the *Virginia*. He knew that it was only a matter of time before the first naval duel between iron-plated vessels would be fought. Seeking to make the most of time, three days after the *Monitor* was towed from Brooklyn, the Confederate naval secretary authorized trials of his splendid new ironclad. Instructed to test the machinery and handling of his vessel on March 8, 1862, Buchanan sent workmen ashore and steamed toward Hampton Roads to do battle with a large squadron of Union vessels stationed there on blockade duty. Since the *Monitor* did not arrive until March 9, Mallory's unauthorized decision to take on Federal warships made March 8 a nearly unequaled day of victory for Rebels.

Buchanan deliberately pitted the *Virginia*, armed with six 9-inch smoothbores plus four rifles of 6- and 7-inch diameter, against vessels of the North Atlantic Blockading Squadron. That meant he would have to fight the 24-gun USS *Cumberland*, the 50-gun *Congress*, the 50-gun *St. Lawrence*, plus the smaller vessels *Cambridge*, *Roanoke*, *Mount Vernon*, *Jamestown*, *St. Lawrence*, *Brandywine*, *Brazilia*, and *Dakotah*. He sailed into battle knowing the mighty USS *Minnesota* was moored a few miles away, and shells from powerful shore batteries could reach the site of battle. In addition to the ironclad, the Confederate expedition consisted of the 6-gun *Patrick Henry* and the *Jamestown* with two guns, plus the little vessels *Raleigh*, *Beaufort*, and *Teaser* with only one gun each.[79]

Pilot A. B. Smith of the USS *Cumberland*, which was lying at anchor, nearly dropped his glass when he turned it upon an approaching vessel.

Conversion of the Merrimac *into the CSS* Virginia *at Gosport Navy Yard.*—CAMPFIRES AND BATTLEFIELDS

"As she came ploughing through the water," he later wrote, "she looked like a large half-submerged crocodile. Her sides seemed of solid iron and at her prow I could see an iron ram projecting straight forward." Though he did not know her name, Smith was positive the iron monster was the brand-new Confederate warship about which there had been so much talk. The tugboat *Zouave*, armed with a 30-pounder Parrott gun, lay near the *Cumberland*; at a signal it raced toward the intruder. After having fired six shots with no apparent effect, another signal from the *Cumberland* took it out of action.[80]

Gustavus V. Fox, who was made assistant secretary of the navy by Lincoln, pushed hard for development of a Federal ironclad.
—NICOLAY & HAY, ABRAHAM LINCOLN

The Confederate vessel moved slowly and ponderously. Its crew paid no attention to the tiny *Zouave*, but opened fire as soon as their vessel was abreast of the *Congress*. By this time, gunners aboard the *Cumberland* were in action, so after delivering a broadside to the *Congress* the *Virginia* moved straight toward the larger Federal warship.

According to Smith, "balls [from our guns] bounced upon her mailed sides like India-rubber, apparently making not the least impression." After men aboard the Federal warship got off a few broadsides, the massive iron ram of the Rebel vessel knocked a hole in the wooden side of the *Cumberland* and set her afire. A member of the Confederate crew calculated that "a horse and cart could have been driven through the hole in the enemy vessel."

Though still firing a few of her guns, the *Cumberland* was taking water rapidly and was clearly out of the fight, so the *Virginia* swung around slowly and turned toward the *Congress*. On "the iron monster" Buchanan knew that his brother, McKean Buchanan, was aboard the *Congress* as paymaster—but this was war. Ordering a desultory fire to continue toward the *Cumberland* and directing occasional shots at the Federal batteries on shore, Buchanan prepared to blow the *Congress* out of the water even if it meant the death of his brother.

By this time, much of the shoreline between Newport News and Fort Monroe was lined with spectators; many of them were civilians who lived nearby, but large numbers of Union soldiers and sailors were also part of the excited crowd. Some of them wondered what Joseph Smith, acting master of the *Congress*, was doing when they saw his ship's jib and topsails set. Minutes later a tug started trying to pull the warship into shallow water where the *Virginia* would not be able to follow, so spectators cheered and threw hats into the air.

Buchanan, who saw what his prey was planning, waited until the tactic was hard and fast. He then moved his vessel to a position about 150 yards astern of the *Congress* and from that point raked her fore and aft with shells for nearly an hour in such methodical fashion that his fire seemed almost casual in nature. While this action was taking place, the USS *Minnesota* ran aground after having steamed five miles to join the fray. Among the biggest and finest of all U.S. naval vessels, this mighty frigate was grounded too far from the scene to take a significant part.

Smith, the *Congress*'s commander, was killed. Lt. Austin Pendergrast took over. A hasty inspection tour revealed blood-covered decks upon which the dead and dying were sprawled everywhere. With most of his

Though relatively small, the CSS Virginia *quickly drove the USS* Congress *from her anchorage.*—BATTLES AND LEADERS

guns out of commission and fires blazing at several points, Pendergrast had his ship's colors struck and raised a white flag; he could do nothing else.[81]

A lengthy French-language account of the action, later published in both its original form and an English-language translation, was written by an especially interested impartial observer who was in command of the French navy's *Gassendi.* Noting that Confederates ceased to fire as soon as surrender was signaled, he wrote: "One of their gunboats, the *Raleigh,* approached [the *Congress*] and ran alongside of her on the starboard side to take

John Ericsson, builder of the Monitor.— NATIONAL ARCHIVES

off the officers and to tell the crew to go ashore in their boats; but at the moment that the gunboat in good faith came alongside the frigate, guns fired by the Federals hid in the edge of the woods, and some also from the *Congress,* killed and wounded many officers and sailors of the *Raleigh.* Some men even on the *Congress* were struck by the balls coming from the land."[82]

Could a veteran seaman who spoke or wrote no English have been mistaken about one of the most bizarre instances of friendly fire during 1862? His account is supported by a *New York Herald* news story about "a most murderous fire" as well as by summaries of later analysts. One of them attributed the first burst of musket fire to a regiment at Newport News Point. Buchanan reportedly was so enraged he demanded a weapon, then personally came out from behind iron shields and returned the fire of the troops until he was hit in the groin and forced to yield command to Catesby Jones.

Aboard the *Virginia,* officer John Taylor Wood noted: "A number of the [Union vessel's] men were killed" by the fire directed at Rebels who were taking off surviving members of the crew of the *Congress.* According to some astonished spectators, Gen. Joseph K. F. Mansfield personally directed two rifle companies of the 10th Indiana Regiment to fire on boats that held sailors from both sides. This observation was supported by a four-sentence report to Gen. John E. Wool, who said that his men

Surviving crew of the Congress *came under fire from their own men as they attempted to escape.*
—CAMPFIRES AND BATTLEFIELDS

had driven the Rebel gunboats away from the burning *Congress.* Some experts later insisted that in addition to Hoosiers, men of the 7th and 11th New York Regiments "fired from the shore in support of the federal ships." Regardless of who was responsible for the musket and rifle fire from shore, nearby batteries soon joined in.[83]

Louis M. Goldsborough, commander of the Union's North Atlantic Blockading Squadron whose vessels were attacked by the *Virginia* on March 8, issued a detailed list of 30 members of the crew of the *Congress* who were wounded that day. He failed, however, to indicate how many were killed by Confederate shells and how many by Federal fire. Total Federal casualties aboard ship and on shore that day were later listed as 409. But no analyst, however skilled, has the source materials needed to determine how many Federals killed or wounded at Hampton Roads were victims of shore-to-ship friendly fire.[84]

The USS *Monitor* arrived too late to aid her sister vessels that day. But the next day the *Virginia* and the *Monitor* fought for hours. It was a head-to-head fight with no shore fire, a battle that had little to do with friendly fire and everything to do with the arrival of a new age in naval warfare.

CHAPTER

10

Nodine Retired in Haste

Pea Ridge, Arkansas—March 6–8, 1862

On March 8, 1862, about the time that men of the USS *Congress* admitted their ship was doomed, far west of Hampton Roads a Union general named Samuel R. Curtis launched an attack that many believed "secured Missouri for the Union." At the Battle of Pea Ridge, Arkansas, forces led by Confederate Gen. Sterling Price and Gen. Earl Van Dorn shattered under the force of Curtis's assault. The Rebels scattered late that day and never rallied.

This fight was also known in some quaters as the Battle of Elk Horn Tavern. It started late on March 6 and lasted roughly two and a half days. Because the conflict ultimately crushed large-scale Confederate resistance beyond the Mississippi River, some later historians came to call it "the Gettysburg of the West." But at Pea Ridge the casualties roughly numbered 1,300 for each side—very modest numbers in the blood-drenched Civil War. Today, it is remembered because it was one of the conflict's longer, most chaotic, and perhaps most colorful fights. A distinguishing feature was the participation of Confederate Indian troops—"Native Americans in Gray."

Brave men, though not familiar with European battlefield tactics, the Native Americans fighting at Pea Ridge served under Gen. Albert Pike. They filled the ranks of Cherokee units that tried, but failed, to follow their sword-carrying white officers' orders—the words of "long knives." For instance, obeying orders, some Indians overran a Federal battery, but once this objective was accomplished, discipline vanished and their commanders found them "all talking, and going this way and that, listening to no orders from any one." On other occasions, when Federal artillery opened on them, the Cherokee units broke ranks, scattered, and began

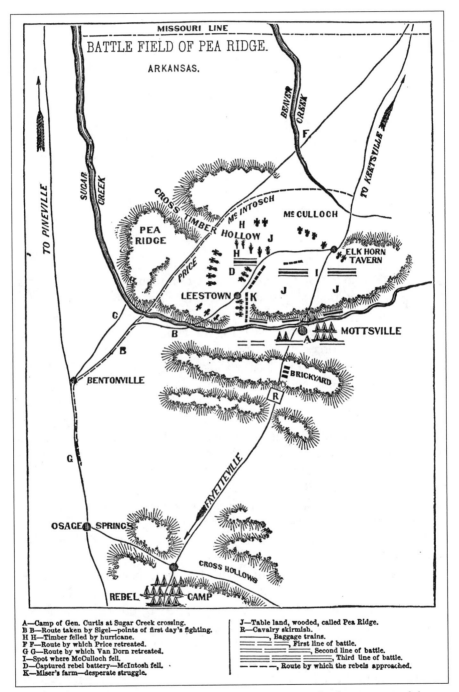

BATTLE FIELD OF PEA RIDGE.
ARKANSAS.

MISSOURI LINE

TO PINEVILLE
SUGAR CREEK
BEAVER CREEK
TO KEETSVILLE

CROSS TIMBER HOLLOW
PRICE
PEA RIDGE

Mc INTOSH
Mc CULLOCH
ELK HORN TAVERN

H
J
H
D
I
J
J
K

LEESTOWN

MOTTSVILLE
A

B
B
BENTONVILLE

BRICKYARD
R

G

FAYETTEVILLE

OSAGE SPRINGS

CROSS HOLLOWS

REBEL CAMP

A—Camp of Gen. Curtis at Sugar Creek crossing.
B B—Route taken by Sigel—points of first day's fighting.
H H—Timber felled by hurricane.
F F—Route by which Price retreated.
G G—Route by which Van Dorn retreated.
I—Spot where McCulloch fell.
D—Captured rebel battery—McIntosh fell.
K—Miser's farm—desperate struggle.

J—Table land, wooded, called Pea Ridge.
R—Cavalry skirmish.
—————, Baggage trains.
═══════, First line of battle.
═══════, Second line of battle.
═══════, Third line of battle.
— — — —, Route by which the rebels approached.

Rough terrain in an isolated corner of Arkansas saw Pea Ridge become one of the fiercest battles in what was then known as the western theater.—The Rebellion Record

sniping at the Yanks from behind the shelter of rocks and trees. This behavior would seem sensible to modern soldiers, but it was not the behavior white officers needed if they were to conduct battles based on the old Napoleonic model. One Rebel officer at Pea Ridge, 55-year-old Col. Stand Watie of the Cherokee Mounted Rifles, was a Cherokee chief. Later promoted, he would go into American history distinquished as the last Rebel general to surrender to Union forces. But at Pea Ridge, both his friends and foes believed his men turned brutal; they were accused of scalping the Union dead.

At Pea Ridge, Union Gen. Samuel R. Curtis was momentarily in such peril that Rebels mistakenly believed he would be captured.—
J. C. BUTTRE ENGRAVING

The Native Americans were just a few of the troops at Pea Ridge that contributed to the chaos. For instance, after two of his chief subordinates were taken out on March 7, Rebel Gen. Van Dorn lost control of his right wing and described it as "thrown into utter confusion." Union and Confederate officers would admit that this was, sadly, typical. Men who made up units on both sides were largely without battle experience or satisfactory training. Maj. Hugh Wangelin of the 12th Missouri Volunteers noted that among Federal units, his was among the least prepared for conflict.[85]

Officers and men repeatedly mistook the identity of units near their positions, and they came close to mowing down comrades or paying with their lives for their mistakes. Confederate Gen. Ben McCulloch had served as a Texas Ranger and U.S. marshal and had dodged bullets in many a fight with Indians. Lost at Pea Ridge, he came face to face with a Union private who dropped him with a single shot. Col. Wells H. Blodgett, advancing with men of the 37th Illinois Infantry, mistook a body of enemies for Federal troops and did not discover his error until they were ready to fire on him at close range. According to the *New York Herald*, members of some cavalry units moved forward, not in the usual orderly fashion, but as "a wild, numerous, and irregular throng."

Orders of Union Col. Jefferson C. Davis and other officers were misunderstood or ignored; men frequently fired at "flashes of light from the muzzles of muskets" without knowing whether the weapons were wielded by comrades or foes.[86]

Following Gen. Curtis's instructions, Lt. J. M. Adams and a companion set out to deliver messages to Gen. Franz Sigel. The two Federals decided to take a shortcut through "a blind wood," and after about a half-mile they heard the shout, "Halt! Who goes there?" Adams responded, "Friends" and was instantly asked to say from which army the friends came. The lieutenant hesitated, then took a chance and replied: "Friends from the Federal army." Commanded to dismount and advance with the countersign, his heart pounded wildly at the realization that he had been given no countersign. Fearfully leading his horse forward by the bridle, Adams found himself facing a detachment of the 3rd Iowa Cavalry. He would not have been surprised to have been taken prisoner by Rebels.

During the night, said Adams later, "There was much confusion in the location of the camp-fires and commands of the contending armies." At one point, Confederates who were pursuing the 37th Illinois suddenly

Soldiers in blue managed to maintain ordered ranks for much of the battle.— THE SOLDIER IN OUR CIVIL WAR

realized they were being followed by a detachment under the command of Col. Thomas Pattison, an officer who identified himself as a member of "the South-western Army."[87]

With men forced to fight in darkness and confusion, beyond the limit of their endurance, it is remarkable that this pivotal battle produced only one specific report of friendly fire. "At one time early in the fighting," according to historian Dee Brown, "confused Union artillerymen shelled their own troops." Brown was referring to the official report of Maj. Frederic Nodine of the 25th Illinois Volunteers, which was probably— but not positively—accurate. Believing he and his men faced three Rebel regiments, Nodine

Defeat of Rebels under Gen. Sterling Price proved to be a mighty setback for their forces in the West.—Nicolay & Hay, Abraham Lincoln

wrote: "Owing to the darkness and thickness of the underbrush I found it impossible to distinguish friend from foe, and from the fact that one of our own batteries was playing upon us from the angle of the brush and road, I thought it best to retire."[88]

Nodine probably did not know whether or not men became casualties when Federal shells began dropping into their ranks. He was so busy trying to find safety that he had no time to inquire about the effects of friendly fire.

Curtis may never have been told that some of his gunners shelled one of his own regiments. But he did express indignation and horror at Indian excesses, sending a letter across enemy lines to Van Dorn, stating that "many of the Federal dead were tomahawked, scalped, and their bodies shamefully mangled." Van Dorn apologized, after a fashion, then countercharged that "many of our men who surrendered themselves prisoners of war, were reported as having been murdered in cold blood by their captors, who were alleged to be the Germans [in Federal ranks]."

Curtis lost no time in answering the charge against his Germans, whom he cited as alleging that some of their number who surrendered were murdered by Confederate captors. What is more, wrote the Federal commander, when a three-gun Federal battery was overrun, "our men serving the guns were surrounded and were shot dead by the rebels although seeking refuge behind their horses."[89]

Utterly different in nature from the naval engagement that took place as the Arkansas battle was winding down, the two conflicts had one significant element in common—the full truth will never be known about either of them.

CHAPTER

11

Eternal Peace . . . for 3,500

Shiloh, Tennessee—April 6–7, 1862

Tiny Shiloh Methodist Church sat about 2 miles west of the Tennessee River and just 25 miles north of Corinth, Mississippi. Soldiers attached its name to the first great bloody battle of the war. Ironically, that name is often translated as "place of peace." Shiloh became a place of eternal peace for 3,500 men who died there. Some commentators have called the battle "little Gettysburg of the West" because the two struggles had some elements in common. But today the battlefields could hardly be more different; Gettysburg is dotted with massive memorials and markers; Shiloh displays trees instead of marble, granite, and bronze. Walking through the national park in Tennessee, it strains the imagination to visualize 119,000 men there, the trees offering them only temporary shelter from flying lead. At one spot, the buzzing of the bullets made some battle veterans call it "the Hornet's Nest."

Gettysburg has so captured the imagination of the world that several books of anecdotes about the Pennsylvania battle are available. Not so with Shiloh. It almost seems wrapped in a conspiracy of silence. Shiloh's lack of popular appeal may stem from the fact that, unlike Gettysburg, the Tennessee national park is not easily accessible to hundreds of thousands of visitors annually. But neglected though it is in many respects, Shiloh has its own bevy of records, distinctions, and oddities.

At Shiloh the nation witnessed the first battle death of a major Civil War field army commander. Rebel Gen. Albert S. Johnston, leader of the Army of Tennessee, on April 6 dropped from the saddle after being hit by an unnoticed shot and died on the battleground. The next day, elsewhere on the field, Arkansas recruit Henry M. Stanley—a recent English immigrant—was captured by Federals; Stanley later walked away from

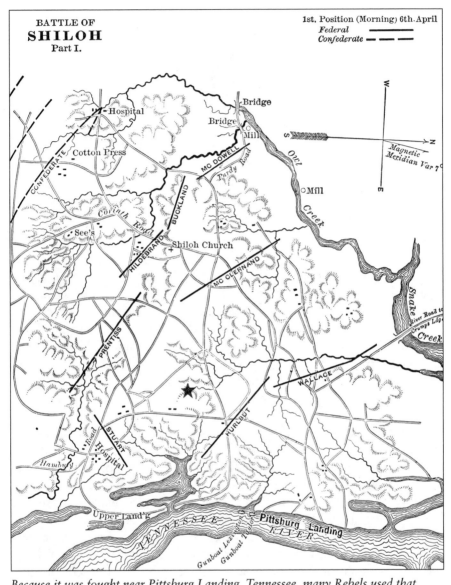

Because it was fought near Pittsburg Landing, Tennessee, many Rebels used that name to designate the battle commonly known today as Shiloh.—BATTLES AND LEADERS

confinement by volunteering for the Union army, then the Union navy, moves that led to a life of adventure, careers in journalism and exploration, and world fame as the man who opened the Congo and who found missing missionary Dr. David Livingstone. On the side opposite Johnston and Stanley at Shiloh, 11-year-old drummer boy John Clem barely escaped death when his snare drum was smashed by a Rebel artillery shell fragment; Clem's youth and bravery won him newspaper notice and a home in the U.S. Army, a career opportunity that saw him stick with the military until 1916 and retirement as a major general.

Shiloh also had some domestic political impact. There, for instance, the sitting Confederate governor of Tennessee—Isham G. Harris—went into battle as a volunteer aide to a general. Observations made by him and other Southern politicians led to the Confederacy expediting its conscription act. This proved to be the first military draft ever approved on the North American continent; it went into effect more than a year before the U.S. Congress adopted a similar law to bolster the size of the Union army.

But far from the least of the Battle of Shiloh's claims to distinction was that it served as the site of three tragic, documented instances of friendly fire—and it may have been the site of a fourth. The first of these, however, did not involve artillery or small arms. The deadly weapon was a steamboat.

On April 5, a day before the Battle of Shiloh began, Union Gen. William "Bull" Nelson—a 300-pounder from Kentucky—led a body of Ohio volunteers into the hamlet of Savannah, Tennessee, a spot across the Tennessee River from the place that would become the Shiloh battleground. Then, early on April 6, word that a fight had started at Pittsburg Landing near Shiloh church reached the citizens and soldiers in Savannah. About 1:30 P.M. that day Nelson's Ohioans were sent seven miles down the east bank of the Tennessee. At that point Bull was directed to cross the river and go through Pittsburg Landing toward the area where the fighting was heaviest. By the time the hefty general began his crossing, however, the river was dotted with the flailing bodies of frightened Union soldiers who had dropped their rifles and tried to swim to safety.

The pilot of the steamer on which Nelson and his men were crossing stopped her engines in order to avoid hitting swimmers. Nelson angrily countermanded the pilot's action and gestured for full speed ahead. An unidentified officer turned his head to avoid looking as the boat began hitting men in the water, men whose faces revealed their confusion and terror.[90]

Nelson later reported that men of his 6th Ohio and of the 35th Indiana Regiments "drove back the enemy and restored the line of battle at 6:30 P.M." Once this was done the outsized general turned his attention back to the men who had thrown down their muskets and fled. Estimating "7,000 to 10,000 men frantic with fright and utterly demoralized" had sought refuge under the riverbank, he wrote, "[These runaways] received my division with cries, 'We are whipped; cut to pieces.' They were insensible to shame or sarcasm—for I tried both on them—and, indignant at such poltroonery, I asked permission to fire upon the knaves."[91]

There is no record that "Bull" was given permission to have his men shoot down frightened refugees from battle.

Individually, rifled muskets were less lethal than an oncoming riverboat, but collectively they were formidable. A few hours before Nelson's boat plowed into fleeing Federals, Rebels of the Orleans Guard had rifles turned upon them by comrades. Sporting bright blue uniforms that contrasted vividly with their red caps, these men returned the fire when comrades in gray took them as targets. An unidentified member of the guard, who saw a fellow drop when he fired at him, allegedly remarked, "It was just like shootin' rabbits—except that these rabbits were shootin' at us." Gen. P. G. T. Beauregard was the Rebel second in command at Shiloh.

Temporarily routed, some Federal forces raced to safety under the river bank at Pittsburg Landing.—HENRY LOVIE, FRANK LESLIE'S ILLUSTRATED NEWS

When he caught a glimpse of the smart-mouthed Confederate—who by then had turned his jacket inside out to show its white lining—the general thought he belonged to some other brigade. What the cranky foot soldier may not have known was that the angry Beauregard—himself a proud Louisianan—was also a member of the all-volunteer guard.[92]

How many casualties resulted from Nelson's haste or the failure to properly dress Rebels from Louisiana is unknown. That was also the case with Shiloh's strangest instance of friendly fire. During the night of April 6, the Federal gunboats *Lexington* and *Tyler* were ordered to shell scattered areas believed to be held by the enemy. Because a variety of distances were involved, fuses were cut at 5-, 10-, and 15-second lengths. Whether fuses were improperly cut or the aim of gunners who threw shells at 15-minute intervals was poor is not known, but Rebel Gen. Patrick R. Cleburne castigated their fire as an instance of "reckless inhumanity" that had few parallels in history.

Many of the Federal wounded had been carried from the field on hand litters or mule-drawn carts, but hundreds still lay where they fell. Numerous shells from the two gunboats dropped on clusters of wounded men in blue, "who were strewn thickly between my camp and the river," Cleburne reported.[93]

The military significance of all who were killed or wounded by their comrades during these incidents is far less than that of Shiloh's most debatable case of friendly fire. On that occasion, Federals who had taken possession of a spot called the Peach Orchard, fought so stubbornly that the Confederates pitted against them seemed ready to give up. In this emergency, Gen. Johnston sent aide Isham Harris to give a brief speech of encouragement to the wavering troops. But words from the Tennessee governor seemed to have little or no effect. At that point, Johnston, the man regarded by many as the most able of all Confederate generals, arrived at a rash decision.

Climbing aboard his fine bay horse Fire Eater about 2 P.M. Johnston signaled that he would personally lead these men into the fight. His reckless exposure to danger was later derided by Beauregard. Believing a modern general's place was behind his troops, manipulating the big strategic picture, Beauregard said that Johnston's style constituted "leadership from the front instead of the [protected] rear." With his men following closely behind, Johnston moved close to the enemy line before permitting soldiers in gray to surge ahead of him. He returned from the fray in a jubilant mood—despite having been hit by three spent bullets that failed to break his skin—and boasted: "They didn't trip me this time."[94]

Gen. Albert S. Johnston, C.S.A., may have been the first commander of an army to die from friendly fire.—THE CENTURY WAR BOOK

On the heels of having proclaimed victory at the Peach Orchard, Johnston began to sway in the saddle. By the time he was lifted down, he was semiconscious, and about 2:30 P.M. the Confederate commander at Shiloh breathed his last. His body was shrouded in a blanket to conceal his death from officers and men, but aides who took this action knew the cause of his unexpected death. A ball had hit him behind his knee at the precise spot where the big femoral artery runs from the thigh to the leg. Since Johnston wore very high boots, the wound was not noticed until too late; when the boot was removed, a river of blood soon ran from where the general lay.

Historians have known for many years that the fatal shot did not hit the front of Johnston's knee, as presumably would have been the case had it been fired from a man in blue who was crouched in the Peach Orchard. Johnston was a superb horseman, and his Fire Eater obeyed signals so swiftly and well that man and animal seemed almost to be one. It is possible, but highly improbable, that the horse's rider might have wheeled about and been hit in a split second at some time during his forward movement. Historian Wiley Sword seems to have been the first nationally known scholar who dared suggest that the fatal ball was "quite possibly fired by a Confederate whose aim was wild in the confusion." Racing behind his leader while whooping and firing his musket as rapidly as possible, many a Rebel probably did not take careful aim during the fateful half hour that the charge lasted. Significantly, historian William C. Davis echoed Sword's verdict in 1991.[95]

The theory that friendly fire from the rear caused the death of Johnston cannot be proved, but it is strongly supported by documented evidence. He was hit by three Union bullets and these—fired from a great distance—had barely enough force to leave imprints on his skin. The fatal shot landed with a great deal more force, so it well may have been fired at a considerably shorter distance.

An unidentified Rebel following his charging leader may have been responsible for taking out of action a man whom President Jefferson Davis trusted implicitly and whose long prewar career had prepared him to fight Yankees like no other general officer in gray. While Federals also lost a general officer at Shiloh—W. H. L. Wallace—and, collectively, 24,000 or so men in blue and in gray were killed, wounded, captured, or missing in the fight, no Shiloh casualty meant more to the outcome of the conflict than did the single minié ball that severed the femoral artery of Johnston.

12

Lincoln under Fire

Sewell's Point, Virginia—May 8, 1862

At the Executive Mansion, where the drive for restoration of the Union was launched soon after Lincoln's inauguration, hope for an early end to secession vanished during the first month of 1862. All signs now pointed to a protracted struggle. The president prepared to take steps designed to compel the cautious Gen. George B. McClellan to act agressively. Personal tragedy intervened, however, and Lincoln—as commander in chief—was forced to postpone plans to take direct charge of some Federal forces.

William Wallace "Willie" Lincoln was the apple of his father's eye—and of his mother's. Bright, lovable, and studious, the boy of 12 years was remarkably different from his younger brother. Thomas "Tad" Lincoln (so called by his father because at birth "he looked just like a tadpole") was much harder to love. Tad suffered a serious speech defect and a condition that today might be diagnosed as hyperactivity. Abraham and Mary Todd Lincoln tried to treat the boys alike, but found that impossible. When in early February the boys came down with what doctors called "bilious fever," the president and first lady took turns sitting at their sons' bedsides.

By the turn of the century, historians generally accepted that the boys contracted typhoid fever from drinking the contaminated water piped into the Executive Mansion from the Potomac River. Even if their sickness had been diagnosed accurately, however, in 1862 physicians could do little to save a victim of typhoid. Tad's recovery was followed by Willie's death on February 20. His parents were plunged into mourning so profound that the chief executive canceled plans to participate in the celebration of George Washington's birthday—in these years a significant and symbolic affair.

On the evening of February 22, Federal buildings in the capital remained dark as a symbol of public sympathy for the president and the first lady. A simple but dignified funeral service conducted by Dr. Phineas D. Gurley on February 24 failed to put an end to the Lincolns' grief. Willie's mother remained in seclusion for an entire month, and his father was unable to concentrate sufficiently to proceed with his scheme to subdue Rebel forces. Immediately, plans to visit commanders in the field were shelved; it took all of the grief-stricken president's strength to maintain his dignity in public and to try to comfort his wife in private.[96]

Lincoln's first trip outside the capital after Willie's funeral was

Willie Lincoln, age 12, died on February 20, 1862, from typhoid fever probably contracted from the drinking water of the Potomac River.—BRADY STUDIO, NICOLAY & HAY, ABRAHAM LINCOLN

made more than a month later, when he went to Alexandria to confer with McClellan. On the following day the presidential party stopped at Mount Vernon, but Willie's father remained on the steamer. Not until May 5 did Lincoln regain sufficient emotional strength to embark on a military mission that he planned to direct from Fort Monroe, one where he expected to demonstrate to McClellan that "the slows" never won a battle. Accompanied by Cabinet members Edwin M. Stanton and Salmon P. Chase, he boarded the revenue cutter *Miami* about dusk. Because the night was extremely dark, the little steamer tied up at a point only 15 miles below Alexandria.[97]

It was nearly 10 P.M. on May 6 when the *Miami* finally docked at Fort Monroe. Following protocol, the president paid a brief formal visit to the commandant, John E. Wool. A veteran of both the War of 1812 and the Mexican War, Wool at age 78 was the oldest general in active service and fourth in seniority in the U.S. Army. Immediately after having left Wool, the president went to the flagship of Louis M. Goldsborough, commander of the North Atlantic Blockading Squadron. Observers who

On the day he barely escaped gunfire from Federal warships, Lincoln was haggard and drawn.—LESLIE'S ILLUSTRATED WEEKLY

noted his visit lasted so long that he did not return to the *Miami* until about midnight took it as a sign that Lincoln would be guided by the naval officer, not by Wool.[98]

Early the next morning the president moved into Quarters No. 1 of the fort, after which he inspected the yacht *Vanderbilt*, the USS *Monitor*, and the 192-ton *E. A. Stevens*. During the afternoon he visited the ruins of Hampton, Virginia, then conferred with Goldsborough again. Members of the party intimately acquainted with the president guessed that he was pondering an important move of some sort and thought that the Confederate-held Norfolk might be its objective.

On the morning of May 8 the president conferred with Goldsborough for a third time, then began to exercise his role as commander in chief of U.S. armed forces. Hearing from a Rebel deserter that all-important Norfolk might soon be evacuated and that the ironclad CSS *Virginia* was likely to be sunk by her crew, Lincoln planned and directed an attack on enemy batteries located at Sewell's Point that were meant to protect Norfolk.[99]

About the middle of the morning, a hastily assembled squadron moved toward the objective designated by the president. Carrying 15 guns, the paddle sloop *Susquehanna* was the most heavily armed conventional vessel of the group, though the accompanying screw sloop *San Jacinto* with 11 guns and the 9-gun *Seminole* were formidable. Two screw sloops, the *Dacotah* and the *Oneida*, mounting six guns each (and in earlier decades the little *Stevens*), would have been considered powerful. Far more threatening to the enemy than all of the wooden vessels combined, however, the ironclads USS *Monitor* and *Naugatuck* were judged strong enough to move toward their objective even in the face of withering Rebel fire.[100]

No longer following military action from a distance, but in the middle of it as its director, Lincoln steamed toward Sewell's Point aboard the tug *Tigress*. She was not far behind the *Seminole* when she began firing on the enemy from a distance of about three miles. At least a mile to the rear, men aboard the *Stevens* simply could not wait until they were closer to their target to get into the action. Oblivious of the fact that a single fuse cut too short could drop a Union shell on the tug and change the course of the war, they fired shells from their Parrott gun over ongoing vessels. Shrapnel from the *Stevens* rained on the deck of the *Monitor*, but it did little or no damage to the ironclad. Subjected to the same friendly fire that may have been caused by defective ammunition, the *Susque-hanna* was not so fortunate. A direct hit from the gun of the *Stevens* took off one of her gaff-headed sails; miraculously, no casualties were reported from this wildly erratic fire.[101]

Though Lincoln was not directly exposed to the friendly fire that erupted from a nearby gunboat, he came into the line of enemy fire. That made largely forgotten Sewell's Point the first place at which a sitting president was exposed to the artillery of hostile forces. This early and potentially fatal experience for the Union's leader is virtually forgotten, though his subsequent exposure during Gen. Jubal Early's 1864 raid on Washington is widely remembered.

The ammunition of some of Lincoln's vessels was almost gone when the CSS *Virginia* rounded a bend and under the command of Capt. Josiah Tattnall steamed ponderously toward the scene of action. About 4:30 P.M. the Federal vessels withdrew. They had not silenced Rebel batteries, but they had at least let them know that plenty of fire power could be trained upon them.

That evening Lincoln consulted local pilots, looked at charts, and personally selected the spot at which troops could land in order to march on Norfolk. When Federals reached the city on May 9, they found it deserted. What's more, the enemy had destroyed the *Virginia* to prevent its capture.

Louis Goldsborough later became a rear admiral.—J. C. BUTTRE ENGRAVING

Union Gen. Egbert Viele was made military governor of the vital Norfolk base, and celebrations were held throughout the Union.[102]

Touring the captured naval center, the president may have congratulated himself on his success as commander of a joint expedition. Naval and army forces had followed his orders and had achieved their goal. Many a man wearing stars on his shoulders would have been proud to have planned and executed the movements by which Norfolk came back into Federal hands and by which the *Virginia* was neutralized.

When Lincoln visited Fort Stevens, one of Washington's defenses, more than two years later, he came under the fire of rifles wielded by Rebels. After having been ordered down from the parapet, allegedly by Maj. Oliver Wendell Holmes Jr., the future U.S. Supreme Court justice, perhaps Lincoln mused on one of the singular coincidences of the war. His life could have been snuffed out earlier at Sewell's Point by a Rebel bullet, by erratic fire from a Union vessel called the *Stevens*, or that day at a Federal fort also named Stevens—instances he could regard only as having been providential.

13

Death from the River

Secessionville, South Carolina—June 16, 1862

Federal victories elsewhere did not reduce Washington's eagerness to take "the seed bed of secession," Charleston, South Carolina. The first guns of the Civil War were fired there—not once, but twice. President James Buchanan's attempt to resupply Fort Sumter in January 1861 was foiled by military cadets from Charleston's Citadel academy, boys who fired cannon that frightened off a relief ship. Lincoln's effort to achieve the same goal brought on the April 1861 artillery duel that is generally regarded as having started the war.

By the second year of the war, Charleston was much more than the symbolic spot from which the conflict's first shots were fired. Second in importance only to New Orleans as a rebel port, the city's immense harbor fostered the arrival and departure of blockade runners in great numbers. Despite a naval blockade and attempts to take the city from the sea, Charleston remained firmly in Confederate hands. Some Northern newspapers referred to it as "a festering sore in the side of the republic," and others used only printer's marks to indicate applicable adjectives.

After Port Royal and Hilton Head in the Carolinas were taken by Federal forces in November 1861, Union army and navy commanders practically drooled at the prospect of adding Charleston to their list of coastal captures. Since warships were judged incapable of reducing the city and its fortresses, men in high places began thinking and talking about a land-based assault in order "to punish that city by all the rigors of war."[103]

At Hilton Head, the Federal command center, officers pored over maps and charts. A chain of islands roughly south of Charleston was found to extend all the way to the harbor. Kiawah Island was listed as uninhabited, and maps showed no roads on it—but it appeared to have an unusually wide and level beach. Troops landing at this point would not be observed by Charleston's defenders; they could march along Kiawah and easily cross a channel that separated it from larger St. James Island. Only one village was known to be located on St. James— a cluster of summer homes known as Secessionville, believed to be well defended.

Union Gen. Henry W. Benham seems to have been the first to put a plan of attack in writing after having discussed it with Gen. David Hunter and the navy's Capt. Samuel F. DuPont, a flag officer of the blockading fleet. Benham submitted a detailed proposal that called for him to lead about 10,000 soldiers, ten cannon, and a small detachment of cavalry against Charleston. Kiawah Island would not be needed, he urged; many troops could be put ashore "at the landing on John's Island." Other units could march 12 or 15 miles from their existing camps, cross the Stono River by pontoon bridges, and join those brought by water. Once troops gained control of James Island, immense Columbiad cannon could be hauled into position and used to shell Charleston. According to Benham's plan, ships of the blockading squadron could assist his men by "a fire of shot and shell" leveled at Confederate batteries on St. James Island.[104]

Gen. Isaac I. Stevens, commanding Federal installations not far from Charleston, was "utterly opposed" to the plan, but on June 7 he agreed

Though minor by comparison with Antietam and Gettysburg, the Battle of Seces-sionville was of great importance to Charleston and her residents.—SOUTH CAROLINA STATE ARCHIVES

to cooperate with Benham. He suggested "arrangements be made with the gunboats to open cross- fires," noting at the same time that it would be essential to have a clear system of signals. When the assault got under way, men from Connecticut, Pennsylvania, Michigan, Massachusetts, New York, New Hampshire, and Rhode Island moving against Rebel positions could be put in harm's way.[105]

Aboard the USS *Pawnee*, Commodore Percival Drayton fine-tuned plans for gunboats to operate in the Stono River. No U.S. Navy officer was more hated by residents of the region than Drayton. A Charleston native, he went North with his father in prewar years and joined the U.S. Navy some time before his brother, Thomas Drayton, donned a Confederate uniform. At the battle of Port Royal, Percival was aboard the USS *Pocahontas* when navy guns silenced defending fortresses commanded by his brother.

As the movement against Charleston took final shape, the Union member of this pair of brothers ordered both the the USS *Ellen* from her Hilton Head base and the USS *E. B. Hale* into the Stono River. Formerly a side-wheel ferry, the *Ellen* carried two 32-pounders and two 30-pounder Parrott rifles. The *E. B. Hale,* a 220-ton screw steamer, had about the same fire power—four guns total, all 32-pounders. Aboard, gunners were eager to put all of their weapons to use.[106]

When Benham's troops reached Secessionville at first light on June 16, they whooped with delight on finding they faced just 500 Rebels under the command of Col. T. G. Lamar. Officers in blue were dismayed, however, when seven artillery pieces opened fire on them. Befuddled, Benham ignored the marshes abounding in the region and ordered a brigade to charge the Secessionville works in line of battle— an impossible movement because the area's solid ground was no more than 200 yards wide. Their configuration forced soldiers to move very close to one another; as a result many of them became confused "and the battle line became a tangled mess" in which the 46th New York, 28th Massachusetts, and 7th Connecticut were soon intertwined.[107]

On the Stono, both gunboats opened fire as planned. Soon after, 2,000 members of the South Carolina militia came to the aid of Secessionville's defenders. Then "shells from the gunboats a mile away began to land short, among the charging Federals." Drayton, estimating that the vessels threw about 100 shells, noted that "some of them came much nearer our own men than those of the enemy, as would be very likely to happen from the very vague and unintelligible directions telegraphed to us." In another report penned one day later, the naval officer stressed that "it was not a very easy thing to know when to fire

Commodore Percival Drayton was born and reared in Charleston, but fought for the Union.—U.S. NAVAL HISTORY INSTITUTE

with our own troops supposed to be mixed up with those of the enemy, particularly as the signal officer on board [the *Ellen*] could not get into communication with our people."

Aboard the *E. B. Hale,* Lt. James H. Gillis noted that after having fired only nine rounds from his Parrott guns, Lt. Melancthon B. Woolsey of the *Ellen* signaled for him "to come within hail." As soon as communication was established, Gillis was warned that "the shells from his guns were stripping and the pieces were falling around" men in blue on their sister ship. Gillis moved his vessel to a spot well away from the *Ellen* and there delivered "8 15-second shells plus 6 solid balls"; seeing that troops were being withdrawn, he then stopped using his big guns.[108]

By the time the gunboats ceased their fire, the pushover that was expected at Secessionville had turned into a debacle. Confederate Secretary of War Judah P. Benjamin reported 667 Federal casualties, a total close to DuPont's on-the-spot estimate of "a loss of killed, wounded, and missing approaching 700."[109]

Angry subordinates joined in castigating Benham, accusing him of having staged the contest without orders. He repeatedly produced evidence that Hunter had given specific orders, and he blamed his superior for the Federal failure. Hunter responded by relieving him and making a formal report to Washington. The dispute was referred to Judge Advocate General Joseph Holt, who collected many pages of evidence and concurred in the revocation of Benham's commission. A friend of the former general appealed to President Lincoln, who canceled the revocation and restored the loser at Secessionville to his former rank.[110]

Months of controversy and reams of paper were devoted to the question of Benham's role in the Federal defeat; a few lines penned by Drayton and Gillis constituted the only recorded admissions of gross negligence on the part of U.S. naval personnel. The Confederate victory brought formal Thanks of Congress to Col. Thomas G. Lamar "and the officers and men engaged in the gallant and successful defense of Secessionville." In Washington, nary a written word pointed out that during the struggle, friendly fire hit members of the crew of the *Ellen* as well as dozens or scores of soldiers in blue.[111]

14

"For God's Sake, Stop!"

Malvern Hill, Virginia—July 1, 1862

Beginning on June 25, 1862, the Army of the Potomac and the Army of Northern Virginia slugged one another for a solid week. Their clash at Oak Grove, King's School House, and the Orchard cost Federals about 600 casualties and Rebels about 400. The following day the two forces met at Mechanicsville, where Confederate casualties numbered about 1,000—the Federals about 400. At Gaines's Mill on June 27 and 28, nearly 7,000 men in blue were lost, and Confederate regiments left the field with about 8,000 gone from their ranks.

Fought almost simultaneously with Gaines's Mill, at Garnett's and Golding's Farms fewer than 900 casualties were suffered, with Lee's army again suffering slightly more than McClellan's. At Savage's Station and Allen's Farm on June 29, it was a different story. There, nearly 2,000 men were killed, wounded, or missing at the end of the day. Exhausted after six days of continuous fighting and their ranks depleted by about 20,000 men, both Robert E. Lee and George McClellan briefly leaned toward belief that there might be a lull in the action.[112]

Lee, however, quickly dismissed the idea of pulling away from the enemy. Aware that numerous stragglers and wagon trains of the Army of the Potomac had gathered nearby on top of a small hill, he received from his subordinates a series of reports convincing him that the strategic spot could be easily taken. In Confederate hands this hill would be a major barrier to McClellan's progress toward the James River, about two miles to the south.

Named for an old plantation, Malvern Hill was located about 14 miles south southeast of Richmond, McClellan's primary target during the entire Peninsula Campaign. After Lee and McClellan fought for it on

As Confederates charged, gunners of this Federal battery deliberately fired over two battle lines manned by their comrades.—ALFRED R. WAUD, LIBRARY OF CONGRESS

July 1, the red brick Malvern house, built in the eighteenth century, was converted into a hospital into which "two hundred and fifty wounded Yankees in all conditions of horrible mutilation" were crowded. There, more than 160,000 Rebels and Federals—in nearly equal numbers—fought during most of the day and well into the night.[113]

Malvern Hill rose only about 150 feet. Before the fight, Lee may not have realized that the Federal 5th Corps, commanded by Gen. Fitz John Porter, was already established on top of it. Clearly, he did not know on the night of June 30 that Gen. Henry J. Hunt was already at work arranging an estimated 100 guns along the slope of the eminence. For his part, Hunt was confident that no infantry, however well-disciplined and eager to fight, could face his batteries—or the 150 other guns he was holding on his flanks and in reserve.[114]

Looking up at Malvern Hill, Lee had to place his faith in some tried-and-tested subordinates, all old U.S. Army "regulars": Gens. Thomas J. "Stonewall" Jackson, James Longstreet, John Bankhead Magruder, and Ambrose Powell Hill. Lee was not as familiar with some of the other commanders he would have to count on, such as William Mahone, a tavern-keeper's son, Virginia Military Institute graduate, and former railroad president; or Lewis Armistead, an old army regular who still had many good friends in Union uniform. Armistead had tough Mexican War experience, but had worn Confederate general's stars for just 90 days.

Though he was a mere brigade commander, Armistead carried the outcome of the Malvern Hill fight in his hands. His men were to signal the final rush on the hill's Union positions; the child-simple plan called for Armistead's troops to shriek the Rebel Yell as loudly as possible, then race uphill on the double. Everyone else was to follow them. For it to work, however, everyone needed to be in their proper positions.

When their scheme was hatched, neither Lee nor Armistead knew Stonewall Jackson had been delayed by having to march his men around a sizable swamp, or that Magruder and his troops had taken the wrong road across the battlefield and had had to retrace their steps to show up in the expected position.

The reason for the Confederates' elementary ploy was that Hunt's Federal artillery had been in action since one o'clock that afternoon. Among the 14 Rebel brigades slated to run at his guns, there was already much confusion since Union cannon smoke was so heavy that no Rebel could make out visual commands.

When they charged about 3:30 P.M.—without artillery support of their own—many Southern soldiers faltered. In the face of Hunt's fire,

Fighting at Malvern Hill was so furious that some survivors called it "murder" rather than "war."—HISTORY OF THE CIVIL WAR IN AMERICA

they looked for low spots on the ground where they could take shelter until nightfall. As an example of the Yankee guns' ferocity, just one of the Union cannon raining shells on the Rebels let go 1,392 rounds during the course of the fight. Those Rebels who escaped artillery fire had to deal with Federal sharpshooters; deployed in larger numbers than in some other engagements, these experts took their time and dropped a man with nearly every shot.

Most commanders did not let the blizzard of lead stop them. Rebel Col. John B. Gordon raced toward the Federal guns along with his men, then endured a bizarre hit when Yankee shell fragments tore off his pistol, canteen, and his coat without hurting him. Magruder, late to the dance, showed up where he was expected after Armistead's men had already taken off uphill. Though he had lost 10,000 of his troops on the march to the hill—they kept wandering in for hours—Magruder sent the 5,000 he did have with him up the hill in a valiant, doomed second assault.

Concurring with modern military analysts who call the Malvern Hill charge one of Lee's most tragic mistakes, Rebel campaign veteran Gen. Daniel H. Hill summed up the bloody event in a single sentence: "It was not war; it was murder."

Hill, whose verdict was based on the slaughter of Rebels, probably had no idea that both forces suffered casualties from friendly fire during the afternoon and early evening. In the Union's Army of the Potomac, gunners atop Malvern Hill fired artillery over their own battle lines, even when such lines were close to the enemy. This practice, common on both sides, rested on four assumptions: that no ammunition was defective; that every battery had been informed of the precise location of its target; that officers and men seldom wondered whether their guns were set at the proper elevation; and that men working the guns never cut a fuse too short.

Thousands of troops were probably hit by their own artillery as a result of these palpably false assumptions. But in the heat of battle it was nearly always difficult or impossible to make note of such occurrences.

In the case of naval gunners who took part in the fray at Malvern Hill, the story is markedly different. Gen. George B. McClellan, who used the USS *Galena* as his headquarters during the last battle of the Seven Days, had secured the full cooperation of the U.S. Navy. Under the command of Commodore John Rodgers, a number of river steamers and vessels from the North Atlantic Blockading Squadron were sent up the James River from Newport News to anchorages below Malvern Hill. About 600 Federal wounded were dispatched to City Point aboard the steamer *Stepping Stones* on June 30, and the *Spaulding* brought a

During a period of intense fighting, a member of the U.S. Signal Service sent a message asking soldiers in blue to stop firing.—Harper's Weekly

shipload of badly needed supplies on July 1. Incomplete records indicate Rodgers's little flotilla of armed vessels included at least the *Monitor*-modeled *Galena* and the USS *Mahaska*, *Aristook*, and *Port Royal*. The *Galena* carried four 9-inch Dahlgren guns and two 100-pounder Parrott rifles; the smaller *Mahaska* had only one 100-pounder Parrott, one 9-inch rifle and four 24-pounder howitzers. The howitzers, however, were not suitable for use on targets more than two miles away. Though the *Aristook* carried two 24-pounders, one 11-inch Dahlgren, and one 20-pounder Parrott, there is no certainty that it took part in the battle.[115]

Some time after 3 P.M., gunners aboard the *Galena* and the *Mahaska* began firing at Rebels they could not see. Under the leadership of Albert J. Myer, tragic situations like that at Hatteras Inlet seldom prevailed. Signal officers in both the army and naval services had mastered a system of communication by use of flags. Hence, a signal corpsman, straddling the comb of the roof of a farmhouse, was in touch with naval signal officers stationed on mast-tops of vessels. By means of the "wigwag" system that had come into general use, naval gunners were told what elevations and fuse lengths to use.[116]

Maj. Albert J. Myer, serving as chief signal officer of the Army of the Potomac, filed a detailed report of the action. Despite his low rank, Myer headed the entire U.S. Signal Corps. Had he been in an artillery or cavalry or infantry unit, he might not have had the temerity to report: "The fire of the Navy covered the left of our army. It was turned upon our enemy, more than 2 miles distant from the ships in the woods and invisible from the vessel, with precision. It was not the fault of naval officers or men that *one or two of the shells struck in our own ranks.* The guns had been trained in obedience to signal messages closer and closer to our lines, until the *variations usual in such long flights of the shell caused the accident."* [117]

Gen. Fitz John Porter, who later endured one of the longest courts-martial in military history, seems to have paid little attention to unwritten codes that governed what a commander might or might not report. Writing for *Century* magazine, he said of Malvern Hill's Federal friendly fire: "Almost at the crisis of the battle . . . the gunboats on the James River opened their fire with the good intent of aiding us, but either mistook our batteries at the Malvern House for those of the enemy, or were unable to throw their projectiles beyond us. All their shot landed in or close by [Col. Robert O.] Tyler's battery [of the 1st Connecticut Heavy Artillery], *killing and wounding a few of his men."*

The accuracy of this summary was challenged by a Rebel newspaper correspondent who told readers that "one of the largest of the shells thrown by the gunboats exploded with the most fatal consequences to the Yankees, killing seven men instantly." [118]

Porter credited quick action by members of the signal corps with putting a stop to this slaughter. According to him, the message, "'For God's sake, stop firing' promptly relieved us from further damage and the demoralization of 'a fire in the rear.'" This may be the only instance of Civil War friendly fire that was independently reported by officers of two separate Federal services. Though the currently used label does not appear in the *Official Records,* Porter's after-the-fact terminology comes close to "friendly fire." [119]

As though the accounts of Myer and Porter were not enough to put Malvern Hill into a class by itself, two other generals admitted "fire in the rear"—this time from Confederates. In a rare departure from conventional reports devoted largely to troop movements and accomplishments, Ambrose R. Wright of Confederate Gen. Benjamin Huger's division wrote, "[with] night setting in, it was difficult to distinguish friend from foe. *Several of our own command were killed by our own friends,* who had come up on our immediate left, and who commenced firing long before they came within range of the enemy. This firing upon us from our friends, together with the increasing darkness, made our position peculiarly hazardous. . . . The fire was terrific now beyond anything I had ever witnessed—indeed, the hideous shrieking of shells through the dusky gloom of closing night, the whizzing of bullets, the loud and incessant roll of artillery and small-arms, were enough to make the stoutest heart quail.

. . . Detachments were ordered to search for water and administer to our poor wounded men, whose piercing cries rent the air in every direction. Soon the enemy were seen with lanterns busily engaged in moving their killed and wounded, and friend and foe mingled on that gloomy night in administering to the wants of wounded and dying comrades." Additional details were provided by a lieutenant in the 12th Virginia, which was in Mahone's command.[120]

Meanwhile, Union Gen. Paul J. Semmes, who called the struggle the battle of Crew's Farm, on July 4 penned an account of his action. He and his men did not get moving until they received orders from Magruder late in the afternoon. Some time after nightfall they charged 150 yards in the face of withering artillery fire from two batteries. It looked as though they might reach the enemy position "when, unfortunately, the right of our line was fired into from the rear by troops of other brigades of our own army." Fire from both the enemy and friends was too much; the Confederate line wavered, then broke, and its members sought "partial shelter behind a number of farm-houses not more than 60 yards from the enemy's guns." Details of troop movements suggest that this was not the incident to which Wright briefly alluded.[121]

In other chaotic struggles, "fire in the rear" is known to have cut down comrades even more frequently than at Malvern Hill. But Malvern Hill stands alone in one respect; officials acknowledged that artillery and muskets thinned the ranks of their users. In no other Civil War battle is this problem mentioned in separate accounts by four distinguished officers.

Though field artillery was puny compared with giant mortars, these highly mobile pieces helped determine the outcome at Malvern Hill.—HARPER'S HISTORY OF THE GREAT REBELLION

15

Six Times in One Day

Baton Rouge, Louisiana—August 5, 1862

When he saw that Baton Rouge might be vulnerable, Confederate Gen. Earl Van Dorn ordered troops to move against the town. Aided by the ram *Arkansas*, he was confident 6,000 men in gray could meet and defeat any Federal force in the region. Rebel Gen. John C. Breckinridge, leading the expedition, heartily agreed. Neither commander knew that the 2,500 soldiers in blue they would face would be supported by the USS *Essex, Katahdin, Cayuga, Sumter,* and *Kineo*.[122]

Having forced his men to move at top speed, the advance guard of the Breckinridge expedition reached the outskirts of Baton Rouge before daylight, August 5, 1862.

Confident that no foes had yet entered the region, Confederate scouts were careless. Hence, men in gray were astonished to become victims of "a terrible misadventure" as dawn began to break. From a field of sugar cane, there came a terrific blast of small-arms fire whose casualties included Gen. Ben Hardin Helm, the husband of Mary Todd Lincoln's half-sister. Helm's horse bolted and fell into a ditch, smashing one of the general's legs. He eventually recovered, only to be killed on another battlefield. Capt. Willis S. Roberts of the 4th Kentucky was one of the most seriously wounded victims of the small-arms fire. But Breckinridge's expedition was set back when the guerrillas' fire caused draft horses to bolt; wrecking gun carriages and caissons of a Kentucky battery. The guerrillas' explanation for their behavior was that they did not know friends had arrived; in the darkness they mistook the Rebels for Federals.[123]

Regarded as a very bad omen, the 4:30 A.M. incident of friendly fire proved to be simply a beginning. Lt. Col. Thomas Shields had led men

Vice President of the United States John C. Breckinridge of Kentucky resigned his office in order to become a Confederate general.—Dictionary of American Portraits

of the 30th Louisiana to a strategic spot on a plank road that linked Baton Rouge with Clinton. There he surprised and routed the 14th Maine Regiment, then advanced on the Federal camp under cover of artillery fire. Withdrawing to a junction with the Bayou Sara road, elated Rebels waited for reinforcements they could see approaching from a distance. "In this new position," Shields reported, "we were unfortunately taken for the enemy and fired upon." He waved the potentially deadly incident aside as unimportant and did not report any casualties from it.[124]

Officers of this regiment tried to exercise extreme caution, emphasizing that their green troops had never been under fire. By noon, weary Confederates were falling out from the blistering heat. At least one comrade in another unit experienced what was then called sun stroke. While advancing on the Federals' second line, men among whom their own shells had fallen earlier got a frantic signal commanding them to halt. At this juncture, according to Col. J. W. Robertson, who was in command of the 1st Brigade, "An officer approached from the right and stated that friends were exposed to our fire." Men of the 30th Louisiana immediately ceased firing, and no record is extant concerning the number of casualties—if any—inflicted during the third Rebel incident of friendly fire at Baton Rouge.[125]

Federal troops debarking from transports at Baton Rouge.—Harper's History of the Great Rebellion

Across the way, Cpl. G. W. Porter of the 4th Wisconsin wrote a brief but telling account of the misadventure suffered by his Union regiment that day. He estimated the enemy to number about 8,000 and wrote that after more than two hours of conventional fighting a fierce melee took place. About the time that the 21st Indiana won glory by repulsing a Rebel charge, Porter was ordered to take the first platoon of his company and skirmish on the extreme left in order to prevent a surprise on the Federal flank. He wrote, "I took a position one mile outside the old picket-lines, in true Yankee style—behind stumps and trees. The rebels did not think it safe to honor us with a

*The death on the battlefield of Gen. Thomas Williams so overshadowed "minor matters" that no official report included mention of friendly fire.—*National Archives

shot. We were fired at, however, by some of our pickets, who were driven in from the front, they mistaking us for rebels. They also reported us to the gunboat *Essex* as rebels, and she commenced shelling our lines. In riding in to correct the mistake, a shell burst directly behind me; my horse taking fright, I broke my stirrup and fell heavily to the ground, and consequently was obliged to retire from the field."[126]

Fitz John Porter, investigating the goings-on at Baton Rouge, seems to have been ignorant of the results of the two separate cases of friendly fire in which men of a single platoon were the targets. He may have overlooked these events because of the overshadowing battlefield death of Union Gen. Thomas Williams.

A third Federal incident took place just before the corporal and his platoon moved to an exposed position at the left. It became one of the most fiercely debated of all such "misadventures." Before the struggle for Baton Rouge reached its height, an estimated 40 percent of the men who made up the 7th Vermont Regiment broke and ran from the field. Contrasting sharply with ragged units from Vermont, the 21st Indiana put ten full companies, largely seasoned veterans, on the field of battle. These men were so awkwardly exposed that their captain, James Grimsley, said many "took cover behind trees and such things as would shield them." At a critical moment, "the Seventh Vermont opened a fire

Mary Todd Lincoln was overwhelmed with grief when she learned that Confederate Ben Hardin Helm had been killed when his horse went out of control.— NICOLAY & HAY, ABRAHAM LINCOLN

in the direction of all engaged, which killed many of our own men outright and wounded several more."[127]

The performance of the Vermonters infuriated Gen. Williams; while Confederates were charging, the general ordered the unit to support the 21st Indiana. When no one obeyed him, Williams waved his sword and ordered the Vermonters to use their pieces. The three volleys that resulted from his angry order, say some analysts, fell directly on their comrades from Indiana.[128]

Williams died shortly afterward from a direct hit. Regardless of whether he was responsible for actions of the Vermont regiment or whether its members acted on their own, their bullets directed into the 21st Indiana's ranks resulted in a formal court of inquiry.

Supplies for Federal troops were unloaded at Baton Rouge from the steamer North Star *(rear), over the deck of the river steamer* Iberville.—WILLIAM R. WAUD, THE SOLDIER IN OUR CIVIL WAR

During lengthy hearings it was established that the only fire delivered that day by the 7th Vermont was on their comrades. Yet members of the court took note of the fact that when the incident occurred, the battlefield was so dense with fog and smoke that "it was quite impossible to distinguish friend from foe." Even more, fire from a federal battery was endangering the regiment to such an extent that a Lt. Col. Fullam had been sent to try to stop it.

Writing for the court, Col. Henry C. Deming of the 12th Connecticut said the 7th Vermont did fire into the 21st Indiana, but had no way of knowing where the Hoosiers were.

William D. Porter cut such a dashing figure that some of his subordinates made unsuccessful attempts to grow facial hair like his.—HARPER'S HISTORY OF THE GREAT REBELLION

As a consequence of this testimony, the colors of the regiment, taken from it after the battle, were restored, the court ruling that no orders communicated to the Vermont unit were disobeyed.[129]

Union navy gunboats were used at Baton Rouge. During the early morning they took no part in the struggle, for fear of hitting their own troops. Later, however, the USS *Essex, Katahdin, Cayuga, Sumter,* and *Kineo* played significant roles in this Federal victory. Cmdr. W. D. Porter of the *Essex* claimed to have stopped the CSS *Arkansas,* steaming to the support of Confederate forces at Baton Rouge. He was severely castigated by Rear Adm. David G. Farragut, however, since evidence indicated that Rebel seamen scuttled their vessel after its engines broke down. There was no Union credit to be taken for the demise of the *Arkansas.*[130]

Interestingly, the end of the *Arkansas* was considered in Washington and Richmond to be of far more significance than the one-day struggle at Baton Rouge. As a result, except for a mild rebuke to men of the 7th Vermont, no retribution seems to have taken place inside the Union army for a day punctuated with one incident of friendly fire after another.

CHAPTER

16

Cover-Up

South Mountain, Maryland—September 14, 1862

aving decided to invade the North, Robert E. Lee planned for his Army of Northern Virginia to move east toward Frederick, Maryland. Rebels marching there had to use one or both roads going around Maryland's South Mountain. Toward the north of the eminence, the National Road snaked its way through Turner's Gap. About a mile south of that point, the Old Sharpsburg Road meandered through Fox's Gap. Both points were vital because of the terrain. Referring to South Mountain as though the gaps cut it into a number of distinct segments, a newspaper correspondent who was present for the battle that took place wrote, "The mountains in the vicinity of the Gap are steep and rugged, and rendered difficult to ascend unless by the ordinary thoroughfares, on account of numerous ledges and loose rocks which afford no permanent foothold. From base to top they are covered with a thick wood, thereby giving protection to the party in possession and making the progress of the attacking force doubly hazardous."[131]

Gen. George B. McClellan moved his Federal army toward South Mountain from the east in two wings. His object was to get in front of Lee's forces. A clash was inevitable; it would involve about 30,000 men on each side.[132]

Believing that enemy forces were scattered over the mountain, Federals marched steadily toward Turner's Gap. Defended at first by only a single brigade under Rebel Gen. Daniel H. Hill, the spot was vital to both armies. Union Gen. Ambrose Burnside, the Federal field commander, arrived about noon. He sent cavalry under Gen. Alfred Pleasanton against Hill's brigade. Then, quickly sensing the importance of Fox's Gap, he directed Gen. Jesse L. Reno to lead his 9th Corps

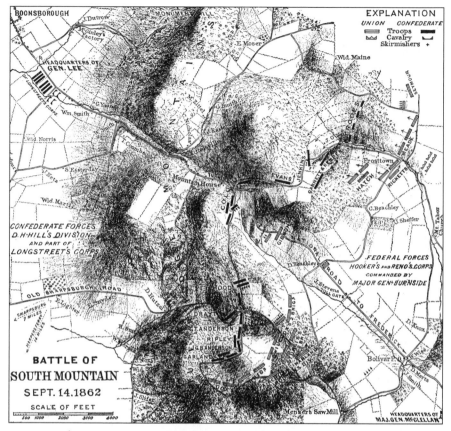

Positions of troops at Fox's and Turner's Gaps, South Mountain.—BATTLES AND LEADERS

against it. That vital spot was not far north of pastureland; there, moving large units was easy.[133]

Gen. Jacob D. Cox, moving through open and relatively level land just south of Fox's Gap, charged the Rebels shortly after 9 A.M. A brigade of North Carolinians took the brunt of this early assault, and Rebel Gen. Samuel Garland soon became the first general officer to die in this campaign. After a period in which weary men on both sides rested on their arms, chaotic fighting broke out again and continued for much of the day. Two future presidents took part in it—Lt. Col. Rutherford B. Hayes and William McKinley of the 23rd Ohio. Fresh Rebel brigades arrived at intervals, led by Gens. John B. Hood, Robert E. Rodes, Roswell S. Ripley, and David R. Jones.[134]

According to Gordon, fierce fighting started again about 2 P.M. Union Gen. Joseph Hooker's corps of Federals reached the region a bit later and about 4 P.M. set out to take Turner's Gap. It took six hours of fierce fighting for this objective to be achieved. Meanwhile, chaos continued at Fox's Gap. There units were often intertwined in woods so dense that one Confederate brigade charged in the wrong direction when ordered to lead a counterattack.[135]

Because it was a prelude to the better-remembered Battle of Antietam, the fight for South Mountain is often treated as having been part of that battle. John M. Priest, author of one of the most detailed and incisive studies of Antietam, long ago devoted special attention to South Mountain. Letters and diaries of survivors, plus detailed reports provided a full generation after the battle, gave Priest documented evidence that the death of a Federal general by friendly fire at South Mountain was deliberately covered up.[136]

By late afternoon, Fox's Gap (sometimes incorrectly listed as Turner's) was being defended by a small Rebel brigade led by Gen. Thomas Drayton. At least six Federal regiments launched attacks that lasted until just before sundown. In this engagement, says Priest, two instances of friendly fire took place. Both were caused by inexperienced, excited men of the 9th New Hampshire Regiment, who "fired into their own troops by mistake." In one case, the victims were men of the 51st

Federals commanded by Gen. John Hatch rushed Rebels who were shielded by stone outcroppings.—NATIONAL ARCHIVES

Pennsylvania; in another, they were members of the 46th New York. Col. Joseph Gerhardt of the 46th reported that when their comrades fired at them, many of his men saved their lives by "throwing themselves down on the ground."[137]

Every account of the battle, however brief, mentions that Gen. Jesse L. Reno died on the field. Born in Wheeling, Virginia (now West Virginia), Reno moved to Pennsylvania with his parents in boyhood and from the Keystone State won an appointment to West Point. He fought with distinction at the Mexican War battles of Cerro Gordo and Chapultepec and was in command of the Leavenworth, Kansas, arsenal when the Civil War began.

This rare portrait of Jesse Reno was actually made after his death.—OLD SOUTH MOUNTAIN INN, BOONSBORO, MARYLAND

Men who knew him in Kansas lauded his unflinching loyalty to the Union, despite despite seeing officers and men under his command throw in their lot with secessionists.[138]

Soon becoming a brigadier, Reno fought under Burnside in North Carolina and was later placed in command of the 9th Corps—the organization he led at Fox's Gap. As night was falling on South Mountain, Union Col. Edward Ferro's men from Massachusetts, New York, and Pennsylvania were sent to relieve front-line units who had been fighting for five or six hours. Accompanied by a pair of orderlies, Reno rode behind the brigade. The soldiers of his 35th Massachusetts Regiment were, however, as green as those of the 9th New Hampshire; they were scattered across wooded ravines and seem to have had no idea of the enemy's positions.[139]

According to massive evidence accumulated by Priest, "a rookie from the 35th Massachusetts" mistook for Rebels the group that included his general. The rookie trained his musket on riders he could barely see. His action triggered a small volley by some of his comrades. One of their bullets hit Reno and lodged in his heart or so close to it that he immediately began to reel in the saddle. Orderly Martin Ficken helped him dismount, then ran for help and soon encountered the general's other orderly, Alexander Wood. Gen. Orlando Willcox encountered the party as Reno, partly covered by a blanket, was being taken toward medical corpsmen. To his comrade, the dying general gasped, "I am killed. Shot by our own men." [140]

Because officers feared the reactions of Reno's men if they should learn how their leader died, orderlies were told to say nothing. They kept their silence for 21 years before Wood decided that it was time to tell the truth about the most notable casualty of South Mountain. [141]

Federal troops who passed through Fox's Gap in the aftermath of the struggle were often shown "the spot at which Reno fell." Later, he was buried in the nation's capital, and a monument was erected close to the place where the man who was "greatly lamented by the entire [Federal] army" died. As a lasting tribute to him, his name was given to a Nevada hamlet that in time became notable as a gambling mecca. [142]

Since the case of Gen. Albert S. Johnston's fatal wound at Shiloh at the hands of his own men remains conjectural, Reno is regarded as the first general officer positively known to have died as a result of friendly fire.

CHAPTER

17

Record Maker

Antietam, aka Sharpsburg, Maryland—September 17, 1862

The Battle of Antietam stands as the deadliest one-day fight in U.S. history. More Americans were killed and wounded on that Maryland battlefield than in all the Mexican War. And before opposing Gens. Robert E. Lee and George McClellan stopped the combat on September 17, 1862, approximately 5 percent of the casualties— 1,150 men—were attributed to friendly fire.

Cannoneers began exchanging shells about 5 A.M., despite the fact that fog completely blanketed some of their targets. This artillery action by batteries commanded by Gens. Joseph Hooker and Stonewall Jackson created an earth-shaking roar. According to one Federal soldier, the thunder of the guns was frequently punctuated by distinct whistles and shrieks from flying shells. He was awed by the stupendous cacophony.

The entire day was one ghastly marvel. Incidents of friendly fire followed so closely on one another that accounts such as this one require that the acts be numbered. But the grimy haze of battle sets the scene for all of them. By 6:30 A.M. most of the fog had burned off, only to be replaced by dense black-powder smoke, sulphurous clouds sometimes so thick that enemies and friends became invisible inside them. Regiments could often identify an enemy's position only by looking for one or two of his flags waving over these walls of smoke.

(1) Soon after infantry moved into action, officers and men of New York and Wisconsin became "fused into a common mass, in the frantic struggle to shoot fast." Two companies of the 6th Wisconsin had been sent to protect the flank of advancing Federals. Men who did not know about this movement or forgot about it in the heat of battle soon turned their muskets and rifles on fellow volunteers from the

Antietam Creek (center) flowed directly through this battlefield, on which the number of ghastly casualties is beyond belief.—

Badger State. Lt. Col. Theodore B. Gates reported this deadly incident as a case of "some disorder."

(2) Moments after it occurred the same Wisconsin regiment took casualties from Federal artillery. Gunners of Battery B, 4th U.S. Artillery, fired so feverishly they overlooked a color-bearer and "almost blew away what was left of the 6th Wisconsin." Lt. Col. Edward S. Bragg, whose account included no language pointing to friendly fire, commended the regiment for holding the ground all night and reported only 90 casualties.[143]

(3) On a portion of the battlefield called the Cornfield, shortly after 8 A.M., Col. Alfred H. Colquitt's Rebel brigade clashed with regiments from Ohio. In an open segment of the field, the 3rd Wisconsin and the 27th Indiana advanced through dense smoke and held their fire for fear of hitting Ohioans. Members of the 5th, 7th, and 66th Ohio were less cautious, delivering everything they had to Rebels. Their wildest shots took out members of the 10th Maine, huddled on another portion of the battleground called the East Woods.[144]

(4) Since the battlefield's West Woods were also shrouded in blue smoke, Federal gunners in batteries located far across Antietam Creek could only guess at their targets. This lack of visibility, however, did not slow the pace of their firing. As a result, their 20-pounder shells landed close to or among men of the 15th Massachusetts.

In the fury and chaos of this day, everything that could go wrong with big guns seemed to do so. One of the batteries commanded by Union Gen. John Gibbon lost so many men that untrained members of the infantry were ordered to take their place. Men who did not know how to elevate a gun moved screws almost aimlessly. Though warned not to do so, these inexperienced troops often rammed double charges of canister into their six-pound pieces. "Double-shooting" light guns often caused them to explode a the breach, killing or injuring crew members. But during at least one dramatic moment, an amateur gunner shone. A 14-year-old bugler was permitted to fire a Federal piece—action for which he was awarded the Medal of Honor.[145]

(5) Gen. Joseph B. Kershaw's men in gray charged the East Woods about 9:30 A.M. Desperate to stop them, Federal gunners became angry when green troops from Pennsylvania's 125th persisted in running between their guns and the enemy. Hastily jotted notes by a veteran artillerist indicate that when it proved impossible to restrain these Union infantrymen, Federals behind the guns opened with everything they had. As a result, noted the diarist, "Some of our men were no doubt killed, but it was better to sacrifice a few of their lives than to allow the rebels to capture the battery."[146]

(6) About 15 minutes after those heedless men from the Keystone State were blown to pieces, some members of Col. Napoleon Dana's 59th New York who were in battle for the first time fired with no idea where their bullets were going. Gen. Edwin V. "Bull" Sumner saw some of their fire hitting the backs of the 15th Massachusetts. Storming to the spot and releasing a torrent of words at least as blue as the smoke that covered the field, he put a halt to the incident. Despite Sumner's inter-

Federal forces crossing Antietam Creek at a ford just north of Sharpsburg.—AUTHOR'S PRIVATE COLLECTION

Gen. Edwin Sumner, who entered the U.S. Army in 1819, was the oldest corps commander in blue.—LIBRARY OF CONGRESS

vention, enemy and friendly fire cost the Bay State regiment 344 casualties on that dreadful day. Uncounted scores of these losses resulted from the New Yorkers' fire.[147]

(7) Minutes later, Rebels had their turn at "fire in the rear." A group of them had massed at the barn of a homestead called the Roulette Farm. There men tried to pick off enemies to their east and northwest. Suddenly a volley hit them from a distance of about 300 yards. They were unable to decide which side had targeted them. But historian Priest later concluded that the shots came from a Confederate brigade led by Colquitt of the 6th Georgia and from survivors of a brigade that had lost its leader at South Mountain a few days earlier, troops of the late Gen. Samuel Garland.[148]

(8) Around 10 A.M., the 14th Connecticut stopped moving as it neared the end of the Cornfield—a spot on a homestead called the Mumma Farm, the scene of one incident of mass killing after another. Unable to see their enemies during a period of "indescribable confusion," these fellows—in combat for the first time—managed to pick off some of Union Gen. Max Weber's men. Even if the field had been clear of smoke and trees, men of the 14th would not have known that numerous Rebels wore blue uniforms that day, suits they seized at Harpers Ferry on their march into Maryland.[149]

(9) A Federal battery, probably belonging to the 1st Corps, found a splendid niche in the North Woods, from which it fired into the West Woods. "Wounded men on both sides staggered blindly between the trees." But from their vantage point, these gunners could not see that great numbers of Federals were racing from the field, dodging heavy fire from Rebel troops who were dogging their heels.

Glimpses of the color gray were enough to trigger action in these Union gunners; "double-shotted rounds of canister were loaded and fired, point-blank, into the hoards of fleeing Federals and pursuing Confederates."[150]

(10) After 4 P.M. three Ohio regiments led by Col. Hugh Ewing moved into a new position in the Cornfield. In doing so, they passed spots held by members of the 16th Connecticut and by Capt. Asa M. Cook's battery of light artillery from Massachusetts. Before the men from Connecticut stopped moving, a cascade of bullets stripped many corn stalks of their leaves. Mistakenly thinking they knew the origin of the fire, the men from Connecticut pumped slugs into the rear ranks of the 12th, 23rd, and 30th Ohio.

(11) Probably disconcerted at being unable to identify the source of the gunfire, cannoneers in Cook's battery "also cut into" ranks of the Buckeye State regiments.[151]

At this point, identifying these accidents by number no longer serves a purpose. During that awful day numerous cases of mistaken identity included those in which the principals ranged from Union Gen. Joseph Mansfield to the colonel of the 4th Rhode Island, who mistook the 1st South Carolina for an ally and ordered a cease-fire. Thousands at Antietam had never been in battle; half of the 7,200 effectives in McClellan's 12th Corps belonged in this category. Four of the ten regiments led by Union Gen. William H. French had received no training; the experience of his three other regiments was limited to garrison duty. Gunners on both sides repeatedly shot just over the heads of their comrades. Many Confederates entered battle wearing Federal uniforms, and at least one commander—Union Gen. Thomas F. Meagher—was believed so drunk that some claim he could hardly sit in his saddle.[152]

Eighteen generals—nine on each side—became casualties in just over 12 hours, six of them killed on the spot or mortally wounded. According to a careful modern tabulation, 2,108 men in blue died, 9,541 were wounded, and 753 were missing when rolls were called. Lee's Army of Northern Virginia lost fewer men—1,546 dead on the field. But 7,752 of his men were wounded and 1,018 were missing when the shooting stopped. All things considered, it is remarkable that only 11 recorded cases of friendly fire took place during the chaotic day in which 22,710 casualties were counted.[153]

Despite the horrifying statistics, in almost every other respect Antietam was a draw. In Washington, the chief executive firmly believed he was an instrument of providence "who did not so much control events as [was] controlled by them." Since Lincoln regarded signs and omens as being of great importance, he eagerly seized on Antietam's role in thwarting Lee's plan to invade the Northern states. Consequently, he

On the heels of Antietam, Lincoln's political actions evoked this British cartoon showing the Rebel Ajax defying "Uncle Sam Jupiter" who was in the act of throwing the "thunderbolt of emancipation."—LONDON FUN

believed Antietam constituted a great victory.

The slavery issue was always on Lincoln's mind. He toyed with the notion of emancipation long before putting it into effect. Late in July 1862 he drafted a rough outline for a plan under which slave owners might be offered compensation for their losses. Then he began to consider the use of black soldiers. Seizing upon Antietam as an omen, eight days after "the signal victory in Maryland," Lincoln presented to his cabinet a "Preliminary Emancipation Proclamation." When finally issued in slightly revised form, this proved to be the most effective single military move made by the commander in chief.[154]

While Lincoln was debating whether or not to hang emancipation upon McClellan's "victory in Maryland," he faced another issue that could not be avoided. Initial enthusiasm for voluntary military service had waned. Jefferson Davis had succeeded in putting Confederate conscription into effect almost three months before Antietam. Now, Lincoln and his intimate advisors decided it was time for the Union to act. One week after Antietam, the writ of habeas corpus was suspended in the case of persons accused of discouraging enlistment. On the following day, a "Proclamation of the Act to Suppress Insurrection" was issued.

Since Antietam was the hook upon which were hung the first steps toward emancipation and toward a system of drafting men for Union military service, its political impact was tremendous. But no significant military or civilian spokesman in the North or the South decried the record-making number of instances of friendly fire that occurred during that fearful struggle.[155]

Part II
BRIEF BITES

The death of Gen. Felix Zollicoffer at Mill Springs.—THE SOLDIER IN OUR CIVIL WAR

18

Twenty-Five Misadventures

1861–1862

D uring 1861 and 1862 a variety of deadly or potentially deadly incidents took place. Accounts of these events often rest on a single diary, letter, or newspaper dispatch. Even when given incidental mention in an official report, such "misadventures" may be so glossed over that details are lacking. Twenty-five brief summaries of such incidents are presented in chronological order here.

September 8, 1861—Washington: On Monday April 16, 1861, Abraham Lincoln responded to the surrender of Fort Sumter by calling for 75,000 volunteers to serve in Union military forces for 90 days. Though the response was overwhelming and immediate, it took time to get men to the capital. "Why don't they come?" Lincoln reputedly agonized as he waited.

Fearful that secessionists would attack and overrun the capital, he launched a massive program aimed at its defense. Many who responded to his call were assigned to guard Washington for weeks or months. In Yonkers, New York, a body locally known as the Motzart Regiment completed its organization on June 27 and on July 4 left the state headed for the capital. Instead of being attached to the army with which Gen. Irvin McDowell was expected to destroy the Confederate military machine, the regiment remained on guard duty until August 4.

Nearly a month before the unit known as the 40th New York was attached to the brigade headed by Col. Oliver O. Howard, Sgt. William J. Wills of Company A was assigned to picket duty. While watching for the enemy on the night of September 8, he was shot and killed by one of his own men. His death from carelessness so impressed newspaper illustrator James E. Taylor that he executed a painting depicting the accident. In it the dead picket is shown lying in the edge of a woods under a full moon.[1]

October 10, 1861—Paducah, Kentucky: Because of its strategic location on the Ohio River, during the summer of 1861 Union strategists made Paducah, Kentucky, a military target. Reporting to Gen. John C. Frémont from Cairo, Illinois, Gen. John A. McClernand stated that two gunboats and two steamers loaded with Federal soldiers left that town for Paducah on the morning of October 5.

Commanded by Gen. U. S. Grant, this expeditionary force steamed 50 miles upriver and on the morning of October 6 encountered no resistance in Paducah, despite the fact that many secessionist flags flew over the city. Grant was told that these emblems were displayed "in expectation of greeting the arrival of a Southern Army, said to be 16 miles off, 3,800 strong."[2]

Grant put Gen. E. A. Paine in command of the occupied city, left both gunboats and one steamer there, and at noon headed downriver to Cairo. The men in blue he left behind were strictly forbidden to "insult citizens or engage in plundering private property." Paine was told to scatter pickets around the community at distances of four or five miles. In the event of an attack by the enemy, he was authorized to seize all money in the city's banks.

On the morning of October 10, a post manned by a few men of a cavalry regiment was attacked by a band of Rebels. Two of the six pickets were mortally wounded and two were taken prisoner. Yet the most serious damage occurred within the ranks of the enemy. Having divided their force into two separate bodies, "in the excitement [of the attack] Confederates fired into each other." After having suffered an unknown number of casualties as a result of each band of Rebels having mistaken the other for Union cavalry, "they then fled" the place.[3]

Late October, 1861—Northern Virginia: When organization of Pennsylvania's 5th Cavalry Regiment was announced in July 1861, recruitment was going slowly in Philadelphia. The second largest city of the United States had few veteran horsemen. Before its ranks could be filled, the brand-new regiment went to Washington on August 22 and like many others was assigned to guard duty.

Still unattached to the Army of the Potomac, its first military mission came in late October. Accompanied by an infantry force with no more training and experience than it had received, the 5th Cavalry rode into northern Virginia to scout the region. In the darkness, comrades were mistaken for enemies, shots rang out, and "men were killed." This turn of events shook up the riders from the Keystone State so badly that "the

5th panicked, broke, and ran in great disorder, trampling three unfortunate foot soldiers" in the process.[4]

November 7, 1861—Belmont, Missouri: During the late summer of 1861, Confederates established a sizable military camp on the west bank of the Mississippi River. The installation was commanded by Leonidas Polk—the only Civil War character who was simultaneously an Episcopal bishop and a Confederate general. Since Polk's forces were located at a point opposite Confederate batteries in Columbus, Kentucky, there was danger that Union traffic on the Mississippi River might be halted there. Eager to keep the waterway open, Washington launched a joint army-navy expedition. As was customary, the warships and steamers as well as the regiments were all under an army officer's command. On this expedition the officer was U. S. Grant. As on other joint expeditions, he had to deal with an awkward command structure and a poor system of communication between soldiers and sailors.

Grant also had to deal with Col. John A. Logan. An attorney and an ambitious Democratic congressman from Illinois with virtually no military experience, Logan had just received his officer's commission in mid-September, but he expected and lobbied for a position that would bring him as close as possible to a full partnership with Grant on this punitive expedition to Polk's Belmont camp. When victory came—as Logan bet it surely would—this green colonel wanted at least equal credit for securing it.

Grant's strategy for this minor campaign was relatively simple. With navy cooperation, he wanted to transport men south from Illinois on a few vessels, land them a short distance from the Rebel's Belmont tents, then lure the Confederates into a fight in the open. This last detail was prudent because the big Rebel cannon across the river at Columbus were correctly judged capable of hitting "every foot of Belmont."

From the beginning, everything that could go wrong with Grant's operation did so. On November 7, Logan's 31st Illinois Regiment landed on the Missouri side of the Mississippi, and the congressman led it toward the Confederate camp adjacent to Belmont. These men helped bring on the battle about 10:30 A.M., but then many of their muzzle-loading rifles burst. It seems that a number of Logan's raw infantrymen nervously rammed several charges into their weapons before they fired. As for the colonel himself, he was so anxious to show himself brave in the face of the enemy that he had three horses shot out from under him during the course of the fight. Then Grant's horse was shot out from under him. And then he could not find Col. Napoleon Buford and his men of the 17th Illinois.

The night before, en route to Belmont, Buford had had his men bivouac on the Mississippi's Island No. 10. Rising in time to move on to Belmont, he appeared to have accepted bad information from a civilian guide and marched his troops to a place called Bird's Point, not the expected battlefield. Realizing the error, he did march his men to Belmont, arrived there hours late, and then let his men wander through the empty Confederate tents.

Out on the river, gunners aboard the navy's USS *Lexington* and *Tyler* did not know the Rebels had been lured from the scene to take on Grant's and Logan's infantry. When they saw movement in the Belmont camp, they assumed the men in it were enemy troops. They pumped shells into the campground, hitting Buford's Illinois infantry.

Two days later the *Tyler*'s Commodore Henry Walke wrote up a report, noting that both gunboats "fired several shells into Camp Belmont." He did not note the time when the shelling took place.

If any Illinois casualties were incurred during this instance of ship-to-shore friendly fire, they were attributed to Rebel artillery and not correctly reported. No officer in hold of his senses willingly admitted he walked his troops into the path of friendly fire, or that loyal naval gunners had turned their big pieces on friendly troops.[5]

Mid-November 1861—The Virginia Peninsula: Tennessee's *Memphis Appeal* of November 16, 1861, summarized an early "misadventure." It reported that, "Two parties of rebel troops met on the peninsula, above Newport News, Va., and mistook each other for enemies. Brisk firing at once commenced, and a number on each side were killed and wounded before the mistake was found out. Among the killed was Major Bailey [no given name] of Mobile."

December 20, 1861—Dranesville, Virginia: The Federal Army of the Potomac being encamped near Washington and Rebel Gen. Joseph E. Johnston's gray-clad troops lying at Centreville, these forces were only about 25 miles apart. Forage for their thousands of horses began to run low almost simultaneously and both forces turned to the lush fields of Fairfax County for an essential supply.

With four infantry regiments, about 150 cavalrymen, and an artillery battery Gen. J. E. B. Stuart was confident he could protect and fill almost all of Johnston's hay wagons. He had no idea Union Gen. E. O. C. Ord would be found gathering fodder near Dranesville at the head of a force of approximately the same size. Men in blue started loading wagons about noon and worked without interruption for an hour. Men of Stuart's advance guard were then spotted, and many of the Yankees took to the woods for cover.

Small Rebel detachments set out to drive their widely scattered foes into the open, but soon the two groups became so intermingled that it was difficult for Ord and Stuart to distinguish their own troops. In this swirling confusion, neophytes who made up the Cofederate 1st Kentucky Regiment stumbled on what seemed to be a substantial body of Yankees. Firing from within a dense stand of pines without having seen their targets clearly, 800 men from the Blue Grass State unknowlingly mowed down many men of the Confederate 6th South Carolina Regiment.

Reporting on the struggle to Union Gen. Seth Williams, Gen. George A. McCall noted that an unidentified captured colonel told him "no intercourse between different [Rebel] regiments was ever allowed." If that comment was correct when the war was still young, lack of back-and-forth fraternization between the two regiments helps account for the fashion in which one fired on the other.

Though Stuart acknowledged a serious mistake was made, he discounted its importance by saying "only a few casualties occurred in consequence." Significantly, however, the 63 casualties in the ranks of the 6th South Carolina came to more than those in any of the four other Rebel units that took part in the fight.[6]

January 19, 1862—Mill Springs, Kentucky: During this battle, Union Col. Speed S. Fry, of the loyal 4th Kentucky became enraged when Rebels fired on his men in blue from a ravine. With formations having fallen apart and confusion mounting, he left his regiment briefly in order to survey action nearby. On his way back to the regiment he met

Sgt. William J. Wills was shot and killed by his own picket guard.—JAMES E. TAYLOR

a rider without insignia who ordered Fry to tell his men to lay their muskets aside. "You are firing on our own men!" he cried.

Fry obeyed the order seconds before a Confederate officer dashed up to the unidentified rider, yelled that the enemy were all around, and fired at Fry. That shot missed, so Fry pulled out his revolver and fired at the man who had ordered him to cease friendly fire. Some of Fry's men took the unknown officer as a target and emptied their weapons in his direction. Possibly (but not positively) hit first by Fry and then by two or three of Fry's men, Confederate Gen. Felix Zollicoffer was dead before he toppled from his horse. At least one widely used reference book does not describe the Rebel's effort to save himself by using the concept of friendly fire; it reports simply that the general officer died on the field "under peculiar circumstances."[7]

March 14, 1862—New Berne, North Carolina: Shouting with joy at word of early Federal victories in coastal North Carolina, 11,000 troops under Gen. Ambrose Burnside learned from him on March 11, 1862, that they had been selected to take part in a great offensive movement involving 13 warships.

Army and navy movements proceeded as envisioned, and on March 13 troops disembarked from vessels in Slocomb's Creek, about 15 miles from New Berne, North Carolina. They crowed with delight at the prospect of defeating Rebels led by Gen. Lawrence O. Branch, a former newspaper editor with no miliary experience.[8]

Aboard the USS *Philadelphia*, flagship of his flotilla, Capt. Stephen C. Rowan directed men on the warships to begin shelling woods that abutted the Neuse River at 8:30 A.M. on March 14. Despite thick fog, Federal units led by Gens. John G. Foster, John G. Parke, and Jesse Reno swarmed ashore in the dim light. With some of their troops still aboard transports, Yankees began moving toward New Berne about 11:30 A.M. Following Rowan's instructions, naval gunners threw shells into the woods just ahead of their own troops moving on New Berne.

Of the four Rebel fortifications that defended the city, Fort Thompson and its 12 guns was the most formidable. Rowan counted on silencing these and other Confederate guns from the decks of the flagship and its companions, *Stars and Stripes, Louisiana, Hetzel, Delaware, Valley City, Underwriter, Hunchback, Southfield, Henry Brinker,* and *Lockwood.*[9]

Close to their objective, five regiments led by Foster met withering fire from Rebels. Then, complicating things, shells from Union gunboats dropped on them. Rowan knew exactly what was happening. He reported to Louis M. Goldsborough that his gunners threw "5, 10, and 15 second shells inshore" as rapidly as possible. Aware that he ran the

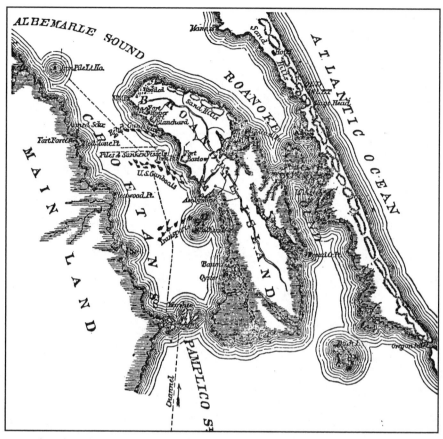

Roanoke Island lay between two bodies of water close to the Atlantic Ocean.—
OFFICIAL RECORDS, 9

risk of killing many Union infantrymen, Goldsborough concluded he would "continue until the general sent word" to stop. He explained this decision, writing, "I know the persuasive effect of a 9-inch, and thought it better to kill a Union man or two than to lose the effect of my moral suasion. The effect was terrible—large pines were cut down like so many twigs."[10]

Regardless of the reasoning by which the career naval officer tried to justify his slaughter of Federal soldiers, the plan was effective. New Berne soon fell, and on the following day Rowan rode over the battle-ground with Burnside. Though he knew he was responsible for some of the wounded in Federal ranks, the veteran seaman described them as "objects of pity, poor creatures, lying exposed and begging a little water." He added that naval batteries were "the boast of the day," but he commended soldiers for their role in "the most gallant affair of the Army that has occurred during the war."[11]

Civil War annals include no other casual admission by a high-ranking naval officer that men of his own forces were knowingly shelled.

February 8, 1862—Roanoke Island, North Carolina: Moving against Rebels entrenched on North Carolina's Roanoke Island, regiments commanded by Gen. John G. Foster were slowed but not stopped by swamps. Their objective was Fort Bartow, located on the western tip of the island. Since the installation had been hammered by big naval guns, resistance collapsed when the 21st Massachusetts reached the enemy's parapet.

Soon several additional Federal units converged on the place. Dense fog and the smoke from muskets and at least 30 cannon almost "shut out the light of day." Apparently unaware that many Rebels had fled, Foster ordered the 9th New York Zouaves, the 51st New York, and the 9th New Jersey to charge the fort. As they began trotting forward, part of the 10th Connecticut emerged from a swamp and fired at the nearly empty Confederate installation. Startled, attackers turned to see the source of the fire. Gray overcoats on the Connecticut men turned them into targets for the Zouaves; some were dropped in their tracks, and others fled.

Near Fort Donelson, a wild shot from a sister warship nearly took out the USS Carondelet.—LESLIE'S HISTORY OF THE CIVIL WAR

Spooked by unexpected events, Col. Edward Ferrero of that regiment had earlier ordered his men to lie down "in order to avoid the shower of bullets from our own troops." His precaution was useless; men of the 9th New Jersey and the 9th New York fired into his ranks. Col. H. C. Lee of the 27th Massachusetts found himself in a similar dilemma. Taking cover in a woods, he found the 23rd Massachusetts "partly in front" of him and the 10th Connecticut "partially covering our rear and firing." Rebel leaders attributed many of the Union casualties to "the indiscriminate firing of the 9th New York when it first panicked; Ferrero blamed both regiments.[12]

Gruff Gen. John G. Foster planned many Federal attacks in North Carolina and carefully covered up blunders made by his artillery units.—LIBRARY OF CONGRESS

New Berne, North Carolina: Charles F. Johnson, a survivor of the battle, added one more account that might have been material for a comic opera, had it not been so serious. Along with other members of New York's Hawkins Zouaves, Johnson took aim at men he could barely see. When his musket failed to fire, he hastily reprimed, then was stopped by an officer who cried: "For God's sake—we are shooting our own men!" Casualties from these two affairs in a single day were not reported by red-faced Yankee officers.[13]

February 15, 1862—Fort Donelson, Tennessee: At Fort Donelson on Tennessee's Cumberland River, Gen. U. S. Grant acquired the nickname "Unconditional Surrender" and started on his road to leadership. All of the credit for the victory went to him, despite the fact that gunboats under his command there also played a significant role in the action.

Flag officer Andrew H. Foote headed a flotilla of four ironclads plus two wooden gunboats; all were small enough to use the Cumberland River on which the Rebel installation was located. Foote's report of the action went not to Secretary of the Navy Gideon Welles but to Gen. Henry W. Halleck, who was then in command of the Army of the West.[14]

Aboard the USS *Carondelet* alone, gunners threw 139 shells into Donelson; fuse length on these shells varied from 10 to 15 seconds. Only 35 Rebel missiles hit the vessel, but in one of his reports Commodore Henry Walke noted "an 8-inch shell, apparently from our flotilla, burst astern of us." Probably fired from the wooden USS *Tyler*, fragments of this shell penetrated the casemate of the *Carondelet*. Had the gunners who fired it from a sister vessel been off target a few more inches, the ironclad might have gone to the bottom of the river and the outcome of the battle might have been different.[15]

February 21, 1862—Valverde, New Mexico: Not far from the extreme edge of the western theater, a greatly outnumbered band of Rebels clashed with U.S. infantry regulars at Valverde, New Mexico. Rebel Gen. Henry H. Sibley's force, made up almost entirely of men who had fought Indians and Mexicans, took cover behind a huge sand ridge described as being nearly parallel to the Rio Grande.

When Sibley's estimated 1,000 whooping Rebels rushed a Union battery commanded by Capt. Alexander McRae, gunners in blue panicked and headed for the opposite side of the river. Following orders, Capt. R. S. C. Lord of the 1st U.S. Cavalry attempted to charge the position now held by the enemy. Federals never made it to their objective. According to Union Gen. E. R. S. Canby's summary of the day, Lord and his men "became exposed to the fire of our own men as well as that of the enemy." Lord's men swerved to the left and fell back.

Castigated in newspaper accounts that made no mention of fire from his comrades, Lord demanded and got a hearing before a formal court of inquiry and was exonerated.[16]

May 1862—Northern Virginia: Elijah V. "Lige" White, member of a prosperous Maryland family, tried without success to get a Confederate commission. This failure occurred despite the fact that when he fought at Balls Bluff as a volunteer; Col. W. H. Jennifer lavished extravagant praise upon him. Eager to fight, the 29-year-old White raised a company of partisan rangers for service in Virginia's Loudon County. He was sometimes called "Captain," but he appears to have had the informal rank of lieutenant colonel. He and his men once attacked a party of 23 Federals; they killed 1, wounded 6, and captured 15.

After a number of successful raids, he led his small band on a scouting expedition west of Virginia's Massanutten Ridge. While returning to his base, he and his men were mistaken for Yankees by civilians and became the targets of gunfire. Hit near the right eye, White may have been the only Rebel who became a casualty from friendly fire by Virginians who managed to stay home rather than don uniforms. The colorful exploits of "Lige" White are mentioned in 11 volumes of the *Official Records.*[17]

June 1, 1862—Mt. Carmel, Virginia: At the head of a sizable force, Stonewall Jackson made contact with Gen. Irvin McDowell's advance guard about a dozen miles from Strasburg, Virginia. With expected Rebel reinforcments led by Gen. John H. Winder having not yet arrived from Harpers Ferry, Jackson warned subordinate Gen. Richard S. Ewell to proceed with caution. But impatient to fight, Ewell had Gen. Richard Taylor send his brigade to the enemy's front, at right angles, in a bid to force Federals to move.

Lt. Col. Elijah V. "Lige" White was noted for his horsemanship and his bravery under fire.—MUSEUM OF THE CONFEDERACY

Ewell said he was "sick of this fiddling about!" and chortled that such action might "stir up" the enemy. Evidently he did not take time to notify his skirmishers of plans, however. As soon as forces led by Taylor reached the Union flank, they came under heavy enfilading fire from Ewell's skirmishers.[18]

May 26, 1862—Corinth, Mississippi: Gen. Henry W. Halleck having decided to move on Corinth, he was taken aback by news learned from a surgeon who had Confederate friends. According to this unidentified informant, the town was held by about 20,000 Rebels. As a result of this incorrect information, Union Gens. William T. Sherman, John Pope, Don C. Buell, and their forces were ordered to advance on Corinth with great caution.

The generals' troops soon made contact with Confederate forces. Sherman reported at one point that pickets conversed with one another instead of using their weapons. With Federal lines drawing closer and closer to Corinth, pickets and skirmishers were thrown out in every direction. Men from the Buckeye State were stationed at the extreme left of Buell's picket lines, very close to Pope's line of skirmishers. At daybreak on a fateful morning, men of the regiment heard someone voice an exceptionally loud challenge. This was followed immediately by a musket report.

Within minutes, it was found that the unidentified general officer of the day of Pope's force had been inspecting picket lines. Approaching the position held by the 14th Ohio, he was challenged loudly, but continued to advance. As a result, witness Frank J. Jones wrote, the common incident in which a picket was killed by one of his comrades was here reversed. Pope's subordinate "paid the penalty of his rashness by receiving a mortal wound at the hands of this faithful soldier" who was on picket duty.[19]

June 7, 1862—South River, Virginia: Near Mt. Carmel, at a point not far from Port Republic, Virginia, opposing forces converged on a bridge over the South River. Rival batteries exchanged a few shots, then two of the three guns manned by Federals were pulled from the field. Shortly, men in blue brought a lone piece of field artillery into clear view of Gen. Stonewall Jackson, who had been observing the action. Turning to Capt. W. T. Pogue, Jackson barked the order, "Fire on that gun!"

"General!" protested the captain, "Those are our own men!"

Heedless of the warning, Jackson repeated his four-word order.

Pogue shook his head and refused to fire. He quickly explained that Jackson's target was a new Confederate battery headed by Capt. E. C. Carrington. Uniforms of Carrington's men, he blurted hastily "almost exactly resemble those of the enemy." Though the gun in dispute was trained on a party of Confederates, friendly fire did not take place. On Jackson's command Pogue's hastily aimed Parrott rifle was discharged at the one battery belonging to Federal forces. Pogue may have been the only subordinate of Jackson who briefly refused an order without being punished.[20]

June 29, 1862—Savage's Station, Virginia: After four days of continuous fighting at different points on the Virginia peninsula, the Federal Army of the Potomac was in retreat. This movement meant a huge Union supply depot on the Richmond & York River Railroad, would be abandoned. Federals, following standard practice, torched the supplies to keep them out of enemy hands. Jubilant at the sight of huge columns of black smoke, Lee dispatched ailing John Magruder and his men toward the fire at Savage's Station.

Before Magruder reached his objective, he learned that his 14,000 men were likely to be confronted by 26,000 under the command of Gen. Edwin V. Sumner. An appeal for Rebel reinforcements brought only two brigades; one of them was constituted of South Carolinians under the command of Gen. Joseph B. Kershaw; the other was made up of Georgians led by Gen. Paul J. Semmes. Magruder hoped to make up for his manpower shortage by using an immense rifled Brooke cannon

At Prairie Grove, artist J. T. Cox made an on-the-spot sketch of Iowa Volunteers who charged a Confederate battery.—HARPER'S WEEKLY

mounted on a railroad flatcar. First of the railroad batteries, it threw 32-pounder shells into Union ranks and created great confusion.

With the sun already having dropped below the horizon, a brisk skirmish broke out in a patch of dense woods. Unable to distinguish between friend and foe, but continuing to fire rapidly, some of Semmes's men shot into the ranks of other soldiers in gray.

A letter from a participant informed the folks back home that in this incident, "The only damage done was that of killing our Major's horse." Whether or not that verdict was accurate is an open question; men in blue suffered 919 casualties during the struggle, and Confederate ranks were thinned by 444 men, many of whom were hit just as the field became enveloped in pitch darkness.[21]

July 7, 1862—Coastal South Carolina: Acting Master D. F. Mosman of the USS *Flag* set out from the Charleston area on the morning of July 7 to find and capture a blockade runner believed to be at anchor in Bull's Bay. Pursuing what he thought to be the enemy, Mosman encountered a vessel that showed no flag. When his men were about to board her, the target vessel "broke out the national colors" and was identified as the U.S. bark *Restless*—inside Bull's Bay on the same mission as the *Flag.*

Soon the *Flag* lookout spotted their target stranded on a mud bank. On boarding her, the *Flag's* men found that the vessel was provided with an English flag and was transporting about a dozen "iron cans of some kind of acid, weighting about 700 or 800 pounds each." Mosman dumped the acid into the bay and put his men to work trying to float the blockade runner in order to tow her into port.

Mosman's work was suddenly and rudely interrupted about noon. According to his report sent to Commander James H. Strong, the newly arrived USS *Blunt* "commenced shelling us and continued to do so for nearly an hour." Mercifully, the *Blunt*'s gunners were inexperienced. They evidently did not know how to cut fuses to the proper length. Every shot sent at the *Flag* fell short. Had they not done so, Mosman confessed, "she would have driven us out."[22]

December 7, 1862—Prairie Grove, Arkansas: With northwest Arkansas and much of Indian Territory firmly in Confederate hands, Union leaders were eager for battle. Confederate Gen. Thomas C. Hindman, believed to have more than 11,000 men and at least a score of cannon, was responsible for defending the region. But Union Gen. James Blunt—commanding the force closest to Hindman—knew himself to be outnumbered and outgunned by the Confederates, and he was reluctant to start a battle. An urgent plea for help induced two divisions under Gen. Francis J. Herron to march 110 miles from Wilson's Creek, Missouri, in three days and make contact with Blunt near a heavily wooded hill known as Prairie Grove. There they hoped to face down Hindman.

An artillery duel with Confederates began there at 9:30 A.M. on December 7. It was merely a prelude to a little-known but significant struggle that lasted all day and saw Col. William D. Blocher's battery of light guns overrun by men from Iowa and Wisconsin. Before the contest was decided, a comparatively insignificant and an especially dreadful pair of "misadventures" were attached to the record of men in blue. The first of these was chalked up to Blunt, who arrived on the field late and promptly opened with his artillery—mistakenly shelling a position held by Herron's men.[23]

Later that afternoon some Union gunners began using hot shot in a desperate bid to start brush fires that might force the foe to retreat. Since they were being guided by signalmen and could not see their targets, the gunners failed to realize that some of their balls fell into an apple orchard where wounded men in blue had found havens of a sort on mounds of straw. When the straw began to blaze, an onlooker wrote, "Two hundred human bodies lay half consumed in one vast sepulchre, and in every position of mutilated and horrible contortion. A large drove of [half-wild] hogs, attracted doubtless by the scent of roasting flesh, came greedily into the apple trees and gorged themselves upon the unholy banquet."[24]

September 13, 1862—Frederick, Maryland: Chasing Robert E. Lee's army, Federal troops began converging on Frederick, Maryland, during the second week of September 1862. An advance cavalry unit arrived on Friday, February 12, and clashed violently with gray-clad troops who already occupied part of the town.

During a see-saw struggle within the community, a few Federal guns were unlimbered. According to a soldier there, a counterattack by Rebels forced McClellan's troopers into chaotic flight. An officer reported that while this action was in progress, a careless rider in blue dashed between the gunner and his piece, "thus drawing the friction primer and discharging the gun full in the faces of our men, killing two outright and wounding half a dozen."

Viewed against the backdrop of "bloody Antietam," it is no wonder that this incident was not described in an official report of a Federal officer.[25]

September 19, 1862—Sheperdstown, West Virginia: Though opposing armies were in shambles after Antietam, a few more clashes took place before that week ended. One centered on Boteler's Ford on the Potomac River. Confederate cavalry reached the steep bluffs overlooking the river's south bank early on Friday. Artillery followed close behind and remained there throughout the day guarding the ford during the retreat of Lee's infantry toward nearby Martinsburg.

The Rebel batteries were gone by the time the 118th Pennsylvania crossed this ford near Shepherdstown well before 7 A.M. September 19. Led by Col. Charles E. Prevost, these men had been at Antietam, but did not fight there since they were held in reserve by McClellan. Regulars of the U.S. Army, led by Gen. George Sykes, crossed the ford soon after the Pennsylvanians, but quickly clashed with an overwhelmingly superior Rebel force and withdrew back across the Potomac.

By the time that men under Prevost had formed a line of battle, they could see the dust raised by Gen. A. P. Hill's 5,000 approaching Confederates. Too stubborn to pull out without a direct order from a superior, Prevost soon found about half of the British Enfield rifles carried by his men were defective and would not fire. Then Prevost was wounded. Lt. Col. James Gwyn assumed command and within half an hour was ordered to withdraw. His green troops scattered and ran for their lives. Some managed to scramble down the 75-foot cliff and take shelter in old lime kilns at its base.

There, the frightened Federals breathed a bit easier—for a few minutes. Across the river, a Union battery decided to shell Rebel forces and went into action so quickly that many of their fuses were cut too short.

As a result, Federal artillery rained fire on Pennsylvanians huddled together in cavelike holes close to the river.

Col. James Barnes, commander of the brigade that included the 118th, chose his words carefully and grimly, writing, "The batteries on the opposite side of the river having been brought into position, opened a heavy fire with good effect upon the enemy, though from the close proximity of the contending forces it was difficult for them to avoid some damage to our own troops. Some of their shot and shell struck in our rear, and some of the casualties of the day may be attributed to that source."[26]

In Washington, a glance at casualty returns showed that of the 362 suffered by Federal forces close to the hamlet of Sheperdstown and in several other minor clashes, 326 were in the brigade commanded by Barnes. He wrote not a word about inept gunners in blue who accounted for "some of them." Three batteries of the 5th U.S. Artillery were engaged at the Potomac River ford, but no commander admitted having fired into Pennsylvanians far below Confederate forces.[27]

October 8, 1862—Perryville, Kentucky: In a desperate bid to bring divided Kentucky fully into the Confederate fold, Gen. Braxton Bragg launched an invasion of the state late in August 1862. By October, Union Gen. Don Carlos Buell had brought 60,000 troops together at Louisville and was sure he was ready to meet and defeat Bragg. Many units from both forces—about 37,000 Federals and 16,000 Rebels—came together near Perryville on October 8.

Marked by an usually high casualty ratio of nearly one man in seven, the struggle was punctuated with instances of mistaken identity in which foes identified themselves as friends.

During the battle, believing some Confederate units were firing into one another, Gen. Leonidas Polk raced to stop the slaughter. Almost too late, he discovered the fire was coming from an Indiana regiment. Some authorities say he demanded and got an instant cease-fire from those men in blue. Other accounts say that on the spot he made prisoners of the Yankees whom he had thought to be Rebels firing upon their comrades.[28]

Col. Michael Gooding of the 22nd Indiana pulled a similar stunt before the hard-fought but indecisive struggle ended. During a time of utter confusion he wandered into enemy lines and was wounded and taken prisoner. Somehow he managed to deceive the commander of the Rebel force and gain time for his brigade to withdraw from a cross-fire.

After darkness fell on Perryville, Gen. St. John Lidell of the Confederate force mistook a Federal unit for one of his own because men in blue cried out, "Stop firing! You are killing your friends!" According to historian Shelby Foote, a similar cry was heard several times on this field when men on both sides gave anguished cries of "*Friends!* You are firing into friends!"[29]

Perryville is notable for having been the scene of a conspicuous example of "acoustic shadow," a natural phenomenon in which atmospheric conditions do not permit sound to travel. At Perryville, the roar of guns could not be heard at a short distance. According to one account, "the six-mile-long scene of action was compartmentalized, each sector being sealed off from the others as if by soundproof walls."

This strange battle that was punctuated by misperceived friendly fire included at least one real instance of it. Before the action began, Bragg sent a division under Gen. Jones M. Withers to intercept a corps commanded by Union Gen. Thomas L. Crittenden. By chance, men under Withers encountered the advance guard of Rebel Gen. E. Kirby Smith. Smith's men were wearing brand-new recently captured Federal uniforms, so both bodies of Confederates took the other for enemies. According to Maj. E. T. Sykes, their mutual mistake led these bands of Rebels to skirmish and fire upon one another with unknown consequences.[30]

December 13, 1862—Fredericksburg, Virginia: The bitter struggle of this date, one of many on which Fredericksburg's calendar dripped with blood, saw one erroneous and three genuine examples of friendly fire On the fog-shrouded battlefield about 9 A.M., Union Gen. John Gibbon deployed many of his men as skirmishers and charged with protecting the 2nd Maine Battery. The gunners, however, were given a frightful order; they must clear Gibbon's men by just one foot in order to do maximum damage to the enemy.

Capt. Edward D. Hall, commanding the Federal battery, received an urgent message asking him to elevate his guns. He honored this request, but his action came too late. "A shell or solid shot from his battery struck the cartridge box of one of the boys while he lay on his stomach." This victim of friendly fire, seriously injured in the hip, lingered for six days before succumbing to his wound. A comrade wrote, "It was bad enough to be killed or wounded by the enemy, but to be killed by our own guns excited a great deal of righteous indignation."

Hall, who acknowledged having fired over lines of his own infantry, expended 1,100 rounds of ammunition and had two men killed—but said nothing about havoc wreaked upon Federal skirmishers.[31]

Fredericksburg: About 11 A.M. a correspondent of the *Cincinnati Commercial* was heartened that Federal batteries on the left opened fire after a long period of inaction. His hope soon turned to dismay, however, and the reporter wrote that he "saw with horror that at least half the sells were bursting behind our own men, and that they were certainly killing more of them than the enemy."[32]

Fredericksburg: Rebel Gen. Maxcy Gregg made a mistake of another kind. When a band of yelling Yankees stormed onto the spot at which his 1st South Carolina Rifles were resting, Gregg, partly because of his deafness, thought they were friends instead of foes. He tried to prevent his men from "firing upon their comrades." But these men were actually their deadly enemies.[33]

Robert E. Lee is the authority for facts concerning the third instance of friendly fire on December 13. During the evening, men under Stonewall Jackson succeeded in pushing the Federal left back a considerable distance. Their foes retreated so rapidly that pursuing Rebels became greatly confused, and bodies of them fired into one another.[34]

December 16, 1861—Whitehall, North Carolina: Vastly superior Federal forces under Gen. James H. Ledlie, chief of artillery for Gen. John G. Foster, smashed Rebels at Whitehall, North Carolina, two weeks before 1861 ended. Col. Charles A. Heckman of the 9th New Jersey, in the thick of the fight, later reported that his men lay on the ground to avoid heavy fire from Confederate batteries. Refusing to give his commander the title that had been bestowed on him and describing this terrifying situation, he wrote, "To add to our discomfort, Colonel Ledlie of the Third New York artillery, from the bluff in our rear, opened (senselessly) several of his batteries with fuse shell, which bursting overhead, showered their fragments upon my men, wounding a number."[35]

With 18 months of fighting behind them, it would seem that leaders in both blue and gray would have to take the necessary steps to prevent additional instances of friendly fire. But they did not. Comrades continued to kill and maim comrades.

19

Friends Keep Killing Friends

1863

January 2, 1863—*Stones River, Tennessee:* Usually regarded as a drawn battle in which 35,000 men in gray were pitted against 42,000 in blue, at Stones River the horrendous casualty list of 24,000 came close to that of Antietam. During three days of carnage and maneuvers that began on December 31, 1862, battle veteran Sgt. Henry R. Freeman of the 74th Illinois recorded incidents of human interest and one of friendly fire.

As night fell after the second day of hard fighting, men from Illinois heard a wounded Rebel begging for help. Found close to the battery that he had helped serve and unable to walk, he was carried to the rear and given a drink of water. His only request was that his mother be informed of his end. Late in 1865, however, a letter sent to "Relatives of M. W. Wildy, Davis Creek Postoffice, Fayette County, Alabama," was never delivered because of its inadequate address.

Three Confederate flags and eleven cannon were captured during the evening in which Wildy was rescued by his foes. On the same night, an unidentified Federal infantryman managed to avoid wading the river around which the fighting swirled. As horses started to pull a battery across ice-cold water, this fellow jumped on one of the guns to ride it across. Capt. James H. Stokes of a light battery funded by the Chicago Board of Trade ordered him off. Clinging to his perch, the still-dry hitchhiker rode "his metal horse" until it reached the opposite bank, at which point he hopped off and dashed into the woods.

On the next morning Freeman's diary began: "To-day rain, rain, rain. No shelter, and rain all the time." When the sun came down after a day of light fighting, the conflict intensified. Men from Illinois drove a body

119

of Confederates from its position and then fell back. Freeman noted that once he and his comrades were in a spot that seemed beyond the reach of Confederate bullets, "The First Tennessee Union Regiment fired into some of our men by mistake."[36]

January 30, 1863—Kelly's Store, Virginia: Taking the offense against the Rebels, Federal forces under the command of Gen. John J. Peck prepared to march shortly after midnight on January 30. From their camp at a signal station near Suffolk, Virginia, they hit the road at 1 A.M. Union Gen. Michael Corcoran marched at their front. A native of Ireland, active in the New York City militia in prewar years, Corcoran had gained national fame as a distinguished prisoner of war following the First Battle of Bull Run.[37]

Most of the men in eight regiments, plus parts of three batteries, headed toward a meeting with Confederates led by of Gen. Roger A. Pryor. After a 16-mile march, about 3:30 A.M., the Federal advance

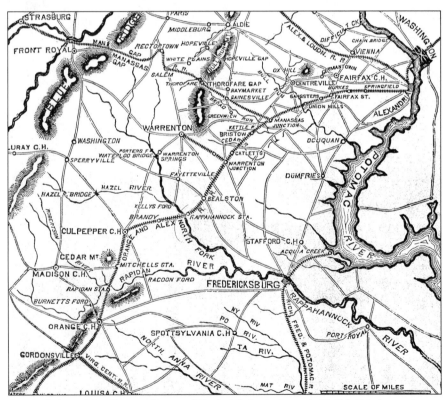

Located about 25 miles northwest of Fredericksburg (center), Kelly's Ford was an important spot at which to cross the north fork of the Rappahannock River.—
HARPER'S HISTORY OF THE GREAT REBELLION

encountered enemy pickets in a clump of trees near a spot called Deserted House, or Kelly's Store. Within ten minutes, artillery was deployed and a fight was under way. When Corcoran ordered his infantry to charge at 5:15 A.M., thick woods and a marsh forced his formations to disintegrate into a confused mass.

During seven hours of fighting, Corcoran's batteries fired 1,140 rounds of shot and shell—to little avail. When Rebels pulled out, leaving most of their 38 casualties on the field, an elated Corcoran claimed victory despite 133 casualties of his own.

According to a garbled newspaper report, some Union losses were occasioned by a predawn mishap. Two of Corcoran's com-

Irish-born Gen. Michael Corcoran led Federal forces toward Deserted House, Virginia.—AUTHOR'S PRIVATE COLLECTION

panies fired at one another instead of at the enemy, reputedly killing three soldiers in blue and wounding four others.[38]

March 17, 1863—Kelly's Ford, Virginia: Key Washington leaders and top Army of the Potomac brass were slow recognizing the importance of cavalry or ways to make good use of mounted troops. Soon after a cavalry corps was organized, the division led by Gen. W. W. Averill was sent to challenge Rebel horsemen, commanded by Gens. J. E. B. Stuart and Fitzhugh Lee, around Culpeper, Virginia.

The Federal advance guard reached Kelly's Ford, located on the north fork of the Rappahannock River, early on the morning of March 17, 1863. The Yanks found it defended by a only handful of Rebels who soon received reinforcements. It took members of Col. Alfred N. Duffie's 1st Rhode Island Cavalry fully an hour and a half to force their way across the rapid stream, after which Averill's entire force followed. After fighting most of the day with three-to-one odds in his favor, the Federal commander withdrew.

Averill lost only 78 men during the entire day, and the bulk of them were members of the 1st Rhode Island Cavalry. This unit suffered 41 casualties, all but one "ordinary results of battle." The extraordinary casualty was an unidentified lieutenant "partially decapitated by a solid shot fired by his own artillery."[39]

April 9, 1863—St. Helena Sound, South Carolina: During much of the siege of Charleston, Federal warships and gunboats were stationed at nearly every safe mooring. But only the bark USS *Kingfisher* was in St. Helena Sound. James Hutchinson and William Bailey, identified as "contrabands"—runaway slaves—were brought aboard the 97-man vessel on the morning of April 9. From Hutchinson, Acting Master J. C. Dutch learned that Rebel pickets on Edisto Island were reporting movements of gunboats and troops to Confederate headquarters.

The next day Dutch notified Rear Adm. Samuel F. DuPont of the South Atlantic Blockading Squadron that he regarded it as "a safe and easy matter to capture them." Arming 35 of his men with rifles, and allowing 10 contrabands to go along, Dutch and Swabs slipped quietly to "the estate of Mr. Whaley." There they captured nine members of the 3rd South Carolina Regiment "with their arms and accouterments."

One of Dutch's men, Noel Blakeman, filled in details that his leader seemed to deliberately omit. According to Blakeman, the Whaley residence was quietly surrounded, after which three officers and a contraband "walked up to the veranda and there saw the guard fast asleep." After slipping his musket away without awakening the fellow, they pushed their way into the main room of the house. A cry by someone in that room "caused our whole force surrounding the house to open fire, ignoring the fact that their own officers were within." This unplanned volley, said Blakeman, "did no harm" despite the fact that it could have taken the lives of one or more U.S. Navy officers.[40]

April 19, 1863—Carrion Crow Bayou, Louisiana: On the last day of 1862, Federal authorities created a new division in Gen. Nathaniel P. Banks's 19th Corps and put Gen. Cuvier Grover in command. He and his regiments spent the next few months prowling western Louisiana, living largely off the country and making occasional contact with small enemy forces. Grover's report concerning this period reveals his total disgust with his command: "On April 15 this brigade marched to New Iberia. The scenes of disorder and pillage on these two days' march were disgraceful to civilized warfare. . . . Negro women were ravished in the presence of white women and children. These disgusting scenes were due to the want of discipline in this army, and to the utter incompetency of regimental officers."

The night after having reached New Iberia "some soldiers got hold of Louisiana rum" and created great disorder. Heading for Vermilion

Bridge on April 17, a wagon train belonging to the enemy was seen, and 3 of its 30 wagons were captured. The following day the brigade reached a burned bridge, which gave the Federals an excuse to stop. The brigade's commander, Grover, then reported: "The following day the brigade marched to Carrion Crow Bayou. The pillage on this day took the form of shooting poultry on the open prairie. Stragglers from the front of the column fired to the rear in such a way as greatly to endanger the lives of the soldiers in rear of them."[41]

Samuel F. DuPont, long commander of the naval yard at Washington, was for a time at the head of the South Atlantic Blockading Squadron.—HARPER'S HISTORY OF THE GREAT REBELLION

Grover, a Maine native from a distinguished family and a West Point graduate, seemed deliberately vague about the events of April 19. Though he did not say so, this officer implied that his unruly stragglers shot at their comrades as casually as they stripped Rebel civilians of their valuables and killed birds on the prairie.[42]

April 19, 1863—Opelousas, Louisiana: During the first months of 1863, west Louisiana seemed like a playground for men in uniform who did not really want to be soldiers. Except for a skirmish at Indian Village on January 28, Col. Richard E. Holcomb's Unionist 1st Louisiana saw no combat. However, its batteries were used on occasion. This unit was temporarily attached to Gen. William Dwight's brigade in Gen. Grover's division.

Headed for Opelousas from Vermillion Bayou on April 19, "stragglers who were engaged in plundering" used their rifles freely. About 1 P.M., while the brigade was halted, shots fired by these fellows "came whistling" over Col. Holcomb and his men. One shot struck very close to a lieutenant. For this escapade, two soldiers were arrested, and Dwight ordered them shot. After a detail of "six men with loaded muskets" had been selected for the execution, Dwight changed his mind and let the culprits remain with the regiment, under guard.[43]

Gen. Alfred Napoleon Alexander Duffie, then a colonel, commanded a brigade at Kelly's Ford.—LIBRARY OF CONGRESS

May 2, 1863—Hazel Grove, near Chancellorsville, Virginia: Stonewall Jackson was mortally wounded by Confederates late on May 2 during the Battle of Chancellorsville. At nightfall on the battlefield, Federal Gen. Daniel E. Sickles and his men stumbled onto Rebels who may have come from nearby Catharine Furnace. This accidental encounter in underbrush and evergreen thickets, wrote historian Shelby Foote, "had some of the qualities of a nightmare too awful to be remembered except in unavoidable snatches."

The clash reflected the confusion and terror of a day that had cost the South one of its heroes and many common soldiers their lives. Groping through the dark and fearful of being trapped between segments of Lee's army, Sickles divided his command into two columns and directed them to march toward the nearest turnpike. Despite help from the light of a full moon, both bodies became lost, then bumped into Rebel units in such a way that the Federals seemed trapped within "one vast square of fire."

In this chaos, Federals shot wildly despite cries of "Don't fire! We're friends!" Nearby, men in blue commanded by Gen. Alpheus S. Williams added to the slaughter by firing on Sickles's units. When Sickles effected a withdrawal to Hazel Grove shortly before midnight, his two decimated divisions were reduced by hundreds of men.

Hearing a tremendous commotion and assuming that it signaled an advance by the enemy, Union Gen. Henry W. Slocum ordered 34 of his cannon to open fire. Alone among general officers whose troops were involved in the tragedy, he admitted that night's disaster involved pitting men in blue against fire from troops in both gray and blue uniforms. "I have no information as to the damage suffered by our troops from our own fire, but fear that our losses must have been severe," he confessed. Sickles, who did not report in detail about the melee, said that he lost 4,039 men "during the recent operations."[44]

May 17, 1863—Big Black River Bridge, Mississippi: In this war, streams called Black River were to be found in Louisiana, Missouri, North Carolina, and South Carolina. In Mississippi the pattern of nomenclature varied slightly. There it included the Big Black River. This stream became famous in Civil War history: The Vicksburg & Jackson Railroad, or Southern Mississippi, maintained a bridge over it outside Vicksburg. Falling back from the May 16, 1863, Battle of Champion's Hill, exhausted Rebels led by Gen. John C. Pemberton stopped at the railroad bridge and prepared to defend it from rifle pits that had been dug earlier. During their long night retreat, regiments and companies had become thoroughly disorganized.[45]

Before daylight on May 17, blue-clad troopers under Gens. John A. McClernand and Peter J. Osterhaus were spotted by lookouts. An artillery duel began. Before it ended, Union Gen. Andrew J. Smith and infantry joined the attacking force, and an all-out assault was planned. Desperate Confederates, knowing they were badly outnumbered, fought as long as they could before burning the bridge and retreating.[46]

Just before the structure was burned, Federal regiments raced over a barricade and captured one of Pemberton's guns. In the excitement of the moment, Pvt. James S. Adkins of the 33rd Illinois jumped on the loaded Rebel piece, flapped his arms, and crowed like a rooster. Having absolutely no knowledge of field artillery, he became curious at the sight of a lanyard and pulled it. The shell he fired barely missed men in other Federal units who were racing to the spot, so Adkins became the only casualty of the incident—slightly wounded by being hurled headlong into the gravel.[47]

June 26, 1863—Vicksburg, Mississippi: Subordinates, weary of the Siege of Vicksburg, got U. S. Grant's permission to erect a huge battery. With it, they hoped to batter Rebels into submission. Near the Union front held by Gen. William Dwight's troops, sappers worked at night to prepare the ground. They succeeded so well that the finished site was large enough to mount 17 heavy guns protected by a thick embrasure of cotton bales.

Shortly before 4 P.M. on the thirty-ninth day of the siege "the Great Cotton Bale Battery" went into action. It took just minutes for experienced officers to realize it was a mistake to put so many guns at one point: Cannon smoke nearly blinded the spotters and attracted the concentrated fire of Confederate batteries.

Even worse, from the standpoint of red-faced Federal officers, boiling clouds of smoke confused gunners aboard Union mortar boats on the Mississippi River. Earlier, these veterans and sailors in naval shore batteries prided themselves on firing for hours at two-minute intervals without missing a target. But this smoky afternoon, to the lasting chagrin of naval officer David G. Farragut, many of his gunners missed their marks and shelled front-line Union forces. According to one analyst, "the mortars caused more Union casualties on that one day than they did Confederate losses in the whole siege."[48]

June 28, 1863—Donaldsville, Louisiana: A significant Rebel force was reported to be in and around Donaldsville, Louisiana. Union troops and the warships *Tennessee, Winona, Princess Royal,* and *Monongahela* were sent against the village.

It was the last week of June 1863. Ships of the West Gulf Blockading Squadron shelled the little town and its environs mercilessly. Reporting to Union Navy Secretary Gideon Welles, Farragut casually admitted having destroyed buildings owned by Jeran Fortuni Henri Blanchay during "the partial burning of Donaldsville." Gen. Benjamin F. Butler characterized destruction of Donaldsville as having been a necessity—partly because he believed it to be a haven for "a gang of cowardly guerrillas."[49]

During the indiscriminate shelling of the place, the big Satterlee military hospital was heavily damaged. Fully 15 acres in extent and under the charge of a Catholic nun, Sister Santa Maria Clara of Baltimore, it cared for wounded men on both sides and saw an estimated 50,000 of them come and go before the conflict ended.[50]

Eventually the destruction of the nonpartisan hospital came to the attention of Butler in New Orleans. On September 2 he wrote one of the most unusual letters of his colorful career, saying to the mother superior, "I am very, very sorry that Rear-Admiral Farragut was unaware that he was injuring your establishment by his shells. Any injury must have been entirely accidental. . . . To [the Sisters of Charity] our soldiers are daily indebted for the kindest offices. . . . I repeat my grief that any harm should have befallen your Society of Sisters, and cheerfully repair it so far as I may by filling the order you have sent to the city for provisions and medicines."[51]

Though comparable destruction of other hospital facilities sheltering men on both sides may have taken place, only Farragut and Butler frankly admitted responsibility for this special kind of friendly fire.

June 30, Washington, D.C.: Though news was fragmentary, Washington was thrown into panic when it was learned the Army of Northern Virginia was in or near Pennsylvania. Many of the 35,000 jittery men assigned to defend the capital had no combat experience; some had never fired a rifle. In this tense atmosphere, Gen. Samuel P. Heintzelman wanted an afternoon outing in the countryside. Riding toward the Chain Bridge, he and members of his party were not recognized by pickets and became the targets of musket fire. Soon a nearby battery entered the fray and directed a few shells at the man in command of the capital's defenses.[52]

July 1–3, 1863, Gettysburg, Pennsylvania: During the biggest battle ever fought on the North American continent, commanders and men were too busy making and trying to execute plans to preserve records of minor matters. Dozens of incidents likely occurred in which comrades fired on comrades during the three-day battle, but most were never reported. Despite the "conspiracy of silence" occasioned by the heat of battle, modern researcher Gregory A. Coco has uncovered several incidents that did take place.

For example, on July 1 the Georgia brigade led by Gen. George P. Doles routed the Federal 11th Corps. An unidentified Georgia officer claimed that while his boys chased the Yankees, they were taken to be Unionists "and were fired upon by our own artillery which killed and wounded several men." That evening Col. Charles S. Wainwright of the U.S. 1st Corps Artillery noted in his diary that the 11th Corps was mistaken for the enemy and as a result "Northern guns fired into their own men."[53]

Things did not go much better for the 1st North Carolina on Culp's Hill. The regiment became the target of the 3rd North Carolina. Some members of the 1st may have believed this fire came from enemies; whatever the case, others believed that the Rebel 1st Maryland did the shooting, so they opened fire on it from the rear.[54]

Horse soldiers suffered friendly fire at Gettysburg, too. Some Union units fanned out to hunt enemy riders on Gettysburg's outskirts. Sgt. George W. Barbour noted that during a chaotic moment Lt. Seymour Shipman "was wounded badly by our own Regt." and was left behind when the unit retreated toward the town.[55]

But in this great battle, infantry suffered most of the friendly fire accidents. About 4 P.M. on July 2 the 80th New York was charged by Rebels whose advance was covered by artillery. Hand-to-hand fighting erupted, but few if any combatants used their bayonets. After the charge failed, many men in gray, instead of retreating, dropped to the ground to escape Federal fire. Describing the denouement of this incident, Capt. John S. Cook wrote: "Our men shouted to them to come in and promised not to hurt them, and at the word hundreds rose up and came into our lines, *dropping their arms and crouching to avoid the fire of their own artillery* which was pouring upon our position."[56]

The 12th Georgia's experience was less complex. Just before sunset, its men hunkered down in a comparatively sheltered position while most of

All Federal units made up of black soldiers were initially led by white officers, among whom Col. Robert Gould Shaw gained early lasting fame.—HARPER'S HISTORY OF THE GREAT REBELLION

their army fell back. Col. Edward Willis went on record as being positive that "whilst in this position my regiment was shelled by our own artillery." He regretted that he did not know positively which Rebel batteries fired on his men, but he angrily insisted that "the officer in command should be made to pay the penalty for his criminal conduct."[57]

While the 12th Georgia was suffering, elsewhere on the field the Irish officers and men of the 69th Pennsylvania found shelter in a copse of trees. Since they did not expect to come under fire after dark, they spent some time gathering muskets and cartridges that were dropped by Georgians who attacked earlier. But a single battery "directly in rear of the left companies of the 69th" began playing upon them and kept up its fire for some time. Testifying before the Supreme Court of Pennsylvania, Pvt. John Buckley said that grape and canister from "Cowan's Battery" of Federals killed some of the men in his regiment.[58]

At daylight on the third day of the gigantic battle, this type of deadly incident continued. Gen. Edward Johnson gave orders to his Confederates to ready themselves to charge the Federal right. In a standard move designed to stop the enemy, Federal artillery delivered "showers of hurtling, shrieking missiles" in their direction. Once more, some of the fuses were cut too short or some of the shells were defective. As a result, shots aimed at Johnson's Rebels hit members of the 20th Connecticut and took off both arms of Pvt. George W. Warner.[59]

July 18, 1863—Fort Wagner, South Carolina: Although it ranks among the best Civil War movies ever produced, *Glory* (1989) was not a success at the box office. Some attribute this lack of appeal to the fact that the film deals largely with the once-famous 54th Massachusetts Regiment, a once obscure all-black regiment led by Col.

Chickamauga accounted for "a horrendous number of casualties in a matter of minutes."—HARPER'S HISTORY OF THE GREAT REBELLION

Robert Gould Shaw, a monied white Bostonian. The outfit was destroyed after Shaw led it to Morris Island in May 1863. Its story is moving history. But graphic and dramatic history rarely attracts today's moviegoers.

Located close to Charleston, the capture of Morris Island's Fort Wagner was regarded by Federal leaders as absolutely essential. Failure of a July 11 assault led Federal officers to hold a council of war in which it was decided to soften up the position with the big guns of the USS *Montauk, Ironsides, Catskill, Nantucket, Weehawken, Chippewa, Paul Jones, Ottawa,* and *Patapsco.*

Shells of 11 inches or more fell on and around the Confederate bastion for eight hours on July 18, but the bombardment failed to break the garrison's spirit. During a gallant but futile infantry attack launched at twilight, Shaw was killed and 272 of his 650 54th Massachusetts troops became casualties. Gen. George C. Strong, who insisted on personally leading the charge wearing a yellow bandana and white gloves, received a serious wound from which he died 12 days later.

Many participants and observers wrote descriptions of the unusually brutal struggle. The *New York Tribune* published the most incisive report. Readers of the newspaper were told: "The darkness was so intense, the roar of artillery so loud, the flight of grape and canister shot so rapid and destructive, that it was absolutely impossible to preserve order in the ranks of the individual companies, to say nothing of the regiment. Without a doubt, many of our men fell from our own fire."[60]

Capt. Garth W. James of the decimated unit said that "the whole tragedy [of the futile assault] was a totally inconsistent military maneuver" doomed to failure.[61]

Earlier, white volunteers in blue uniforms were charged with deliberately firing on black-skinned comrades at Ship Island, Mississippi, and at other points. No such action took place at Battery Wagner, however. Writing in detail to Massachusetts Gov. John Andrew, witness Edward L. Pierce assured him that blacks wounded near Charleston were receiving good care at Beaufort and Hilton Head. "Could any one from the North see these brave fellows as they lie here," he said, "his prejudice against them, if he had any, would all pass away."[62]

July 19, 1863—Buffington Island, Ohio River: Three spectacular and successful raids led by Rebel Gen. John H. Morgan made his name feared by Yankee civilians and some military leaders. The most famous of these took place when Gen. Braxton Bragg authorized a raid into Kentucky and the cavalry leader and his men instead decided on a more ambitious project. They rode out of their camp on July 2, 1863, headed for Louisville and for Cincinnati. Passing through Unionist towns and villages and defeating several small bodies of green volunteers, they terrorized the region.

Union Gen. Ambrose Burnside called out all available Federal troops and militia units, but seemed unable to find and stop the raiders. After having spent a night close to or in Cincinnati, Morgan crossed the Ohio River into Indiana. This movement gave his foes an opportunity to patrol the river and try to capture him as he recrossed it. On July 16, Capt. LeRoy Fitch of the U.S. Navy was authorized to put every available riverboat at a point that might be chosen by Morgan for his return to Kentucky.

Aboard the USS *Moose*, and accompanied by the *Allegheny Belle* and an unarmed steamer, Fitch took up a position in a narrow channel between Buffington Island and the Ohio River's shore. On July 19 he spotted his quarry and fired every gun he had at him. Surprised and outgunned, Morgan's Rebels fought for an hour before turning and fleeing toward the hills.[63]

According to Capt. H. C. Weaver of the Union's 16th Kentucky, Fitch's heavy pieces played not only on the enemy but also on comrades who had come there by land. According to Weaver, "at one time General [Edward H.] Hobson and staff, who were upon an elevation next to the hills, were singled out as fair game [for naval gunners]." Since Washington was interested only in Morgan, the man who threw shells at this general officer was never reprimanded. Instead, Fitch was heartily commended for the Buffington Island affair by Gen. Jacob D. Cox and by Secretary of the Navy Gideon Welles.[64]

*Gen. Jacob D. Cox survived the Buffington Island struggle and later marched with Sherman to the sea. He wrote an early account of this epic venture.—*J. C. BUTTRE ENGRAVING

July 13, 1863—Morris Island, South Carolina: Only 3.5 miles long, Morris Island lies close to Charleston and Fort Sumter. This location caused it to become one of the most bitterly contested tracts of land south of Virginia. It loomed in importance when a joint army-navy assault on the city failed in early April 1863. Gen. David Hunter, who led land-based Union forces, was notorious in the Confederacy for once having attempted to liberate slaves in his military district before passage of Lincoln's Emancipation Proclamation. Rebels labeled him a "felon to be executed if captured." Failure of his all-out Morris Island assault led to his replacement by Gen. Quincy Gillmore.[65]

Days before assuming his new command, Gillmore boldly announced it would be relatively easy to "reduce Charleston from Morris Island." To this end, 11,000 infantry, siege guns and field batteries, and a fleet of warships and gunboats were assembled. To facilitate communication, a signal station was erected.

Rebels inside Fort Wagner were at the tip of the island and had just 927 men plus 2 heavy guns and 12 light ones. When two of Gillmore's divisions attacked on July 10, defenders were completely surprised, but somehow managed to hold Fort Wagner in the face of 15-inch shells and a series of furious assaults by infantry.[66]

Gen. P. G. T. Beauregard, who led Confederate forces in the region at that time, sent Rebel gunboat commanders an urgent message demanding the destruction of Federal ironclads. He also implored the governor of South Carolina to send him 3,000 slaves for use as laborers. Little came of Beauregard's demands and pleas, so local commander Confederate Gen. William B. Taliaferro decided to go on the offensive. On July 13 he picked Maj. James H. Rion to lead a hand-picked party of 150 men on a night foray. They were instructed "to push forward, drive in the enemy's pickets, and feel their way" until a heavy force of Federals was encountered.[67]

Taliaferro's terse report of this action noted that Rion's band "pushed the pickets and first reserve back upon a reserve brigade in such disorder that the latter fired upon their retreating companies, inflicting a heavy loss." This case of "fire from the rear" at a once-obscure spot was later confirmed by other accounts.[68]

September 20, 1963—Chickamauga, Tennessee: Already noted for his role at Shiloh, 12-year-old Union trooper Johnny Clem played a much-publicized role at Chickamauga. He rode an artillery caisson to the front and later mounted a cannon from which he wielded a sawed-off musket. Challenged on his perch by a Rebel officer, the drummer boy reputedly shot and killed the unidentified fellow. This incident put the boy into Northern newspaper stories again, where he was hailed as the "Drummer Boy of Chickamauga."[69]

Shortly before or after Clem's exploit (which may have been embellished), Confederate forces scored a significant victory on the afternoon of July 20. Troops under Rebel Gen. William Preston, a Harvard Law School graduate, broke the Federal line and beat up three regiments by inflicting 887 casualties in a matter of minutes. But as twilight faded into darkness, Confederates fired at one another steadily instead of at the enemy. Having occupied positions on opposite sides of a salient, each body believed the other to be made up of men in blue.[70]

December 17, 1863—Bean's Station, Tennessee: Having heard that three Federal cavalry brigades led by Gen. James Shackleford were not far from Knoxville, Confederate Gen. James Longstreet set out to capture them with a mixed force of infantry and cavalry. His infantry marched directly toward Bean's Station, but cavalry under Gen. W. T. Martin and Gen. William E. "Grumble" Jones split into two segments in order for one to attack and the other to cut off the enemy's retreat. Three bodies of attackers having reached their destination at almost the same time, no Confederate leader knew where all supporting troops were.

At the village of Bean Station, men of the 60th Alabama found a refuge of sorts in a stable not far from the tavern into which attacked Federals had packed themselves. Volleys from the tavern caused gunners of three Confederate batteries to shell the place as well as a nearby stable. In what

Little Johnny Clem, who became famous at Shiloh, was reputedly active in the fighting at Chickamauga.—BATTLES AND LEADERS

may have been the last incident of its sort in 1863, shells from Rebel field artillery killed two men in gray and wounded two more.[71]

20

Will It Ever Stop?

1864–1865

January 31, 1864—*New Berne, North Carolina:* Located on the Neuse River, New Berne, North Carolina, was captured and occupied by Federal forces in March 1862. Almost a year later, Confederate Gen. J. J. Pettigrew's attempt to retake the town failed. Since Jefferson Davis badly wanted the strategic place, he consulted with Robert E. Lee and with some naval officers. One of the navy men was a grandson of President Zachary Taylor, who been made a colonel of cavalry and assigned to Davis's staff. This officer, John Taylor Wood, agreed to lead seamen in a joint army-navy assault on the river city and coordinated his plans with local commander Gen. George E. Pickett.[72]

On the last night of January 1864, Wood's hand-picked raiders rowed down the Neuse River and slammed aboard the 325-ton USS *Underwriter,* largest of three gunboats at the station. After a short, bloody struggle, the 186-foot sidewheel steamer was theirs—along with the majority of her 84 officers and men. Wood quickly gave orders for the gunboat to get under way, but his planned movement was stopped short by a shell from a Union battery at nearby Fort Stevenson.

Men in blue had learned of the Confederate capture from members of the crew who managed to swim ashore, so they opened up on the *Underwriter* with all they had—"shot, shell, and small arms fire." Gunners knew that nearly half the men aboard their target were members of the U.S. Navy taken prisoner. However, that did not deter them from using their pieces, so 1864 began with another incident in which men deliberately fired on their comrades.[73]

February 20, 1864—Olustee, Florida: According to a Virginia-born veteran of the Olustee fight, Florida's largest Civil War battle, this encounter saw a special kind of not-so-friendly fire. "The negroes [Union Troops] saw a hard time; those who stood were shot by our men, those who ran by the Yankees." His accusation directed against the enemy may have been accurate—in many instances officers reputedly did shoot their men who tried to flee. This function was the specialty of omnipresent file-closers, usually noncommissioned officers who ran alongside advancing columns with drawn pistols, men rarely mentioned in writing.[74]

February 22, 1864—Okalona, Mississippi: During one of his famous raids, Rebel Calvary General Nathan B. Forrest received a report that a vastly stronger Federal force under Gen. William Sooy Smith was not far away from his hard-riding body. They met near Okalona, Mississippi, not in an "affair," but in a full engagement

*John Taylor Wood, a grandson of Zachary Taylor, made his military reputation as a raider, which today would be called a commando.—*AUTHOR'S PRIVATE COLLECTION

about which 20 reports were filed and preserved. Bluster, good luck, and hard fighting saw men in Union blue lose six guns and suffer defeat in spite of their overwhelming numerical superiority.

Pursuing the enemy late in the afternoon and accompanied by only his personal escort, Forrest and his small party were mistaken for the enemy. At a point about 14 miles from Okalona, men who knew Forrest intimately and had ridden with him for days at a time fired on him. When the shooting from the Rebel command ended, one man lay dead, and Forrest reputedly had bullet holes in his clothing.[75]

April 9, 1864—Pleasant Hill, Louisiana: Confederate troops under Gen. Richard Taylor were in no condition to fight when they reached Pleasant Hill, Louisiana, early on the afternoon of April 9. Having marched 45 miles in two days, all of these men were eager for a good meal and a few hours' sleep. Taylor let them rest for two hours without eating, then ordered an advance on a superior force led by Gen. Nathaniel P. Banks. The ensuing struggle generated official reports by several officers, among whom were Col. George W. Baylor and Gen. E. Kirby Smith.

Gen. William Sooy Smith, whose riders met Confederates under Gen. Nathan B. Forrest at Okalona, Mississippi.—
Library of Congress

Things went badly for men in gray almost from the first. For them, the situation became serious when foes under Gens. A. J. Smith and James McMillan emerged from dense woods.

A Federal charge broke the Rebel center, but Taylor's men stubbornly continued to fight until dusk. Bone tired and suddenly frightened, as the sun began to set many of them took refuge in a patch of woods at their rear. Some of their comrades who failed to notice this movement thought the place was filled with Federals, so they fired on it. In turn, this body of troops received a withering blast from the comrades they had taken for enemies.[76]

May 1–15, 1864—The Shenandoah Valley: Gen. Franz Sigel, a German military academy graduate and stickler for protocol, made his headquarters in Winchester, Virginia, during the final days of April 1864. Perhaps he took May Day as propitious; that day he set out at the head of a body of 13,000 infantry and cavalry. Charles Fitz-Simons, one of his men, said of the subsequent two weeks that "although it was well known that there was no force of the enemy in our front, Sigel developed in this advance a peculiar idiosyncrasy in the matter of cavalry scouting; day and night he kept our cavalry in motion, detailing them in parties of from fifty to a hundred men, and sending them out in all directions, east, west, north, and south, with no definite instructions or apparent object. Indeed, the casualties to the numerous detachments, resulting from their mistaking one another for the enemy, were the most serious losses sustained."[77]

May 15, 1864—Resaca, Georgia: Pushing slowly but steadily into Georgia and generally staying close to the single-track Western & Atlantic Railroad that was his supply line, Union Gen. William T. Sherman found the mountains of north Georgia to be extremely rugged. Fighting one battle after another, he reached the railroad town of Resaca on May 14 and launched a furious assault the following day.

Union Col. Benjamin Harrison led the 1st Brigade of the 3rd Division, 20th Corps. Following close behind, in obedience to orders, was the 3rd Division under the leadership of Col. John Coburn. Initially told to form in close columns of battalions, Coburn's officers were soon ordered to form two lines in the rear of the 1st Brigade. Their action took place "in a narrow ravine, very thickly wooded with low trees and bushs, with steep hill-sides." Simultaneously, men of the 2nd Division moved by the left flank through Coburn's brigade, "breaking and intercepting the lines, and preventing any regimental commander from seeing his own troops" or managing them.

Small wonder that in such circumstances some of Coburn's men fired on Harrison's command. Union Gen. Daniel Butterfield sensed tragedy in the making, so he sent aide-de-camp Maj. Henry E. Tremain between the two bodies in order to stop the fratricide. No record exists of how many of the 156 men lost by Harrison at Resaca fell before Tremain arrived. Congress later took note of the matter, however, and in 1892 issued to Tremain a Medal of Honor for having stopped the lone recorded case of friendly fire that was directed on a future president and his command.[78]

May 23–26, 1864—North Anna River, Virginia: For nearly four days, fighting around Virginia's North Anna River was so fierce and continuous that hardened veterans on both sides said they had not seen anything like it except at Gettysburg.

Despite the running struggle between these large bodies of men, events transpired that later made good anecdotes. Advancing to take up a picket post, Sgt. Jonathan C. Kirk of the 20th Indiana walked into a band of more than a dozen Rebels from the Carolinas. Shouting over his shoulder as though to his followers, Kirk then turned to the Carolinians and demanded their instant surrender. They meekly relinquished their weapons, and Kirk marched them back to his regiment. In 1897, lawmakers awarded him the Medal of Honor for this exploit.

No plaudits came, then or ever, to gunners of an unidentified Federal battery located on the river's bank. Late on the first day of fighting, Gen. Samuel Crawford managed to get an entire brigade of Pennsylvanians across the river without incident. Supported by artillery, Rebel Gen. Cadmus M. Wilcox moved his division toward the point at which men in blue had crossed the North Anna; at his signal, 20 Confederate guns opened up simultaneously. This Rebel barrage was bad enough, but things soon got worse for men from the Keystone State. Federal guns on the north bank of the river responded to the Confederate artillery with everything they had. Poor aim, the excitement of combat, or carelessness in cutting fuses caused many of their shells to fall on the Pennsylvanians who were looking to them for rescue from their precarious situation.[79]

Gray-clad riders under Gen. Nathan B. Forrest charged Federal guns at Tupelo, Mississippi.—HARPER'S NEW MONTHLY MAGAZINE

June 25, 1864—Kennesaw Mountain, Georgia: William T. Sherman's numerically superior forces, having pushed Gen. Joseph E. Johnston's Confederates slowly south from camps below Chattanooga, discovered their arrival at Pine Mountain seemed to offer them a splendid defensive position. But shortly afterward at Kennesaw Mountain, a bit farther south, Union artillerymen went into the Civil War equivalent of the doghouse. On June 25, Gen. M. D. Lagged received from Gen. Frank Blair a terse message: "An officer from General [Walter Q.] Gresham's command has been sent to these headquarters to inform the major-general commanding that shells from your advance battery have been thrown immediately in the locality held by General Gresham's skirmishers. You will please see that it is discontinued, and that your fire is directed more to the front or left. Several men have been wounded, and much embarrassment occasioned on this account." [80]

July 14, 1864—Tupelo, Mississippi: The careless or zealous Federal gunners who cut down comrades at Kennesaw Mountain were not identified. A month later, men of Battery G of the 2nd Illinois Artillery were less fortunate. At Tupelo, Mississippi, where Rebel cavalry under Nathan B. Forrest charged Federal guns, Maj. Thomas S. Tate decided to move the 12th Kentucky. He ordered his men back from the front despite the certainty that this move would bring heavy enemy fire down on them. "Seemingly not content with the speed that the enemy were slaughtering us," he wrote afterward, "one of our own batteries commenced a heavy and destructive fire on us."[81]

July 18, 1864—Atlanta, Georgia: From his headquarters, Sherman scolded Gen. Oliver O. Howard about as gently as was possible under the circumstances. He said that Union Gen. John M. Schofield had sent a messenger to Peachtree Creek, but the communication did not arrive. Howard's pickets fired on Schofield's men—the general's messenger among them—and wounded an orderly. The lot returned to Schofield without delivering the message. Insignificant except for the fact that it came to Sherman's attention, this incident was overshadowed by major friendly fire accidents during battles around Atlanta.[82]

August and September 1864—Petersburg, Virginia: During the long Petersburg siege, troops also clashed many times outside the city. One of these incidents took place August 19 when both sides converged at a spot on the Weldon Railroad. Shortly after 4 P.M., the brigade led by Rebel Gen. William Mahone swept through Union Gen. Gouverneur K. Warren's line. Men who halted momentarily to cheer soon found themselves running for cover. According to Gen. Samuel W. Crawford, at the very moment of the Federal breakthrough, Union gunners "opened fire upon friend and foe, the shells bursting among our men."[83]

Before a month passed, Union Gen. August V. Kautz was central to another Petersburg area friendly fire incident. It took place near the Chickahominy River. Having been ordered to conduct what most commanders would have regarded as a foolhardy attack—launched about midnight—Kautz saw his men become hopelessly confused. After a period in pitch blackness, there followed an "ineffective round of firing at one another as much as at the enemy," so the Federal force "mounted up and rode back to the south."[84]

August 21, 1864—Grubb's Crossroads, Kentucky: During a spectacular but unsuccessful Confederate raid into Ohio in July 1864, Confederate Col. Adam R. Johnson commanded one of John H. Morgan's brigades and swam the Ohio River to avoid capture. Three years earlier the Kentucky native planned and executed one of the most daring exploits of the war. Erecting logs plus lengths of stovepipe on the south bank of the Ohio, the Confederate raider crossed the great river into Indiana with only two men. The trio entered Newburg, now a suburb of Evansville, and captured the place by pointing to those "Quaker guns" and convincing locals they were outgunned.

Made a brigadier in June 1864, Johnson was stuck with the nickname "Stovepipe" because of his nervy ruse. His luck held until mid-August that year. During a Henderson County, Kentucky, raid that took place in "fog so dense that there was no visibility at all,"at a spot called Grubb's Crossroads, one of his own men took him for an enemy. A rifle shot hit Johnson in such fashion that it cut out his right eye before plowing through his forehead and destroying his left eye. As a result of a single shot from friendly fire, this general was blinded and forced to end his military career. He went to Texas and in postwar years "became a prominent and successful man, and founded the city of Marble Falls."[85]

October 3, 1864—Mt. Jackson, Virginia: Though he entered the war as a Missouri State Guard company captain, John H. McNeill soon became a partisan ranger. Like Stovepipe Johnson, he received a regular Confederate commission, but never rose above the rank of captain. His outfit went by the bogus name of Company E, 18th Virginia Cavalry, but it was an informal guerrilla organization.

Operating in Virginia on an independent basis, McNeill staged one raid after another on the Baltimore & Ohio Railroad before joining the command of Gen. Jubal Early. During an assault on Mt. Jackson

Use of "Quaker guns" started before Bull Run and continued throughout the war.—
AUTHOR'S PRIVATE COLLECTION

planned and executed by Early, the partisan leader was hit by a shot from one of his own men. At his own instruction, he was left behind by his raiders. McNeill's wound was mortal.[86]

November 19, 1864—Covington, Georgia: Capt. James R. Ladd of the 113th Ohio reached this railroad village 25 miles east of Atlanta on Friday, November 18. A foraging expedition led by Ladd that evening delivered "several chickens, honey, sweet potatoes, flour and meal" to the headquarters mess, enough for "a splendid supper."

When the regiment marched east on Saturday, Ladd left the corps again to forage. His little band traveled only about a mile "when two men of the party were accidentally shot, or rather carelessly by their comrades while shooting chickens." Ladd sent a messenger for a surgeon and an ambulance. No diaries or letters are known to include another instance in which men in blue managed to wing their comrades when engaged in plundering Confederate chicken yards.[87]

November 29, 1864—Sand Creek, Colorado Territory: Seeking to put an end to Indian raids, members of the 1st and 3rd Colorado Cavalry launched an organized hunt for Native Americans on November 20. During ten days they covered 300 miles, one-third of these in snow two feet deep. Having discovered a 130-lodge Cheyenne village, they attacked at daylight on November 29.

Col. John M. Chivington, a parson who had become a soldier, recorded with satisfaction the killing of Chiefs Black Kettle, White Antelope, Knock Knee, and Little Raven plus the slaughter or capture of an estimated 500 tribe members. Men in blue suffered 47 casualties, of which only 9 were fatal. Chivington's glowing report of the action says nothing about the fact that many or most white cavalrymen who were left on the field were probably felled by the fire of their own comrades who were "drunk with victory."[88]

November 30, 1864—Franklin, Tennessee: About 25,000 men were engaged on each side at Franklin, Tennessee. It ranks as one of the fiercest battles of the war: Five Confederate generals were among the 8,500 casualties of the day. According to participants, some on both sides suffered death or wounds from the fire of comrades on comrades.

The first assault by Rebels had been checked. Union troops were dug in around Franklin. Then men of the 72nd Illinois began "rearranging themselves in good form." "To our surprise and chagrin," wrote Capt. James A. Sexton, "one of the new regiments in our rear opened fire, killing and wounding scores of our own men. Lying flat in the pits and on the ground, we sent word to them time and again to cease firing, but without avail." Though "scores" is far from an exact number, Sex-

Gen. Alfred H. Terry's mission was of top importance; Fort Fisher was the last Confederate installation of any importance on the Atlantic coast.—NICOLAY & HAY, ABRAHAM LINCOLN

ton's use of the term suggests that this incident must have been a major misadventure.[89]

A Confederate soldier, George B. Gordon, and some comrades fought for a time behind log breastworks at Franklin. Largely shielded from the enemy, they came under fire from the Rebel corps commanded by Gen. Alexander P. Stewart. Gordon said that fatalities from fire in the rear as well as from men in blue caused him and his friends to "cross the works and surrender."[90]

January 14, 1865—Fort Fisher, North Carolina: Determined to subdue the last Confederate fortress on the Atlantic Coast, Grant assembled a force of 8,000 men and put Gen. Alfred H. Terry in command. Simultaneously, he enlisted the aid of Rear Adm. David D. Porter for still another joint army-navy expedition.

Covered by fire from warships, men of four divisions established a beachhead close to the fort during the afternoon of December 13. On the morning of Thursday, December 14, all 44 of Porter's warships opened on the Confederate bastion and continued the cannonade for hours. Precisely at 4 P.M. a land assault was launched by three brigades of infantry plus 1,600 sailors and 400 marines. Union Col. Galusha Pennypacker, age 20, led an assault in which the Rebel parapet was scaled and a national flag was planted.

Some of the fiercest hand-to-hand combat of the war followed the raising of the Stars and Stripes and continued until nearly dusk. According to youthful Federal cannoneer Augustus Buell, Porter's gunners could not have failed to see the all-important flag, but they continued to throw shells into the tightly packed mass of men in blue and in gray wrestling in heavy smoke. About 9 P.M., conflict inside the fort subsided, Porter's 15-inch guns fell silent, and his ships "began signaling with different-colored rockets." For his role in this struggle, during which Federal fighting men were fired on by ships of the U.S. Navy, Pennypacker was made a brigadier at age 21.[91]

March 29, 1865—Near Petersburg, Virginia: Gen. John B. Gordon, a Georgian, studied every available map of the region around Petersburg in search of a Federal "soft spot." He decided it would be possible to break through the siege lines at Fort Stedman before dawn on March 29.

His plan worked. Gordon's men overran Fort Stedman. But then they were halted by rows of trenches and dugouts to the north. Turning south to nearby Union-held Fort Haskell in dim early light, they were within 100 yards of it before being recognized as enemies.

Inside the fort, Capt. Christian Woerner commanded a battery of four Napoleon cannon, three of which were loaded and ready for use. As soon as he opened with them, his fire was answered by Confederate artillery. Soon guns to the rear entered the fray. Lt. Julius G. Tuerk of the 3rd New Jersey Artillery, awed by the cannonade, said burning shell fuses in the sky looked like "a flock of blackbirds with blazing tails beating about in a gale."

At Fort Haskell, several Yankees were killed or wounded and their flag was shot away. When the national banner disappeared, far-off comrades assumed that the fort had fallen, and they turned their artillery on it. In this desperate situation, an officer called for volunteers to lift a flag where it could be seen. Of the eight men who responded to this challenge, four were killed by their own big guns before cannoneers could be signaled to stop firing at the fort.[92]

April 2, 1865—Selma, Alabama: A sharp two-day engagement at Selma, Alabama, generated 27 reports by officers such as Union Gens. George H. Thomas, Emory Upton, and James H. Wilson. One report spoke of friendly fire.

One Confederate battery defending the town held six guns and was manned by about 60 troops from Mississippi whose pieces had been lost in the December 1864 Battle of Nashville. Of this bunch, James A. Turpin and 22 of his gunners were captured by the enemy and soon found themselves marching toward Federal lines. Behind him, Turpin's remaining active troops, who seem to have been temporarily unable to see any color except blue, fired on both the prisoners and their captors. Shells that continued to play on the mixed band would have led to the death of every man in gray, Turpin believed, had not a Federal officer guided the prisoners to the rear.[93]

April 5, 1864—Amelia Station, near Petersburg, Virginia: Three days after Lee's forces left Richmond, Yankees captured his chief supply train near Painesville and burned 180 wagon loads. All roads leading from the Rebel capital became choked with deserters, stragglers, and civilian refugees. After dark, things were even more chaotic. Men of the 20th Maine had no notion that they slept close to unidentified Confederates, troops probably belonging to Gen. James Longstreet's force.

Long after darkness fell, a horse tied close to the Rebel camp broke loose and created a commotion, dragging the fence rail to which he was tied. Hungry and dog-tired men in gray took the noise to mean that they were being attacked, which caused them to start shooting. Some of their comrades who were on the march "returned the fire, and before sanity could be restored, several men had been killed or wounded."[94]

April 7, 1865—Farmville, Virginia: Col. Hiram Berdan, the U.S. military's top rifle shot, organized a unit of sharpshooters in the autumn of 1861 and led it until early 1864. Late in the war, Gen. William Mahone decided to form a battalion of Confederate sharpshooters and became head of "the most renowned shock troops" of the Confederacy. One of its officers, Capt. John E. Laughton, wrote a comparatively detailed account of the last days of the Army of Northern Virginia.

While marching from Chester, Virginia, toward Lynchburg, Mahone's unit of picked men had their last fight on April 7 at a point about two miles from the village of Farmville. Though records treat it only as an engagement, Union Gens. Francis C. Barlow, George G. Meade, and Philip H. Sheridan, Rebel Gen. Fitzhugh Lee, and 43 other officers filed reports about Farmville. None of their accounts include information jotted down by Laughton, who lamented that a captain in his outfit "was instantly killed by a fragment of shell fired by one of our own [Rebel] batteries."[95]

April 6, 1865—Sayler's Creek, Virginia: Logic suggests friendly fire "misadventures" should have ended close to the time that Lee surrendered. But nothing about the Civil War is logical.

Nearly a month after Lee's Appomattox Court House surrender, Rebel flags captured at the battle of Sayler's Creek led to one of the largest mass decorations ever. Each man in blue involved in the capture of nearly 50 Confederate banners received the Medal of Honor.

The ceremony brought out this strory. During the Sayler's Creek melee, Pvt. Charles A. Taggert of the 37th Massachusetts stumbled onto a small band of Confederates. Somehow he managed to get off a quick shot and seize their emblem before he was identified by his enemies. When he began racing toward his own lines, hotly pursued by Rebels, men of the 37th Massachusetts believed they were facing a Confederate charge. Their hasty fire wounded Taggert. Fortunately, his comrades were poor shots. The flag-capturer soon recovered and received his award.[96]

May 10, 1865—Near Irwinville, Georgia: Having successfully eluded pursuers for five weeks, fugitive Confederate President Jefferson Davis was finally discovered in southern Georgia. Union Gen. James H. Wilson's seasoned cavalrymen swept the countryside in separate sets of movements; two of Wilson's units converged on Davis's camp almost simultaneously. One unidentified member of the Davis party wrote of the climactic moment: "One regiment, the 4th Michigan, I think, [which] had made a circuit and had got in front of us startled us with their shouts: 'Where is the President? Has he escaped?' [They] were soon answered, for across the road, not thirty steps from where we were, stood a Federal soldier [who demanded Davis's surrender. Our] attention was arrested by rapid firing near us. Another Federal regiment [the 1st Wisconsin Cavalry] coming on in our rear had bumped into the Michigan soldiers and in the gray dawn of morning each fired at the other."

This account could seem like Rebel fiction designed to disparage Yankees, were it not mentioned in numerous accounts of the capture. Some authorities list it as a battle, despite the fact that all participants were in blue uniforms.

Pvts. John Rupert and John Hines of the 4th Michigan Cavalry fell dead in the mix-up and were buried at Andersonville National Cemetery.

Though often described as having traveled on river steamers, Davis and his party actually rode through the South on horses.—FRANK VIZETELLY

Maj. Charles L. Greeno of the 7th Pennsylvania Cavalry reported that an officer of the 4th Michigan and three men of the 1st Wisconsin were severely wounded.

Men of the contending Federal units took up a collection and got "a liberal sum" for relatives of those who became casualties that morning. No member of the Davis party was injured in the brisk exchange of gunfire, and the former Confederate president was sent to Fort Monroe for imprisonment.[97]

May 13, 1865—Palmito Ranch, Texas: Three days after events near Irwinville, the last battle of the Civil War took place far to the west. A force of black soldiers clashed with Texas Rebels at a spot near Brazos Island, a spot often incorrectly identified as Palmetto Ranch.

While the fight was in progress, a boat manned by Rebels came steaming toward the point of struggle, and Confederates "threw two round balls at her" from one of their cannon. These two shots fired from cannon by Southerners, like the first shots at Fort Sumter, brought the story of Civil War friendly fire to a post-official end. Pondering the last Texas fight, a puzzled participant in it noted: "Why, under the existing circumstances, it was brought on and fought, was not explained."[98]

Part III
WEIGHTY MISSILES

CHAPTER

21

Deadly Mortars

Port Hudson, Louisiana—March 14, 1863

S oon after going into the western theater of war, Ulysses S. Grant
notified Washington that Vicksburg, Mississippi, must be taken
regardless of what it might cost in money and manpower. Some
officials in the War Department were less than persuaded by his reasoning, but they gave him the go-ahead for an operation designed to reduce
the fortified Confederate community. They cautioned that a direct
assault on the river city could be made only from a southern starting
point and reminded him that the U.S. Navy had no gunboats capable of
razing Vicksburg from the river.

Grant's first plan, calculated to bypass military obstacles, featured a
long and costly canal to help change the course of the Mississippi River.
When the canal scheme was abandoned, he set out to send warships
toward Vicksburg by means of a turning, twisting, and tedious passage
through waterways and bayous. By the end of February 1863 it was
clear this scheme would also have to be abandoned. So the future lieutenant general made plans to get behind his objective by using the Yazoo
Pass. He doggedly persisted in pursuing this route despite warnings of
river traffic by veterans, who correctly predicted it would not work.

About 300 miles downriver from Grant's headquarters, 62-year-old
U.S. Rear Adm. David G. Farragut had ideas of his own. A native of
Tennessee whose wife hailed from Georgia, his strong Southern ties had
earlier made him suspect in Union decision-making circles. But in Washington, all doubts about his loyalty vanished when he planned and executed a series of moves that led to the fall of New Orleans, by far the
largest city in the Confederacy.

About the time that Grant began preparing to use Yazoo Pass, Farragut became fighting mad. Rebels, who held the river between Vicks-

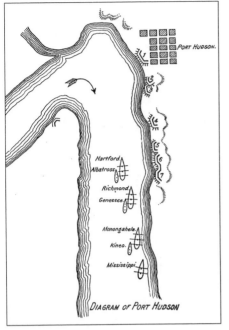

Its location at a bend in the river gave Port Hudson a strategic advantage.—OFFICIAL RECORDS OF THE UNION AND CONFEDERATE NAVIES, 19

burg and Port Hudson, Louisiana, captured the Union steam ram *Queen of the West* and promptly incorporated her into their fledgling navy.

Since Grant seemed incapable of moving on Vicksburg from the north, Farragut decided to strike from the south and crush Port Hudson. Over a span of about two weeks, the naval officer assembled a flotilla near Profit's Island, more than six miles below his target. Knowing his plan involved a great deal of risk, he managed to persuade Gen. Nathaniel P. Banks to authorize a joint operation by which some of his 20,000 troops would move against Port Hudson by land at the same time that Farragut's ships tried to pass.

Confederate spies warned Port Hudson officers that a two-pronged move was about to get under way. Very early on the morning of March 14, men and officers who were under arrest had their charges suspended and were ordered to their respective commands. "The enemy has at last determined to advance against this place to make an effort here to open the navigation of the Mississippi," officer T. Friend Willson warned in General Orders No. 27. Cooks were ordered to prepare two days' rations, and troops were notified that they would be required "to remain continuously at the breastworks."[1]

Farragut knew artillery situated on a bluff about 100 feet high would have difficulty hitting his vessels; it would be almost impossible for Rebels to depress the muzzles of their guns sufficiently to make constant fire possible. But nature gave the Rebels a special advantage. At Port Hudson, the down-flowing Mississippi curved sharply west in such a fashion that a fast-moving vessel was at risk of becoming stuck on mud flats unless she had an exceptionally skilled pilot. This difficulty was compounded by the fact that in order for Farragut to have a chance at success, the operation would have to be conducted in total darkness.

Though postbattle reports of Federal officers fill about 40 printed pages of official records, by far the most detailed single account of the action was written by an unidentified correspondent of the *New York World,* who watched all three hours of it from the deck of the sloop-of-war USS *Hartford.*

Guns of other warships aside, *Hartford*'s 24 nine-inch Dahlgrens were more than a match for the 21 pieces of artillery in Confederate batteries—if the ship's guns could be elevated sufficiently to go into use. Two other oceangoing sloops, the *Richmond* and the *Monongahela,* would follow close behind Farragut's vessel and would be trailed by the paddle wheeler *Mississippi.*

Since fire from Rebels would come from starboard, Farragut decided to lash a small gunboat to the side of each of his first three vessels to shield them from shells. However, it was impossible to shield the *Mississippi* in this way since her paddles would be in constant motion. Some Federals were surprised to learn this old vessel had crossed the Pacific Ocean twice. It was on her deck that Commodore Matthew Perry stood when he swept into Tokyo Bay a decade earlier. Unless the noise of engines driving vessels against a five-knot current aroused sentries, the flotilla had a chance not to be noticed by the enemy.[2]

Fate was against Farragut on the Saturday night in which he put his plan into operation. About 9:15 P.M. his little fleet was under way. But the move was detected almost at once. Rockets fired by Confederates signaled the beginning of "a thundering roar, equal in volume to a whole park of artillery." Stokers on the flagship poured on coal as rapidly as possible. The *Hartford* soon began moving a bit faster, but she emitted immense clouds of thick black smoke so dense that the river's surface was soon covered. Smoke was so conspicuous that the reporting newspaper correspondent incorrectly decided it might be intended to "confound Rebel gunners."

Bringing up the rear, *Mississippi* was completely enveloped in smoke before she came in range of shore batteries. Aboard the paddle wheeler, Capt. Melancton Smith saw his gunners preparing to fire into swirling columns of smoke without having elevated their guns. With horror, he realized they had mistaken the *Richmond* for a Rebel craft and were taking aim. Reporting this incident, Smith wrote that his veterans "were with difficulty restrained from firing into her."[3]

Though the *Hartford* suffered no severe damage, both the *Richmond* and the *Monongahela* were soon out of commission, although their guns were still in use. Largely undamaged and pushing her engines to the limit, the *Mississippi,* with her guns blazing, caught up with and then passed the *Richmond*. Gunners on the *Richmond*, who could not see their sister vessel, briefly watched the flashes of fire she emitted and then took her as a target. Hit from both shore batteries and the *Richmond*, the steam-paddle veteran of many a voyage slammed into the mud and could not get out.

Lt. George Dewey, executive officer of the crippled *Mississippi*, displayed the initiative and courage that later made him the hero of Manila Bay during the Spanish-American War. He put 64 casualties into small boats, directed them downstream, and then reported to Smith that only uninjured men were still aboard. When he received this report, Smith reluctantly ordered the vessel to be fired so she could not be used by the enemy.

Among the Union vessels, only the *Mississippi* went up in flames. It was shortly after 2 A.M. Sunday. With the gunboat *Albatross* still lashed to her side, the flagship *Hartford* steamed north toward Vicksburg. Though his force suffered about 120 casualties, of whom half were *Mississippi* crewmen, Farragut had demonstrated his reasoning was sound. It was, indeed, possible to run past Rebel shore batteries at night—at a cost. Months later, experience gained at Port Hudson would enable Federal forces to move southward past Vicksburg to ferry across the river the troops that Grant would lead in his campaign against the city.

Up and down the river in the aftermath of what one of Farragut's men called their "splendid adventure by night," much of the talk among Rebels was about "cross-eyed Yankee gunners who couldn't tell one of their own warships from a lumber scow."

Every exaggerated account of "how Yanks blew their own paddle-wheeler out of the water" brought cheers and guffaws from people who

Farragut's fleet before Port Hudson.—F. B. SCHELL, THE SOLDIER IN OUR CIVIL WAR

heard the story of the *Richmond* versus the *Mississippi*.

Writing for his New York newspaper, a correspondent whose name was not attached to his extremely long dispatch challenged the truth of this story. He gave great emphasis to denying that the two vessels fired into one another—but said nothing about shots from the *Richmond* that went unanswered from the *Mississippi*.

If the reporter knew what carnage was caused by mortars aboard the gunboats, he said nothing about it. Smoke plus poor aim caused a great many shells from these special guns to fall on Union infantrymen who had set out to take the city by land. Men aboard most or all Federal warships learned about the deadly work of Farragut's mortars at Port Hudson, and some shuddered at the prospect of being under his direct command. Lt. F. A. Roe of the USS *Pensacola*, who

David G. Farragut, shown here in the main-rigging of a warship, became a hero at Mobile Bay, Alabama.—
AUTHOR'S PRIVATE COLLECTION

kept a detailed diary, wrote: "It is strange that the admiral does insist upon such reckless and useless exposure of officers, men, and ships. . . . We are all losing confidence in Admiral Farragut, for he displays no judgment or prudence. He is wasteful of life and blood to a criminal degree."[4]

Unlike army officers, men of the U.S. Navy frequently compiled detailed lists of casualties. Surgeon Robert T. Maccoun reported 25 men aboard the *Mississippi* were killed and four suffered "severe" wounds—a euphemism for "wounds believed to be fatal." Three members of the crew were known to be slightly wounded, and an unknown number of others who were hit by Rebel or Federal shells were reported as having "jumped overboard, fearing to fall into the hands of the enemy." No such list of casualties among Federal land forces was prepared and preserved.[5]

Sooner or later, veterans of war on the water had agreed, an enterprise undertaken at night was all but certain to involve an exchange of fire among vessels of a fleet or flotilla. Too bad that the first major target of such fire had to be the old *Mississippi,* long "the pride of the U.S. steam-driven navy."

CHAPTER

22

Mighty Stonewall

Chancellorsville, Virginia—May 2, 1863

At Port Hudson hundreds of pounds of Federal iron rained upon infantry and the USS *Mississippi,* causing an unknown number of casualties. At Chancellorsville three missiles from weapons in the hands of North Carolinians brought down mighty Stonewall Jackson. Loss of the man whom Lee called his "strong right arm" affected the subsequent course of the war and possibly its outcome. The historian Douglas Southall Freeman summed up the Confederate debacle at Gettysburg in a single sentence, pointing out that it stemmed from the fact that the South's finest strategist, mortally wounded by friendly fire, had been buried before the biggest battle of the war was waged.

In late spring of 1863, established in The Wilderness with tiny Chancellorsville as their center, Union troops were within striking distance of Fredericksburg. To Lee, that meant he must attack in spite of the enemy's numerical superiority. He and Jackson conferred at length on the night of May 1 in a setting so informal that it has been dubbed "the cracker box conference." Reputedly sitting on hardtack crates, the generals talked and developed a risky plan. Jackson would make a long march and attack with his entire corps. Lee, meanwhile, would hold Union Gen. Joseph Hooker in check with only two divisions.

Riding through dense fog on May 2, Jackson joined Lee and Longstreet for another council of war at about 3:30 A.M. Splendid in a brand-new uniform presented to him by Gen. J. E. B. Stuart, Jackson tersely proposed to deal with the 75,000 Yankees they faced by giving them the bayonet. Both he and his fellow commanders knew that he was not speaking in literal fashion since he would be using more than 100 pieces of field artillery. Soon his entire corps plus Stuart's cavalry

Gen. Robert E. Lee and Gen. "Stonewall" Jackson reputedly sat on cracker boxes for a prebattle conference.—W. L. SHEPPARD

moved off at the standard rate of two miles an hour, headed toward a spot where Jackson believed one wing of the enemy's army could be forced back upon Chancellorsville and the Rappahannock River.

Long lines of men in gray often had to change their course in order to avoid thickets so dense that rapid passage through them was impossible. Here, bayonets were wielded if not used; at the rear of each regiment, guards brandished these weapons at every man who was inclined to lag behind his unit. After conferring with Gen. Fitzhugh Lee, who had seen the enemy clearly that morning, Jackson revised his plan slightly to march about 14 miles in order to attack at a point 2 miles from Chancellorsville. Well on his way toward his objective by noon, he turned to his cavalry leader, Stuart, and voiced typical optimism. "I trust that God will grant us a great victory," he observed. Some time after 3:30 P.M., he began deploying his troops for the planned assault upon the flank of the Federal 11th Corps.[6]

Shortly before 5 P.M., 28,000 hopeful Confederates prepared to advance. It had taken their commander almost an hour to get them into a mile-long line on both sides of a turnpike. Their presence less than a mile from the Federal line seems to have gone undetected by the enemy. Possibly because of the phenomenon called acoustic shadow, Hooker, at his Chancellorsville headquarters, had no idea a battle was about to commence.

Gen. O. O. Howard, whose men took the brunt of the first assault, never forgot how startled they were when it began. Animals fleeing through the woods gave them the first sign that Jackson's men were about to hit the only two regiments that fronted the approaching Confederates. When men under Col. Leopold Von Gilsa fell back rapidly, the division immediately behind them was pushed upon forces led by Union Gen. Carl Schurz. Unable to stem the tide of retreat, the division under the German-born commander folded into another unit that was encamped close to its rear.

By 7 P.M., many positions held by men in blue had been overrun. Hooker's line had been pushed back at least two miles, but the Confederate line had become extremely ragged. Riding toward the front to re-form his line after having learned that heavily wooded terrain had caused some units to become intertwined, Jackson and a band of no

Riding away from his great victory at Chancellorsville, Lee paused to write a note to Jackson in which he attributed the win to his wounded subordinate.—LIBRARY OF CONGRESS

more than 30 companions heard the roar of Federal artillery. It was so loud that they briefly took shelter, aware that nearby Confederate troops were its targets.

Having sent members of his personal escort on an errand from which they had not returned, Jackson launched his inspection of the front about 8:45 P.M. After passing his picket line on the turnpike, he scoffed at danger and told members of his party that it was clear the enemy had been routed.[7]

Suddenly, scattered shots rang out, and Gen. Ambrose P. Hill realized that they came from men in gray. At the top of his voice he shouted: "Cease firing! Cease firing!"

Gen. Joseph Hooker boasted to subordinates that "the Rebel army is about to be smashed by the Army of the Potomac."—HARPER'S MAGAZINE

A momentary pause followed, during which Little Sorrel, Jackson's horse, bolted into the dense thicket that bordered the trail used by riders. Lt. Joseph G. Morrison quickly repeated and amplified the warning by shouting to men he could not see that they were firing on their own men. His first response was a taunt challenging the order as a lie, after which Maj. John D. Barry of the 18th Carolina shouted: "Pour it into them, boys!"[8]

That command was quickly followed by a volley fired from a line of men who probably knelt in order to take steady aim. Jackson's right hand was hit and wounded by a smoothbore musket ball that was left embedded in the flesh. His left wrist received a nasty but nonthreatening cut from a second missile. It was the third hit, almost certainly from a minié bullet, that did the serious damage. A bone in his left arm was broken and the large artery in it was cut; as a result, he bled profusely.

Feeling himself rapidly growing dizzy, Jackson did not protest when Capt. R. E. Wilbourne and a Lt. Wynne insisted on helping him from his saddle. By the time his feet were on the ground, he was close to fainting, so aides helped him stagger to a small tree and lie down. Wynn raced off

"Stonewall" Jackson received wounds that were not initially considered to be fatal.— VIRGINIA STATE LIBRARY

to find the corps surgeon, Dr. Hunter McGuire; fast losing consciousness, Jackson swallowed a mouthful of whiskey and asked for water. No one knew better than he that he was outside his own lines and very close to a Federal position.[9]

Fearful that a Federal charge might take place at any minute and engulf the spot where the wounded general lay, aides helped him to his feet and guided him to a litter. Two officers and two privates seized the litter and tried to hurry from the dangerous place, but John H. Johnson of the 22nd Virginia soon took a hit that ripped off both his arms. A second litter bearer released his grip and bolted toward safety in the woods; officers who were forced to put Jackson on the ground did so as gently as possible. Joined by a comrade, three of them lay down and tried to form a protective shield with their bodies.[10]

When fire from Federal batteries slackened, Jackson was moved slowly to the rear. Gen. W. Dorsey Pender, who encountered the little party, expressed sorrow that his commander had been wounded and muttered something about "the necessity of falling back." Some authorities insist that despite his loss of blood, Stonewall managed to order Pender to hold his ground. Moving quickly to the Stony Ford Road, men who surrounded and assisted the stricken general found an ambulance, put him in it, and sent him toward safety.[11]

After jolting four miles to a field hospital, Jackson was put in bed and covered with blankets before receiving more whiskey and water. Though he was obviously in great pain, his condition did not seem to be life-threatening, so McGuire did not give him a thorough examination until the wounded general recovered somewhat from shock considerably later. About 2 A.M. on Sunday, May 3, the surgeon informed his patient that amputation of his left arm just below the shoulder was advisable and should be performed at once. When the procedure was finished and Jackson recovered from the chloroform that had been administered, he conferred briefly with Maj. A. S. Pendleton. After learning of the amputation, Lee made his often-quoted observation about having lost his own "right arm." By 9 A.M. on Sunday, Jackson was feeling so much better that he sent his brother-in-law to Richmond to tell his wife of his condition.[12]

A few hours after Jackson's splintered left arm was removed, a man who commanded opposing troops was injured. A shell from one of the guns brought to the scene of battle by Jackson scored a hit on a post against which Hooker's head was resting. Impact of the missile was such

Artist A. C. Redwood painted this version of the wounding of "Stonewall" Jackson by fire from North Carolina troops.— BATTLES AND LEADERS

that the Federal general almost certainly suffered a concussion, for his aides initially believed he had been killed. When revived, he grimaced with pain that he later described as being so intolerable that he seems briefly to have considered relinquishing command of the force.[13]

Though Jackson's wounds were not initially considered life-threatening, he soon developed pneumonia and physicians were unable to cope with it. His death came on May 10, when the 1,400-day national conflict was close to its halfway point. Had he survived, Freeman's debatable appraisal of his impact on Gettysburg would have been put to the test.

Relatively few officers on either side stepped forward to accept responsibility for incidents in which comrades fired on comrades. Gen. James H. Lane of North Carolina wrote a detailed account of circumstances under which his men believed that they had a group of enemies in sight when they glimpsed Jackson's party. Members of the 18th North Carolina, said Lane, were soon under the impression that they had hit both Jackson and Hill and had killed some members of their staffs. Top Confederate authorities seem to have believed the Tarheels acted properly in a confused situation. Barry, who may have given the order to fire on his commander, was promoted in the aftermath of Chancellorsville. When Lane was wounded at Cold Harbor, Barry took over his command and briefly functioned as a brigadier.

Despite the fact Lane's account is detailed and specific, a few authorities do not accept it. Pointing to matters not mentioned by Lane, it has been suggested that the 33rd North Carolina, rather than the 18th, may have been at the spot from which men fired on riders they could not clearly see. Regardless of which regiment of Tarheels delivered a few ounces of lead, their deadly fire affected the North-South conflict much more severely than did many a full-scale cannonade from batteries or warships.[14]

23

Hotchkiss Shells

Vicksburg, Mississippi—May 22, 1863

E very gun in every Federal battery opened fire promptly at 5 A.M. on May 22, 1863. Smarting from heavy losses during an assault on defenses of Vicksburg three days earlier, U. S. Grant had ordered a rain of metal on the city.

Four times he had failed in attempts to get within range of his objective. With the estimated 43,000 men of his three army corps scheduled to strike at 10 A.M., the man from Illinois was confident that before the day ended he would send a triumphant telegram to Washington.

Grant was vividly conscious of every detail of the elaborate operation that enabled him to finally approach the Confederate bastion by land. Cmdr. David D. Porter's Mississippi Squadron had succeeded in a desperate gamble that took a small flotilla past Vicksburg's guns. Only then was it possible for Grant's forces, long massed south of the city on the west bank of the great river, to cross to the east bank and move toward their objective.

Marching north after their crossing and fighting at Raymond and Port Gibson, they met spirited resistance on May 17 at the Big Black River bridge. But after having suffered just 279 casualties there, the men pushed forward and broke the back of the Rebels' defensive effort. Two days later, an all-out assault on Vicksburg failed miserably and cost Federals almost 1,000 men.[15]

After a five-hour cannonade seldom punctuated by silence, Grant was confident that the enemy was sufficiently battered to offer only token resistance. Pennsylvania-born Rebel Gen. John C. Pemberton, who commanded the Vicksburg garrison, had only about 20,000 men. All of them were bone-tired and hungry before the cannonade began;

Gen. U. S. Grant correctly regarded Vicksburg as the most important Confederate bastion on the Mississippi River.—HARPER'S ENCYCLOPEDIA OF U.S. HISTORY

despite his reverses on May 19, Grant was sure that this sorry pack of Rebels would give way when his well-rested, well-fed, and eager men moved on fortifications gaping with holes made by Federal artillery. Bugles sounded promptly at 9:55—a signal that the massive assault would be launched in five minutes.[16]

As commander of the Military Division of the Mississippi, Grant was poised to throw all he had against the Confederate bastion that Capt. C. N. Lee of the 22nd Iowa called "the Gibraltar of the Southern Confederacy." Led by Grant's political archenemy Maj. Gen. John A. McClernand, ranks of the attacking Federal 13th Corps included Gens. Peter J. Osterhaus, Andrew J. Smith, Eugene A. Carr, and Michael K. Lawler. Though small in number, the 13th Infantry, U.S. Army, could be counted on to put some iron into the backbones of the other 24 regiments that made up the corps. Support from big guns was relatively weak, however; only one battery from each Ohio and Indiana Light Artillery had been assigned to the force.[17]

Veteran reporter Sylvanus Cadwallader sent a telegram to his editors describing what happened precisely at 10 A.M. "The whole Federal army was transformed into a monster serpent which began to writhe and twist and turn and undulate. Brigades broke off and advanced right or left or left oblique—divisions moved up squarely to the front, the hoarse shouts of officers were echoed along the line, columns closed up, the earth began to shake and tremble."[18]

Even after having carefully surveyed the terrain through which his troops must pass, Grant failed to realize how formidable the obstacles were. Capts. Frederick E. Prime and Cyrus B. Comstock of the U.S. Corps of Engineers noted the ground over which their troops must pass was made up of "an intricate net-work of ravines and ridges," some of which had sides "so steep that their ascent was difficult to a footman unless he aided himself with his hands." Hundreds of the trees that once flourished here had been felled to form "in many places entanglements which under fire were absolutely impassable."[19]

Crawling up the steep slopes of ravines and stumbling through brush while under withering fire, a few men in blue succeeded in reaching Confederate defenses. Col. Thomas K. Smith of the 54th Ohio found that he could not advance his entire brigade, however. In some sectors it was impossible to move forward except in single file. Little hills, he wrote later, were "exceedingly precipitous, intersected by ravines in three directions, the bottom treacherous [and] filled with sink holes concealed by dried grass and cane." Hence, he watched in awe and admiration as a few of his men "advanced their colors to the very base of the [Rebel] parapet." Wave after wave of Grant's men clambered and clawed their way to points where they lay eyeball-to-eyeball with the enemy, then fell back or crawled to safe spots in gullies and stayed there until nightfall.[20]

Three especially dramatic incidents occurred some time during the late afternoon. In bold but clumsy attempts to achieve results that would come only after hand grenades were perfected, men on both sides lit the fuses of shells and simultaneously tossed them toward the enemy. Men

Principal defensive installations plus location of Federal ships just before the surrender of the city.—OFFICIAL RECORDS, 21

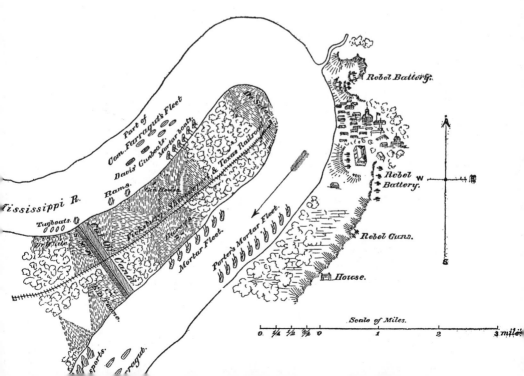

Vicksburg's defenders were under the command of a Yankee—Pennsylvania native John C. Pemberton.—Vicksburg Historical Society

under Capt. J. J. Kellogg of the 113th Illinois fixed bayonets when within 300 yards of the Rebel bastion "and charged point blank for the rebel works at a double quick." Kellogg, who realized too late that "it would take only a stumble of some lubber behind" to skewer him, soon saw his veterans "swept back to the temporary cover of a ridge."[21]

Col. Thomas K. Smith's men of the 55th Illinois, hardly aware of what they were doing at the height of the fray, fired so continuously that they completely ran out of ammunition. In this emergency, Orion H. Howe volunteered to go for a fresh supply and soon the 14-year-old drummer was on his way toward Sherman. Though he was wounded in one leg, he managed to reach the corps commander and saluted before asking that .54 caliber bullets be sent to his unit. Sherman reputedly failed to act on the request, perhaps because Howe stipulated ammunition of the wrong caliber. Wrong caliber or not, in 1896 "the boy hero of Vicksburg" received the Medal of Honor for his heroism.[22]

Incomplete records suggest that two separate instances of friendly fire may have occurred on that bloody day, but logic suggests that a single case was reported in two markedly different fashions. Writing three days after the struggle, Sgt. W. W. Gardner of the 13th U.S. Infantry said Capt. Edward C. Washington was cut down by a "most terrible cross fire" while in a deep ravine. Professional soldiers, said Gardner, "pressed forward to within 50 yards of the [Rebel] fort," then had to try to find shelter behind trees and stumps. In this exposed position, he said, "We were now under fire from our own batteries, and infantry in our rear."

Gardner's account implies that Federals in the rear of the U.S. Army regiment fired too low and therefore cut down some of their comrades. Cadwallader, who had taken refuge in a gully, saw things differently. A trained observer, he was city editor of a Milwaukee newspaper before deciding to report the movements of Grant's forces for the *New York Herald* and the *Chicago Times*. The journalist wrote: "The cannonading from both sides was terrific. The air was filled with hollow shot, percussion shells, and about every kind of missile ever thrown from heavy guns. At this time we [of Grant's forces] were using many Hotchkiss shells having wooden bases fastened to metal points with wires and strips of tin. These were so imperfectly manufactured that the wooden base was blown off a larger proportion of them before they reached the enemy. When fired over the heads of our advancing columns, it was a common remark that they killed more of our men by flying to pieces prematurely than they killed and wounded of the enemy combined."

This rain of death on Union troops probably came from the 1st Illinois Light Artillery. But it is possible some other battery was responsible for it.[23]

Though regarded by some experts as extremely reliable, the 3-inch Hotchkiss shell as described by Cadwallader was one of the worst things gunners could fire toward the enemy when their own men were underneath their trajectory. No big guns were immune from aberrations that could cause their fire to go astray. Even the cup or sabot of the famous Parrott projectile was prone to fail to grip the barrel's rifling in proper fashion. "The result was at best an erratic trajectory; at worst it meant a hopeless tumbling round."[24]

Even Grant's most ardent admirers acknowledged that his second frontal assault on Vicksburg was a bloody failure. In the 13th Corps, to which the U.S. Army's 13th Infantry was attached, 1,275 men suffered casualties in about eight or nine hours. It is impossible to determine how many of these were caused by friendly fire. With the other two corps included, Federal casualties on May 22 ran to 3,199 men. This made it the fourth costliest Federal assault of the entire war, topped only by Fredericksburg, Cold Harbor, and the Battle of The Crater at Petersburg.[25]

24

Warhorse Down

The Wilderness—May 5–7, 1864

U lysses S. Grant and Robert E. Lee crossed swords fiercely when forces they commanded fought savagely in The Wilderness, not far from Fredericksburg. Both the Army of the Potomac and the Army of Northern Virginia suffered casualties from comrades firing on comrades in the struggle where a common foe was fire. Losses among Grant's forces were trivial compared to Lee's. The Rebel general's loss was on a level not far below that which he suffered when men in gray accidentally killed Stonewall Jackson.[26]

After getting his divisions across the Rapidan River on May 4, Grant

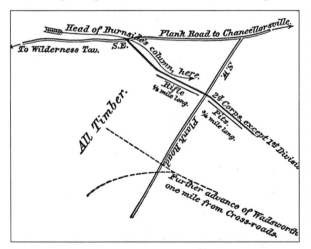

paused long enough to perch on a log and scribble a message to Washington. In it, he informed the Union's leaders that "Forty-eight hours now will demonstrate whether the enemy intends giving battle this side of Richmond." Since he had little stomach for fighting in the maze of underbrush and trees that constituted The Wilderness, he had his men on the

Well-named, The Wilderness included large areas that were virtually untouched by human hands until they became the sites of battles.—AUTHOR'S PRIVATE COLLECTION

move before 5 A.M. on May 5 without having any idea of what the day might bring.

One of his aides, Col. Horace Porter, noted that before sunset his commander expected to become involved in "either a fight or a foot-race." Following orders, Union Gen. Winfield Scott Hancock moved his 2nd Corps south from Chancellorsville on a path that would take it below the Orange Plank Road. From his headquarters in a tavern, Union Gen. Gouverneur K. Warren directed his men westward along a narrow trail that intersected the plank road at a tiny general store.

Warren's forces proceeded slowly because their lane was bordered by dense forests that sometimes made it impossible for more than eight men to march abreast. Two hours after men in blue got in motion, Grant and Gen. George Meade conferred at the Wilderness Tavern. They then sent orders for the southward thrust to stop because Rebel cavalry had been seen. Warren was ordered to attack with everything he had. One of Warren's forces was led by Gen. James Wadsworth, age 56, educated at Harvard where he had studied under Daniel Webster. But Wadsworth did not learn from Webster or anyone else how to guide troops through the semidarkness of a great forest.[27]

Since Lee had only a small segment of his army with him, he wanted to avoid combat until the arrival of Gen. James Longstreet's 1st Corps. Knowing the two Rebel bodies could not be united before the following day, about noon Lee directed one-legged Gen. Richard S. "Old Baldhead" Ewell to move slowly. Ewell's men received the directive only a few minutes before being assaulted by Federals whose advance wave was made up of the 140th New York and segments of five U.S. Army regiments. New Yorkers wearing uniforms festooned with red shouted "Zou! Zou!" as they charged into heavy fire. While they advanced, Lt. W. H. Shelton of the 1st New York Artillery hurriedly took two light guns to a point at which he could support the Zouaves.[28]

Almost as soon as the Federal guns were in place, Confederate sharp-shooters began taking out Shelton's men. Badly rattled, Shelton had both of his brass Napoleons loaded and fired hastily. Their charges plowed into the backs of men who made up the 140th New York and accounted for part of the 255 casualties suffered by this noted regiment during the battle.[29]

By the time Shelton's terrible mistake became widely known among men who had been fighting hand-to-hand, leaves and underbrush had been ignited by munitions, and men who had survived friendly fire found themselves fighting a forest fire.

*Pausing from his whittling, Gen. U. S. Grant told a reporter to inform Washington, "There will be no turning back."—*LIBRARY OF CONGRESS

Wounded men who lay in the path of flames were heard begging for water and screaming. A few were rescued by comrades, but dozens or scores burned to death. Despite spirited moves on both sides, men battling terrain plus foes plus fire openly yearned for the coming of darkness. Members of both armies threw up improvised defensive works and dug in for the night. Sitting by his campfire, Lee assured himself that Longstreet's corps and a division under Gen. Richard H. Anderson would reach the site of battle very early on May 6.

A native of South Carolina who spent much of his boyhood in Georgia, James Longstreet was appointed to West Point from Alabama. It made for a very Southern upbringing. During his first tour of duty near St. Louis, he became acquainted with Lt. U. S. Grant and soon introduced Grant to his future wife, Julia Dent. During the Mexican War, Longstreet fought at Palo Alto, Resaca de la Palma, Monterrey, Veracruz, Cerro Gordo, San Antonio, Churubusco, and Molino del Rey and soon was made captain. In 1858, then a major, he was sent to Albuquerque, New Mexico, as paymaster. On the heels of Fort Sumter he resigned and went to Richmond, offering to serve the Confederacy in "the pay department." Instead, he was made a brigadier on July 1 and sent to fight at First Bull Run.[30]

Just 16 months after having terminated his stint as a Federal paymaster, Longstreet was a lieutenant general in charge of Rebel defenses on Marye's Heights at Fredericksburg. A few months later, he survived Antietam as a result of chance and indecision. Sgt. Charles Fuller and Pvts. Porter A. Whitney and George Jacobs of the 64th New York were sent into the cornfield to watch movements of the enemy. When a small band of mounted Rebels was spotted, the New Yorkers debated among themselves whether to betray their presence by using their pieces. While they conferred, Longstreet and his comrades rode out of range.[31]

Responding to a message delivered at the edge of The Wilderness by courier, Longstreet and his men moved at top speed, and before dark on May 5, 1863, they were within ten miles of the battle. Eager to meet the enemy, they pulled out at 1 A.M. on May 6. Headed for the Orange Plank Road, they reached their destination just as Federals under Gen. James Wadsworth began pushing back Rebels led by Gen. Ambrose Powell Hill. Longstreet somehow managed to form his line in a dense thicket where Hill's men were retiring in great disorder. The new arrivals checked the Federal advance and a period of relative quiet ensued.[32]

Men under Gens. William Mahone, Richard H. Anderson, and William T. Wofford having been assigned to support part of Longstreet's front, a line of attack was formed. According to Mahone, "three brigades, in imposing order and with a step that meant to conquer, now rapidly descended upon the enemy's left." During their successful sweep to the plank road, Union Gen. Wadsworth was mortally wounded and survived only two days. Warren incorrectly believed that he died on the spot from "a bullet through his head." Wofford was less severely wounded and soon recovered; many Confederate officers began to smell victory and to shout their elation.[33]

A lull in the fighting lasted until noon, giving Longstreet an opportunity to dispose his troops in order to deliver a smashing and decisive blow to enemy units that were giving ground. According to Col. Charles S. Venable of Lee's staff, his commander in chief ordered David M. Gregg's Texas brigade forward, then spontaneously guided his horse behind the line in order to take part in the assault. This action precipitated the famous "Lee to the Rear!" incident when Texans shouted that they would not go on unless their commander turned back.[34]

As the pace of the action accelerated, many Federal and some Confederate regiments became hopelessly entangled, separated from their brigades, and lost in what seemed to be an impenetrable forest lighted only by blazing fires. In the midst of confused fighting during which only occasional periods occurred when men could see clearly, the lieutenant general and a number of his officers and aides were caught in fire between two Virginia regiments. Longstreet was hit in the throat and right shoulder by a minié bullet; many of his muscles and nerves were cut. Some of his companions saw him lifted from the saddle by the blow of the bullet and concluded that he was dead.

They were wrong; he lived to become revered as "Lee's War-Horse." But he never recovered full use of his right arm. Maj. Andrew Dunn, an aide-de-camp, left the general on the ground where he fell and raced to find medical help. When Drs. Dorsey Cullen and Randolph Barksdale reached the stricken commander, they were surprised and delighted to find him breathing.[35]

Lee, who seldom lost his capacity to view a battlefield almost as though he were a distant, impartial observer, did not come up to his own standard in the aftermath of the tragedy. He took personal command of the part of the line where his officers and men were felled by their fellows, then countermanded Longstreet's announced plans for a concerted advance. Seeking to "make more perfect dispositions of his troops," the lull in fighting that he created lasted until 4 P.M. By then, it was too late to score the great victory that seems to have been within his grasp.[36]

Grant's army suffered about 18,000 casualties and Lee lost at least 7,500. A Rebel who called himself a deserter, but who may have been sent into Federal lines by superiors, reported that both Lee and Gen. George E. Pickett were seriously wounded. Relayed to Washington, this false story led to a brief outburst of rejoicing.[37]

Observers were quick to note the strange set of coincidences involved in the death of Stonewall Jackson and the permanent injury of Longstreet. Both were hit by fire from their own men at spots not far

So many men were wounded that all conventional devices for transporting the wounded were exhausted and men resorted to using poles and canvas.—AUTHOR'S PRIVATE COLLECTION

distant from one another, and the two incidents took place just four days more than one year apart.[38]

These fatal misadventures had still another element in common. As in the case of Jackson's mortal wounding, the casualties that took place on and close to the Orange Plank Road brought no reprisals, and some who were involved did not mention the incident in their reports. Happy that "no blame attached" to fellow Rebels, Gen. Charles W. Field meditated on "the unfortunate accident" of May 6. He concluded that "no ordinary forethought" could have prevented it, so wrote that the entire matter "must be considered one of those mysterious interpositions by the almighty in the affairs of men deemed necessary to shape for His own purposes the course of human events."

Gen. James Longstreet was lauded by Robert E. Lee as his "war horse."—HARPER'S ENCYCLOPEDIA OF U.S. HISTORY

In Washington, President Lincoln never learned the full details of the day on which Grant was given an unexpected and inexplicable reprieve. Had he known of events in The Wilderness, Lincoln almost certainly would have echoed the verdict of Field that they reflected "the mysterious impositions of the almighty."[39]

25

"Fire Gun Number One!"

The Wilderness—May 6, 1864

In response to that terse order, very early on the morning of January 9, 1861, George E. Haynesworth of Sumter County, South Carolina, pulled the lanyard he had been holding for two hours or more. The ball he delivered skipped across the waters of Charleston harbor, well in advance of the sidewheel steamer *Star of the West.*

Chartered by authorities in Washington at a cost of $1,250 a day, the vessel was loaded with provisions designed to enable the Federal defenders of Fort Sumter to hold out for many weeks. Staying below decks and well out of sight, 200 hand-picked men of the U.S. Army were under the command of Lt. Charles R. Wood of the 9th Infantry. Once the steamer reached its destination, Wood and his men expected to pour out and more than double the effective strength of the fort's garrison.

Haynesworth held fire until he was positive his piece was carefully aimed well ahead of the bow of the *Star.* Soon a second shot was delivered. This time it was aimed directly at the vessel that had come from New York. Then a rain of metal from secessionist guns forced the steamer to turn around and go back North. Haynesworth would be remembered as the man who fired the first shot of the Civil War, had it not been for the fact that President James Buchanan did not want armed sectional strife—and therefore did not dispatch warships to Charleston when his January expedition was turned back.[40]

The youthful gunner whose name failed to get into history books was a cadet at South Carolina's Citadel Military Institute. He and fellow students were in charge of a battery hastily erected among the sand dunes of Morris Island. Established 19 years before the brief appearance of the

Star in Charleston harbor, his school was one of many that helped persuade Southerners they could easily defeat Northerners, though Northerners' numbers, money, and industrial power were much greater.

Military schools and institutes were scattered throughout much of the Cotton Belt, and in addition to the Citadel some of them played significant roles in the conflict that officially began three months after cadets fired on the *Star of the West.* At least 50 students left the North Carolina Military Institute early in order to enroll in Confederate units. Located in Lexington, the Virginia Military Institute threw

Gen. Micah Jenkins rode toward Federal lines after having assured subordinates that his men would "smash the enemy now."—Author's Private Collection

nearly 2,000 students and faculty members into the conflict; along with Prof. Thomas J. "Stonewall" Jackson, 16 of them rose to the rank of general. Later, cadets still on the VMI grounds played a heroic and memorable role in the Civil War battle of New Market.[41]

Micah Jenkins, son of a wealthy planter, graduated with first standing in the Citadel class of 1855. In partnership with a classmate, he immediately launched the King's Mountain military school in York County, South Carolina. With sectional strife looming, Jenkins helped to organize the troops of his state. He then became colonel of the 5th South Carolina and left for Virginia under the command of West Point graduate and Mexican War veteran Gen. David R. Jones.

Before the end of 1861, as a colonel of the Palmetto Sharpshooters, the Citadel graduate was commanding a brigade and had won the favorable attention of James Longstreet. Soon, the older officer whose South Carolina roots were strong was pushing for Jenkins to be made a

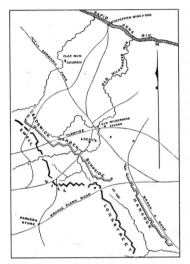

Large numbers of opposing troops converged just southwest of the Wilderness Tavern.—

brigadier. Though his recommendations were supported by P. G. T. Beauregard, the Charlestonian fought at Williamsburg, Seven Pines, Gaines's Mill, and Frayser's Farm as a colonel. Without explaining his reasons, Jefferson Davis twice rejected Longstreet's recommendation that his young protégé be made a brigadier.[42]

The August 1862 Second Battle of Bull Run was the first fight during which Jenkins wore stars. After fighting at Fredericksburg, Chickamauga, and Knoxville, he led his brigade of seasoned veterans into The Wilderness. On the second day of fighting there, he rode by the side of Longstreet during the morning and expressed great optimism about the outcome of the struggle. According to one analyst, throughout the Army of Northern Virginia, men "enjoyed a thrilling surge of adrenaline" as a result of having "won a clear-cut tactical victory."[43]

Trees and shrubs, which grew so close together that visibility was limited to a few yards, proved to be more deadly in some respects than Yankee muskets. Realizing they had become separated from their comrades, some of the Rebels in Mahone's brigade who were north of the plank road turned around and moved toward the vital thoroughfare. Simultaneously, other regiments from their brigade pushed rapidly toward the road from the south. Still more men in Jenkins's brigade were marching toward the plank road from the west and were fast approaching the spot at which other units would converge. Along with Gen. Joseph B. Kershaw, Longstreet and Jenkins and several of their staff officers rode with Jenkins's command.[44]

Smoke from forest fires and batteries of field artillery was so thick that Union Gen. Winfield Scott Hancock took note of both smoke and heat in his formal report, and a participant said "no one could see a hundred paces in any direction."

More confusion resulted from the color of the uniforms worn by most of the men under Jenkins. Though their outfits were dark gray, under trees among which columns of smoke swirled, their Rebel uniforms appeared to be blue or black. Having been held in reserve during the morning, men from the Palmetto State were eager to fight. Their officers knew that they would be expected to launch a fresh attack whose objective would be to clear the Orange Plank Road of the enemy.[45]

Headed toward the plank road from the north and separated from their brigade, men of the 12th Virginia were taken to be enemies by the 41st Virginia. Peering toward what to them seemed to be a column of foes, men of the 41st began sporadic firing, which was quickly followed by a volley. George S. Bernard, a soldier present that day in the ranks of the 12th Virginia, said afterward that

Gen. Joseph B. Kershaw.—Carolina Museum

when firing began he had just one thought: *"The enemy are in our rear, and we are in a bad box."* Some members of the 12th managed to escape injury by throwing themselves to the ground. Gray-clad riders just ahead of the unit whose uniforms appeared to be blue were caught in the fire from the 41st Virginia.[46]

Rebel Lt. Col. G. Moxley Sorrel, also present, insisted that he never knew positively who started the onslaught. Lt. Col. Everard M. Feild of the 12th Virginia was certain one or two regiments to his right opened fire. Lt. John R. Patterson of the same unit insisted that the line of comrades who "were at the time pouring a deadly fire into us" were less than 50 yards away. If his recollection of the incident is correct, general officers and their aides were caught in fire from the 41st regiment as well as the 12th.[47]

Gen. Charles W. Field, riding with Jenkins, saw that men who followed them "instantly faced the firing and were about to return it." He later reported that in this crisis he dashed his horse into their ranks, crying, "They are friends!" Some accounts insist that his actions prevented still more fire. Substantial evidence indicates, however, that Field failed to stop the shooting until after many of Jenkins's men knelt and "aimed blindly into the bush." If that was the case, their actions represented still another lethal incident of the sort that took the life of their commander. Kershaw is credited with having shouted "Friends!" at the top of his voice, and he always said that by doing so he helped save the life of Longstreet.[48]

Prior to rejoining the Army of Northern Virginia, Longstreet's corps had been separated from it for more than six months; his seasoned veterans cheerfully scrambled up steep slopes against the enemy.—LIBRARY OF CONGRESS

In the utter confusion that followed sudden tragedy, no one compiled a complete list of casualties that resulted from this friendly fire accident. Hit in the head and mortally wounded, Jenkins lingered only briefly. Capt. Alfred E. Doby died on the spot; so did Pvt. Benjamin B. White of the 12th Virginia and "a couple of couriers." There is no record concerning the number and nature of wounds suffered by other officers and men.[49]

The death of Jenkins was mourned throughout much of the Army of Northern Virginia. He was lauded by Longstreet as "intelligent, quick, untiring, attentive, zealous in discharge of duty, truly faithful to official obligations, [and] abreast with the foremost in battle." Years later, a brief but poetic biographical profile of his last day in uniform read, "In a moment of highest earthly hope, he was transported to serenest heavenly joy; to that life beyond that knows no bugle call, beat of drum or clash of steel."[50]

Authorities differ concerning the date of Jenkins's birth; some say 1839; others insist that he was born four years earlier. Regardless of the correct date, when the South Carolinian drew his last breath in the aftermath of "the mistaken fire of another body of Confederates," he was no older than 28. That made him the youngest general officer on either side to be killed by his comrades.[51]

CHAPTER

26

Fifty Officers, Fifty Days

Charleston, South Carolina—June 12–August 3, 1864

On June 12, 1864—the thirty-ninth day of the siege of Charleston as counted by the city's officials—a contingent of 50 Federal officers reached the city. Their arrival was noted two days later by both the *Daily Courier* and the triweekly *Mercury*. Edited by a fire-eating secessionist, the *Mercury* gleefully informed readers, "For some time past, it has been known that a batch of Yankee prisoners, comprising the highest in rank in our hands, were soon to be brought hither to share the pleasures of the bombardment [by Federal warships]. They accordingly arrived on Sunday. . . . These prisoners, we understand, will be furnished with comfortable quarters in that portion of the city most exposed to the enemy's fire. The commanding officer on [Federally held] Morris Island will be duly notified of the fact of their presence in the shelled district, and if his batteries still continue their wanton and barbarous work, it will be at the peril of the captive officers." [52]

Readers of the *Daily Courier* received the sanctimonious assurance: "We do not expose or confine these prisoners in a fortress or walled town or city or thrust them forward in our battles as the Yankees do with the unfortunate Negro, who has now, under God, no true friends but in the 'Confederate States.' We place them in our city of Charleston, among and near by our wives and children, and old men and our hospitals. . . . If the Yankees have a rule or code of war which justifies them in throwing shells—incendiary shells and other Yankee variations—into a city whose outer works are still in great part actively defiant, we leave them to the enjoyment of that right [since they will risk the death of a Yankee officer every time a gun is fired]." [53]

According to the newspapers, big naval guns threw 21 shells on Saturday, June 11, and 44 on the day Federal officers arrived to be placed under the fire of their own warships.

A poem of eight four-line stanzas was published in connection with the triumphant announcement that the prisoners had arrived. Titled "The Beleaguered City," it boasted that "the fearless city" still stood despite "Yankee hate."

Prisoners were duly listed by rank and by name. Five generals, 11 colonels, 25 lieutenant colonels, and 9 majors were on the list. Eliakim P. Scammon had been a prisoner longer than any other general officer sent to Charleston. An 1837 graduate of West Point, dismissed from the U.S. Army in 1856 for disobedience, he put his uniform back on as colonel of the 23rd Ohio. He fought for nearly three years before being captured by partisan rangers in West Virginia.[54]

Gen. Henry W. Wessells was captured at Plymouth, North Carolina, less than three months before being shipped to Charleston. Gen. Charles A. Heckman became a prisoner of war about the same time, but he was taken at Drewry's Bluff in Virginia. Both Gens. Truman Seymour and Alexander Shaler fell into Rebel hands during the Battle of The Wilderness. Last to be captured among the general officers who became unwilling visitors to the port city, these four generals were openly hopeful that an early exchange could be arranged.[55]

Charleston, fourth largest city in Colonial America, as photographed by Matthew Brady.—LIBRARY OF CONGRESS

Many Charleston residents celebrated the news that the five generals and 45 other Federal officers had arrived. It was hoped their presence would change the ways of gunners on occupied Morris Island and on Federal naval vessels. Had they not been given constant reminders by their newspapers, many residents would have long since lost count of the number of days during which shells rained down on their beloved city.

Many of today's readers who retrieve sections of newspapers from microfilm find themselves surprised. In June 1864, Charleston's residents had many things on their minds in addition to hostages who had been selected to come under friendly fire. A section of *News from the United States* and of *Northern Intelligence* informed them that Abraham Lincoln had been renominated in Baltimore and that Grant was besieging Richmond. Some slave owners became angry when they spotted a notice that required them to "deliver one fourth of their slaves" for work "at the railroad depots nearest their residences."

Considerable interest was shown in "the Cleveland ticket" of Independent Republicans who were avowedly against the continuance of the war. Their candidate for the presidency, John Charles Frémont, was quoted as having declared the Lincoln administration constituted a military dictatorship. Reelection of Lincoln, said his former general, "would be fatal to the country."

A dispatch from Richmond by a correspondent of the *Mercury* was published the day after the 50 Federal officers became involuntary Charleston residents. Readers who turned to this report could hardly fail to see in the next column a lengthy list of casualties experienced by the 20th South Carolina Regiment at "Gaines' Farm, Virginia." Patients in all ten of the city's hospitals—of which half were filled with soldiers from the Palmetto State and Louisiana, North Carolina, Georgia, and Virginia—were listed two or three times a week.

The April report of the captain of police to the mayor showed that 728 white males and 17 white females were known to have been arrested during the most recent month. Only 130 black males and 18 black females were thrown into jail during that period. Four-horse wagons with wooden axles were offered for sale at $500, and a person willing to work could earn five cents by shelling 56 pounds of corn into a sack furnished by the government. With officers below the rank of brigadier still being elected by their men or appointed by the governor, a group of "many voters" wanted Maj. Rumph of Orangeburg to become colonel of the 3rd Regiment of reserves.[56]

One day after the arrival of the 50 hostage officers, Confederate Gen. Samuel Jones notified his Federal counterpart at Hilton Head that

Admiral John A. Dahlgren's big naval guns failed to pound Fort Sumter and the city of Charleston into submission.—H. WRIGHT SMITH ENGRAVING

these prisoners of war were in Charleston "for safe-keeping." Jones told Gen. J. G. Foster that "[officers will be given] commodious quarters in a part of the city occupied by non-combatants, the majority of whom are women and children. It is proper, however, that I should inform you that it is a part of the city which has been for many months exposed day and night to the fire of your guns." A similar notice went simultaneously to Gen. Alexander Schimmelfennig, commander of Federal forces on occupied islands near Charleston.[57]

Foster voiced his vigorous protest at such an inhumane action by fellow Americans, and he immediately ordered Confederate prisoners shipped to him from Johnson's Island, Ohio. He must have 5 Confederate generals, 15 colonels, 15 lieutenant colonels, and 15 majors, he said. They were needed in order to be placed under Confederate fire and must exactly match the contingent of officers held in Charleston.

Reporting to Gen Henry W. Halleck in Washington about developments on the Carolina coast, Foster enclosed "an extract from the Charleston Tri-weekly Mercury of the 14th instant, giving a list of the names of our officers now in confinement in that portion of the city of Charleston most exposed to our fire."[58]

Col. Joseph T. Tucker enlisted in the Rebel forces from Winchester, Kentucky. Captured during Gen. John Hunt Morgan's Ohio raid in July 1863, he was initially held as a prisoner in the Ohio State Penitentiary. After having been transferred to Fort Delaware south of Philadelphia on June 26, 1864, he became one of the 50 Rebel officers sent south to be placed under Confederate guns in retaliation for the Federal officers confined in Charleston. Like its Federal counterpart, this contingent of prisoners was headed by five generals.[59]

Gen. James J. Archer, a prewar Maryland attorney with Mexican War experience, directed his brigade from an ambulance at Antietam. After winning glory at Fredericksburg and Chancellorsville, at Gettysburg he became the first general officer in gray to be taken prisoner since Lee had assumed command of the Army of Northern Virginia. He was imprisoned at Johnson's Island, Ohio, for about a year before being selected to be placed under fire by Foster.[60]

Rebel Gen. Franklin Gardner, born in New York, was in command of Confederate forces when Federals fired on their own men at Port Hudson, Louisiana. A West Point graduate in the class of 1843, he surrendered to Gen. Nathaniel Banks in July 1863. Gen. Edward "Allegheny Ed" Johnson of Virginia graduated from West Point five years before Gardner. He fought under Stonewall Jackson in the Shenandoah Valley, and after Jackson was mortally wounded by friendly fire he took over the division and led it to Gettysburg. He was captured at Spotsylvania, Virginia, on May 12, 1864.[61]

Though Gen. George H. Steuart of Baltimore was also a West Pointer, he entered Confederate service as a captain of cavalry. Like

Though Charleston was heavily bombarded, sections in which Federal officers were housed were not hit.—AUTHOR'S PRIVATE COLLECTION

Johnson, he fought in the Shenandoah Valley and at Cross Keys, where he received a severe wound that took him out of action for about a year. He, too, was captured at Spotsylvania. Meriwether J. Thompson was turned down at West Point, and by Virginia's Gov. Clairborne F. Jackson on the outbreak of war. Determined to fight the North, he organized a band of irregulars and as their leader became noted as "Swamp Fox of the Confederacy." Claiming to be a general and widely hailed as having that rank, despite the fact that he did not hold a Confederate commission, after being captured his self-bestowed rank led captors to send him south when Foster's call was received.[62]

Along with 15 colonels, plus an equal number of lieutenant colonels and majors, the 5 top Confederate officers selected for retaliatory treatment seem to have gone to Hilton Head for a brief stay. They were shipped to Charleston on June 26 aboard the steamer *Dragoon*. Foster had made elaborate plans to place them in jails that were to be erected on Morris Island—the target of heavy Confederate fire because Fort Wagner was in Federal hands. Problems soon developed; it was found that the jails would have to be constructed at Hilton Head, dismantled, shipped to Charleston harbor and reassembled for use on the island. In Washington, Gen. Henry W. Halleck hit the ceiling when he received a newspaper clipping indicating that the Rebel officers had not been placed under fire of Confederate guns, as planned. Foster patiently explained that when his jails were finally ready for use, he had received authorization to effect a special exchange.[63]

Weeks before Foster tried to appease Halleck, he relayed to Washington a plea received by way of Jones from the 50 Federal officers who were under fire from their comrades. Speaking for the entire band, the five captive generals in blue addressed Gen. Lorenzo Thomas, adjutant general of the U.S. Army. In their document, the quintet expressed their "firm belief that a prompt exchange of prisoners of war in the hands of the Southern Confederacy is called for by every consideration of humanity." The Charleston captives insisted they were situated "as pleasantly and comfortably as is possible for prisoners of war" and that they were not being unnecessarily exposed to fire.

In transmitting this letter, Jones stressed his personal conviction that "there should be an exchange of prisoners." Foster expressed interest in an exchange, but he wrote that it must be preceded by removal from Charleston of "the United States Prisoners of War" then in the city. At the same time that he erected this barrier to an exchange, Foster requested from Halleck the authority to work one out. Apparently something went wrong with the communications system—a frequent occurrence—for

Halleck seems to have authorized a special exchange as early as June 19. Seeking face-to-face dialogue in lieu of the continuous transmittal of letters, Jones sent Maj. J. F. Lay to Hilton Head. Talk progressed rapidly, for on July 20 Foster notified Jones that the U.S. secretary of war had authorized the proposed exchange, "rank for rank, or their equivalents." This exchange, he stressed, must be treated as "a special one."[64]

Gen. John G. Foster—NICOLAY & HAY, ABRAHAM LINCOLN

The exchange of prisoners erupted as an extremely sticky question when the war was very young. Lincoln objected to the practice on the grounds that engagement in it would constitute recognition of the C.S.A. as a sovereign nation. Lacking a mechanism by which to effect exchanges, many commanders resorted to time-honored but complex European practices and offered paroles to prisoners. A person who entered into such an agreement swore he would not fight again until after having been "regularly exchanged."[65]

Arrangements for prisoner exchanges were eventually worked out, but the process frequently broke down. After U. S. Grant became the head of the Union military effort, exchanges became more difficult, for he correctly reasoned that he had a virtually unlimited pool of manpower, while prisoner exchange was the enemy's chief method of replenishing decimated units. After all exchanges ceased by order of Grant, increasingly large numbers of Federal prisoners had to be housed and fed and clothed in the impoverished Confederacy. This factor contributed mightily to the horrible conditions that developed at the Rebel prisons such as Andersonville, Georgia, and Salisbury, North Carolina.

Jones and Foster were keenly conscious that the exchange of Federals in Charleston for an exactly equivalent group of Confederate prisoners constituted a special one-time arrangement. Grant did not consent to resumption of exchanges on a routine basis until January 1865, when it was clear to most observers that the South was tottering toward an end of the war.[66]

Once he was positive that he was authorized to effect the special exchange, Foster contacted Rear Adm. John A. Dahlgren of the South Atlantic Blockading Squadron. He wanted exchanged Federal officers to be brought to Hilton Head on the USS *Cosmopolitan,* Foster said. With all her flags flying and her band playing, this vessel should "round to under the stern of the Pawnee" so that a salute could be fired from the warship's immense guns.[67]

Security having been greatly relaxed as soon as definite plans had been made for an exchange, 50 Federal officers were taken into Charleston harbor on August 3. That morning they were swapped for the 50 Confederate officers who had remained under guard aboard their steamer, but not under fire. Along with a few other Federal prisoners who were simultaneously released or exchanged, they did not go to Hilton Head. Instead, they obeyed orders to "proceed North on the steamer Fulton, under command of Henry W. Wessells."[68]

Exchange of 10 generals, 30 colonels, 30 lieutenant colonels, and 30 majors, half of whom had been under the fire of Federal guns for 50 days, went without a hitch. Enemies who conveyed them to the waiting steamer talked profusely about the marvelous fact that no prisoner was wounded despite the fact that shells rained on Charleston every day they were in the city.[69]

No man on either side involved in this "special exchange" then dreamed that it did not spell the end of placing men under the fire of guns manned by their comrades. Within days the defenders of Charleston discovered that they had unwittingly opened a Pandora's box. As a result, their shells and balls would soon be directed over the heads of Rebel officers confined in a pen situated so that fire from Fort Sumter threatened to maim or kill many of these special captives.

27

Two Acres of Hell

The Crater, Petersburg, Virginia—July 30, 1864

"**A** slight tremor of the earth for a second, then the rocking as of an earthquake, and with a tremendous burst which rent the sleeping hills beyond, a vast column of earth and smoke shoots upward to a great height, its dark sides flashing out sparks of fire, hangs poised for a moment in midair, and then hurtling downward with a roaring sound showers of stones, broken timbers, and blackened human limbs, subsides—the gloomy pall of darkening smoke flushing to an angry crimson as it floats away to meet the morning sun."[70]
This was a description of the detonation of 8,000 pounds of black powder under the Rebel trenches at Petersburg, one of the most spectacular events of the war. W. Gordon McCabe's eyewitness description of the explosion of 320 kegs of explosives beneath the Confederates is just one of many.[71]
Federal forces had been besieging Petersburg for weeks and seemed to be getting nowhere. Weary of the protracted stalemate, Lt. Col. Henry Pleasants of the 48th Pennsylvania listened with interest when a former miner in his command proposed a novel step. It would be hard work, the fellow admitted, but men who were doing nothing would jump at the chance to tunnel under the Rebel defenses and blow the fellows sky high with a single mighty blast.[72]
Gen. Ambrose Burnside, in immediate field command, reacted to the novel idea with enthusiasm. Gen. George G. Meade said little, but his silence indicated grave doubts. Submitted to Gen. Ulysses S. Grant, the concept won grudging approval. During the siege of Vicksburg, Grant's men had tried a similar experiment that fizzled, but almost any action seemed better than doing nothing.[73]

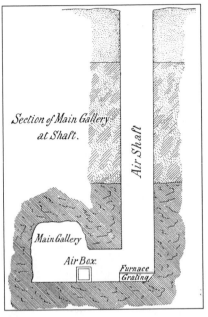

Section of Main Gallery at Shaft.

Air Shaft

Main Gallery

Air Box.

Furnace Grating.

Cross-section of the all-important main gallery at the air shaft.—BATTLES & LEADERS

Digging began on June 25 and proceeded until July 23. The main tunnel created by miners reached 511 feet in length by most accounts; Burnside said it was 522 feet. Maj. Oliver Bobyshell of Pennsylvania was ecstatic that Federals had done the impossible with "no tools, no nails, no plans, and no wheel-barrows." Miners had few complaints, except that they had requested 12,000 pounds of powder, but received just two-thirds that quantity.[74]

Before placement of the charge was begun on July 27, Rebel Gen. E. Porter Alexander, an artillery officer, had become suspicious about strange sounds occasionally heard when nights were exceptionally quiet. He surmised, correctly as events soon proved, the enemy must be trying to dig a lengthy mine whose terminus might be under one of his batteries. He ordered men in gray to sink a countermine, but despite hard work they discovered nothing.[75]

Grant made plans for an elaborate diversion, by which he hoped to draw many of Petersburg's defenders away from the site of the attack. Though this movement did not have its desired effect, Federal troops prepared to make the assault. Divisions under Gens. Edward Ferrero, Robert Potter, James Ledlie, and Orlando Willcox would have the honor of blasting Rebels to bits so that their triumphant enemies could march into the city and make arrangements for Burnside to dine there that night.

Ferrero's black soldiers, who made up the only division of its sort in the Army of the Potomac, were the freshest of the lot. Hence, it was initially planned for them to take the lead. Mead objected that such action might make some civilians and soldiers think they were "shoving these people ahead to get killed because we did not care about them." With Ferrero relegated to a follow-up position, Burnside could not make up his mind which of his three white divisions should be first to follow up the explosion. To solve this dilemma, he had his generals draw straws and by means of this impromptu lottery Ledlie was chosen to lead. The choice of Ledlie meant that men in blue would be guided by "perhaps the least competent division commander in the Army of the Potomac, a known weakling, drinker and coward."[76]

Final Federal preparations were made during the night of July 29, which was remarkably quiet and clear, lighted only by a waning moon. Men selected to light the mammoth charge were in motion by 2 A.M. Saturday, July 30. They touched a small torch to powder at 3:15 A.M.; it sputtered only momentarily before flaring up. The fuse had been lit!

When nothing happened after many long minutes, Lt. Jacob Douty and Sgt. Henry Rees of the 48th Pennsylvania laid their lives on the line by volunteering to see what had gone wrong. Crawling on their hands and knees in total darkness for about 50 feet, they found the spot at which the dampened fuse had gone out; they then relighted it and scurried back to the entrance. At 4:33 A.M. Pleasants notified Burnside: "In eleven minutes the mine will explode."[77]

When the charge went off precisely at 4:44 A.M., it blew a hole so enormous that trained observers disagreed about its size. Its length was reported as having been from 135 to 150 feet; some said it was just 50 feet wide, but others insisted that it measured 97 feet across. Nearly all commentators agreed that depth of the hole was about 25 to 30 feet, and that a 12-foot crest was created around much of its rim. With its likeness to a volcanic crater heightened by that crest, the hole, measuring about two acres, was dubbed on the spot "the crater"; in later

The explosion, as depicted by an artist who did not see it.—THE SOLDIER IN OUR CIVIL WAR

Picks and cracker boxes with which to haul dirt were the chief tools used in digging the tunnel.—Library of Congress

usage, the title became capitalized.[78]

Guns and men of a Confederate battery shot upward as a result of the blast; they came down as fragments of metal and body parts. Four out of every five men who were tending that battery never knew what hit them. But nearly ten minutes passed before officers decided that Ledlie's troops were properly aligned to charge.

With troops moving over broken ground, the assault became chaotic before it reached the rim of The Crater. By the time most of the white troops had scrambled down and discovered that no easy way out of the hole could be found, Ferrero's black troops began pushing in behind them. Rebel Capt. H. A. Chambers of the 49th North Carolina later vowed that enemies of both races poured into The Crater shouting, "No quarter to the rebels!" Soon troops within The Crater were described by Gen. Edward O. Ord as resembling men who had fallen into the bottom of a well. All semblance of order vanished; units were so intermingled that none preserved a pattern.[79]

By the time the immense hole was crowded with an estimated 5,000 men in blue, units were so disorganized that their members were labeled "rabble." Though relatively few Confederates had plunged into The Crater, those who did became engaged in hand-to-hand fighting as soon as their feet hit the ground. About 7:30 A.M., Gen. Benjamin C. Ludlow reported to Butler: "The position looks very encouraging, if they [the Federals] but push along." That overly optimistic verdict was dispelled by the time an estimated 7,000 men inside The Crater were forced so close together that some could not lift their arms. To Confederate marksmen, most of those who made up the trapped and entangled mass were sitting ducks who could be taken out almost at leisure.[80]

Eventually, men of both armies were inside The Crater. They began using their muskets with bayonets attached as though they were whale hunters; since it was seldom possible to lift a weapon so that it could be fired, the air was briefly filled with improvised "harpoons." About 11 A.M., Rebel Gen. William Mahone, who headed a "supporting body" of three divisions at some distance from the site of the explosion, received orders to take his troops into the fray.[81]

Though Mahone's men were soon fighting hand to hand, it is less than accurate to say that they won the Battle of The Crater. By the time they arrived, it was clear to many onlookers that only a few Federals could climb the steep walls of their bizarre prison in order to continue toward Rebel positions. According to Capt. John C. Featherston of the 9th Alabama, a lull occurred in the fighting about noon. Sporadic strug-

Gen. Edward Ferrero, who hid in a bomb shelter while his men raced into The Crater, was censured by a court of inquiry.—LIBRARY OF CONGRESS

gles within small spaces continued until about 5 P.M., when fighting men arrived at an improvised truce. Scores of communications exchanged between Federal officers during the day yield little information; though collectively they occupy more that 40 pages, most are only four to ten lines in length.[82]

By the time that the most compact notable battle of the war ended, it was clear that Rebels had suffered only about 1,500 casualties against 4,400 to 5,000 among Federal ranks. The ratio of wounded to killed among fighting men in blue was remarkably low; in some spots, the dead were observed to be lying on top of one another "eight bodies deep." Following the truce, bodies of an estimated 700 Federals were dumped into a ditch about 100 feet long. Mahone watched the unceremonious burial while wearing a uniform that had been improvised from Federal tent cloth.[83]

Maybe the most colorful story of survival attached to Union Gen. William F. Bartlett. Having lost a leg in The Wilderness, he limped into The Crater on one good leg plus a cork leg equipped with springs. When his cork leg was shot off, he fell to the ground and was almost crushed. Confederates who rescued and then captured him cheered wildly when he stumped out of the hole using two inverted muskets as walking sticks.[84]

In the immediate aftermath of the Federal debacle that created a Confederate triumph, Mahone was made a major general, and two of his captains who sustained wounds became instant brigadiers. Grant, who had headed toward Fort Monroe early in the day, saw little of the action, but described it as having constituted "the saddest affair I have ever witnessed in the war." To Meade, he observed on the following day that "Preparations were good, orders ample, and everything as far as I could see, subsequent to the explosion of the mine, shows that almost without loss the crest beyond the mine could have been carried. This would have given us Petersburg with all its artillery and a large part of the garrison without doubt."[85]

Meade, furious at the actions of other commanders, brought charges against Burnside and a formal court of inquiry was held. It took only a cursory investigation to reveal that neither Ledlie nor Ferrero took any part in the action; both of them took early refuge in a bombproof shelter and spent the day drinking. Ledlie was relieved, and Burnside was never given another assignment; perhaps because of his unique role as

Much of the blame for the fiasco at The Crater was placed on the shoulders of Gen. Ambrose Burnside.—NATIONAL ARCHIVES

commander of black troops, criticism of Ferrero was limited, and he was eventually awarded a brevet as major general.[86]

During the fierce fighting of one of the bloodiest Saturdays of the war, most officers on both sides were far too busy with other things to notice and record details about incidents in which comrades rained their fire on comrades. After the battle was over, fighting men told of having witnessed four such incidents in rapid succession.

The first of these befell a small group of Rebels who somehow escaped death when the Federal charge went off under them. Capt. George B. Lake of the 1st South Carolina and some of his men were thrown into The Crater. Covered with dirt from the explosion, they were dug out by members of a New York heavy artillery unit and were made prisoners. Lake wrote afterward that he and his comrades were kept in the vast hole "for a considerable time," during which they were exposed to shells from their own batteries.[87]

Ferrero described his 4,300 raw troops as having had less than two weeks of training before going into combat. After their confused advance into The Crater, their presence enraged many Rebels who had never before seen a black soldier. Though firsthand descriptions are missing, it is probable some of these men who were unable to defend themselves were shot or clubbed because of the color of their skin.[88]

The protracted Court of Inquiry on the Mine Explosion that began in Washington on August 3 heard several witnesses make guarded admissions that many white men in blue were almost if not quite as angry as their enemies that black troops were involved. An unidentified officer of the 1st Division is quoted as having written, "It has been positively asserted that white men [Federal troops] bayoneted blacks who fell back into the crater. . . . Men boasted in my presence that blacks had thus been disposed of, particularly when the Confederates came back up."[89]

Some Federals surrendered before the fight was over and were promptly ordered by their captors to the rear. According to the *Richmond Times-Dispatch*, Capt. John C. Featherston said, "In their confusion and eagerness, these early prisoners went across the open field, along the same route over which [Rebel troops] had charged them. Their cavalry, seeing them going to the rear, thought it was our men repulsed and retreating, and they at once opened fire upon them, killing and wounding a number of their own men. One poor fellow had his arm shot off just as he started to the rear, and returning, said: 'I could bear it better if my own men had not done it.'"[90]

A third instance of mayhem in Federal ranks seems to have stemmed from the use of so many big guns. One estimate places the number at

Because Gen. William Mahone weighed less than 100 pounds, he was often called "Little Billy."—LIBRARY OF CONGRESS

110 cannon plus 54 mortars strung along a two-mile line. Another observer insisted that at least 200 pieces were fired and that a single "park of artillery" included some 50 guns. Weapons employed by gunners in blue ranged from huge siege guns to relatively tiny Coehorn mortars. Capt. H. A. Chambers of the 49th North Carolina said that "mortars and other artillery threw large shells into huddled masses with great havoc." Maj. William H. Etheridge of the 41st Virginia echoed that report, saying, "every piece of artillery that could be brought to bear" on The Crater was used vigorously.[91]

At least one such incident was remembered by a survivor, Capt. George Clark of the 11th Alabama. Clark asserted that when an informal truce was reached, "The enemy threw down their arms, marched out as prisoners, some being killed or wounded by their own cannon as they filed past where I stood."[92]

Only four instances in which comrades mowed down comrades on July 30 are described here. With dozens or scores of gunners firing simultaneously, even the most skilled of them would have found it all but impossible to avoid hitting their own men. Such slaughter must have taken place many times during hours of chaotic fighting within an enormous hole in the ground. The struggle was so compact, however, that most of the men engaged in hand-to-hand fighting probably had no idea whether canister or grape or balls came from the enemy or from their own batteries.

Chapter 28

"The Immortal 600"

Morris Island, South Carolina—September 7–October 20, 1864

"There is not a darker page in the history of the war than the treatment of the six hundred [Rebel] prisoners at Morris Island and at Fort Pulaski. It is the darkest blot upon the civilization of the American people." Judge Henry Howe Cook of Franklin, Tennessee, delivered that verdict long after he and more than 500 other prisoners spent about 42 days under the constant fire of Confederate guns. They were put there by captors who mistakenly believed they were retaliating for similar treatment of 600 Federal officers.[93]

In June 1864, Rebel Gen. Samuel Jones put 50 captured Yankees into the line of fire from guns of the forces that were besieging Charleston. Federals transported an equal number of Confederate officers to the port city, but they seem never to have put them under the fire of guns in Rebel batteries. A special exchange was effected early in August, and residents of the city believed that the high-level squabble was over.

They were soon found to be wrong. Extremely crowded conditions at Andersonville and other prisons persuaded authorities to move many Federal captives to Charleston, Columbia, and Florence, South Carolina, while waiting for a place called Camp Lawton to be completed. This Confederate prison camp was expected to be suitable for housing 40,000 men, but scarcity of construction materials halted work. The delay meant that "temporary places of imprisonment," among which Charleston was the most notable, continued to hold officers in blue uniforms. Once the men who had been exposed to the fire of guns manned by their comrades were exchanged, Union Gen. John G. Foster authorized bombardment of the city to accelerate. Writing to Washington from his Hilton Head headquarters, Foster told General-in-chief Henry W.

Gen. Henry Halleck probably made the decision to place 600 captured Confederate officers under the fire of guns at Fort Sumter and Charleston.—Battles and Leaders

Halleck that he was adding six 11-inch naval guns to his batteries. He also divulged plans to build two immense "assaulting arks," with which he hoped to make a frontal attack on Fort Sumter.[94]

Many if not most Southerners blamed Foster for the next significant step in the long-standing struggle between forces in and around Charleston. That blame, however, should attach to Halleck. On August 18 he sent Foster a message in which he enclosed a copy of a newspaper dispatch. Published in the *Richmond Examiner* on August 9, an unsigned report informed readers that "the rebel officers who were recently exchanged in Charleston Harbor were never placed under fire by General Foster, and General Sam. Jones, the rebel commander in Charleston, has now a large number of newly arrived Federal officers under the fire of guns being used by Foster's subordinates."[95]

Having earlier berated Foster for his failure to expose the group of 50 Rebel officers to friendly fire, Halleck seems to have become furious at the unsubstantiated report that a new batch of Federals were being subjected to this treatment. But rumors that were taken as truth in Washington were without foundation. Foster queried Jones about the matter on August 15. The Rebel commander sent a lengthy statement to his enemy five days later. Information given to Federals by deserters and officers who were exchanged during the first week of the month was correct in one respect, he noted. Other prisoners of war were confined in Charleston, and some had arrived since the August 3 exchange.

Jones, however, told Foster: "You are mistaken if you suppose those prisoners have been sent here for the purpose of being placed in positions where they may be reached by your shot. They are placed here by the Government simply because it is found more convenient at present to confine them here than elsewhere." They would be removed from the city as soon as "proper arrangements" could be made elsewhere, he promised.

The Federal ordinance yard on Morris Island, where ammunition for the "Swamp Angel" was stored.—AUTHOR'S PRIVATE COLLECTION

In closing, Jones wrote, "They [the Federals then held in Charleston] are certainly as prisoners of war justly entitled to fair and honorable exchange, and that their Government denies them. I am ready at any time to send you every prisoner of war now in this department if you will give me in exchange an equal number of C.S. prisoners, man for man, rank for rank, or their equivalents."[96]

Jones's offer clearly put Foster into a box not of his own making. Earlier, Foster had repeatedly expressed his personal preference for exchanging men instead of holding them prisoner. His hands were tied, however.

On August 21, Lt. Gen. U. S. Grant gave the secretary of war a terse directive that required him to inform Foster "that in no circumstances will he be authorized to make exchanges of prisoners of war." Prisoner exchange, Grant ordered, must be limited to transactions agreed upon by generals on the battlefield. Though Grant did not say so, this directive meant that Federals would not have to accept in exchange any sick and malnourished officers or men who had been held in Confederate prisons.[97]

Halleck, persuaded by a single newspaper clipping that a large number of Federal officers were exposed to the fire of Federal guns in a new bid to protect Charleston, reacted with haste. Though his orders seem to have been destroyed, the Washington official who was serving as intermediary of sorts between Lincoln and Grant set in motion events that caused captured Confederate officers to be called "The Immortal 600" and hailed as martyrs and heroes.

Prompted by his mistaken belief, Halleck directed officials at Fort Delaware to select precisely 600 Confederate officers and ship them to Charleston to be placed under Rebel fire. Located on an island in the Delaware River about 40 miles below Philadelphia, the huge Federal prison then held an estimated 2,500 officers and 8,000 privates. Gen. Albin F. Schoepf, a native of Poland who was then commandant of the prison, arranged for quick lottery of men who would be shipped to Charleston "in retaliation for Confederate atrocities" believed to have taken place.[98]

On August 20, the heavily loaded steamer *Crescent,* escorted by the USS *Admiral,* began a far from routine voyage. Capt. F. N. Graves of the 61st Georgia was among the passengers forced into the vessel's hold who tried to describe it. All of them, he wrote, were "in one small transport, packed like sardines, four on the floor to every six feet square, then a bunk eighteen inches above with four more men, and then another tier above that making twelve men to about every six cubic feet during August, with mercury in the nineties."[99]

En route, Capt. Walter G. McRae and a few acquaintances counted heads. They determined that the *Crescent*'s cargo consisted of 6 men from Maryland, 186 from Virginia, 111 from North Carolina, 24 from South Carolina, 60 from Georgia, 10 from Florida, 26 from Alabama, 22 from Mississippi, 31 from Louisiana, 5 from Texas, 27 from Arkansas, 8 from Missouri, 35 from Kentucky, and 49 from Tennessee. If their list was accurate, exactly 600 men who believed they were about to be exchanged were on the way to Charleston Harbor to be put under Confederate guns.[100]

Places at which these men had been captured were as varied as their states of birth. Capt. C. C. Grace was made a prisoner at Spotsylvania, as were a number of his shipmates. J. Charles Carson of the Jeff Davis Cavalry was taken at Trevilian Station, and John R. Keane, a captain of heavy artillery, became a prisoner at Port Hudson, Louisiana. Lt. Benjamin H. Hutchinson survived Pickett's Charge at Gettysburg, but was captured immediately afterward; Capt. Edward Carter, who also participated in the futile charge, was severely wounded and left on the field as dead. Picked up by Yankees, after a period of hospitalization he went to Baltimore's Fort McHenry as a prisoner.

Seized by the enemy while recruiting near Lebanon, Tennessee, Lt. C. D. Covington went to Murfreesboro and then to Louisville before being sent to Camp Chase in Ohio. Briefly held at Fort Delaware, he was shipped to Johnson's Island and from that prison to Point Lookout before being returned to Fort Delaware and chosen to go South. Taken prisoner in North Carolina, Lt. W. B. Allen said he was sent to Old Capitol Prison in Washington and while there was visited by famed Southern agent Belle Boyd. He, too, went to Fort Delaware after a period and from that prison was selected to go to Charleston.[101]

A gale drove the *Crescent* into Georgetown, South Carolina, after which the transport made for Hilton Head. So many men were seriously ill that about 30 were taken off the ship and sent to hospitals. Though their number was now reduced, men destined to be put under Confederate fire continued to call themselves "The 600." From the port at which Foster was located, the *Crescent* steamed for

Maj. W. E. Stewart of the 15th Arkansas barely survived imprisonment.—CHARLESTON COUNTY LIBRARY

Charleston. After a 17-day voyage from Fort Delaware, she reached her destination before the stockade designed for her passengers was ready for use. Rear Adm. John A. Dahlgren of the South Atlantic Blockading Squadron used men of the USS *Ottawa* to guard the transport and her prisoners until they could be taken ashore.[102]

The 600 disembarked on September 7, their stench being such that guards who marched with the band grimaced and held their noses as they moved along the sand-covered beach to a stockade fashioned from palmetto logs. Dotted with tents barely big enough for four men, the place was described by one survivor as being about 130 yards square; others calculated its size as about one acre. All accounts insist that a hemp rope about one inch in diameter was stretched ten feet from the stockade wall. After having been warned that anyone who touched the rope dead-line would be instantly shot, men were assigned to tents. Their guards were enlisted men of the 54th Massachusetts, survivors of the Fort Wagner assault. White officers of this pioneer unit of black soldiers did not participate in guard duty; captives were unanimous in believing that the Federal choice of their guards was intended as "an additional humiliation."[103]

Morris Island, today almost washed away by the sea, was in 1864 described as "a small barren island of the shape of a sugar loaf, about 1,200 yards from Charleston, and between Charleston and the Federal batteries." Since the stockade into which the 600 were crowded lay directly in front of Fort Wagner, "the shells and shots from the Federal batteries passed over the inclosure where the Confederate officers were confined and guarded by negroes." Numerous as they were, these shells and balls were not considered a source of danger to the prisoners. Their lives were put on the line, however, every time a gun was fired from Fort Sumter or Sullivan's Island.[104]

Prisoners were positive that about sunrise on their first morning in the stockade, Federals made a calculated effort to goad gunners in gray to fire on them. A colonel of the 63rd Tennessee who was present that morning wrote, "every battery on the island and the guns on the monitors [ironclad Federal warships] were, at a given signal, opened upon the Confederate forts, to which the Confederate batteries promptly replied, and a regular artillery duel ensued, lasting for an hour or more. [Confederate] Forts Johnson, Beauregard, Moultrie, and a battery on James Island participated. Shells from the Confederate batteries were thrown with great precision into Fort Wagner, passing immediately over our pen, and others exploded to our left and front so uncomfortably close to the pen that we, at first, thought our friends were not upon the island. This storm of shot and shell created some consternation among the prisoners, and at first caused something like a panic."[105]

Terror subsided after the firing had gone on for about an hour. Prisoners decided, correctly as events proved, that their comrades were taking great care to avoid dropping a shell into the stockade.

Captors did everything in their power to anger Confederate gunners so that they would become careless. A Federal battery on James Island included one of the best-known guns used in the war. Soon admiringly called the "Swamp Angel" by its users, the 16,500-pound Parrott rifle was first fired at Charleston very early on August 22. From a distance of about 8,000 yards it threw a 150- or 200-pound shell into the city shortly before 2 A.M.; more than a dozen similar charges followed before daybreak. Some of the immense missiles were filled with a combustible liquid known as Greek Fire—until the invention of napalm, one of the most brutal fire weapons known to man. After having been fired about two dozen times on August 23, the immense gun burst. Men who manned it surveyed the now-useless piece ruefully. Charleston was not burning, and return fire drawn by the "Swamp Angel" had failed to kill a single Rebel in the crowded pen in front of Fort Wagner.[106]

On many clear nights the "whole heavens were illuminated" by shells that crisscrossed the harbor. Burning fuses presented a spectacle not unlike a July 4 fireworks display. Rebel Lt. Junius L. Hempstead managed to keep a diary of sorts by writing on blank pages in a textbook. On September 20 he noted "a shell went flying over us just now" and hoped that his comrades would not return the fire; to his great relief, they did not. Gunners in gray were keenly aware that failure to elevate their pieces a trifle more than needed in order to reach their targets could be deadly to members of the 600. They also took special care cutting their fuses, for a difference of one-tenth of a second was potentially crucial.[107]

Capt. W. D. Ballantine of the 5th Florida helped organize the tent city erected for captives.—CHARLESTON COUNTY LIBRARY

According to records and recollections of men who had been put under friendly fire, during eight weeks, only 17 Confederate shells fell short of their mark, and no casualties resulted from them. One shell exploded directly over the pen, and its fragments fell among the prisoners, but no one was injured. No members of the 54th Massachusetts killed or wounded a man who was under their guard. During this entire period of "retaliation," no Federal officer was in Charleston at a spot likely to draw the fire of a gunner in blue. The mistaken belief that men who had surrendered to Rebels had been "requisitioned from Andersonville" in order to serve as living shields for Charleston was not limited to Halleck, Foster, and their colleagues; many Confederates took this tale to be true.[108]

Inmates of the Federal stockade that was under Confederate fire day and night faced the shells of their comrades with more hardihood than the worm-infested food that was doled out to them in meager quantities. Civilians in Charleston occasionally managed to send them a parcel of fresh and tasty food that occasioned a banquet of sorts. One man lamented afterward that he somehow received a large ham, which he entrusted to "one of the negro soldier guards to cook it, as negroes were good cooks by nature." When the delicacy came back in a dish and wrapped in a newspaper, its proud owner lifted the paper and found that "the entire body of the ham had been cut out, leaving only the skin and bone." Water was very scarce, so men often caught and drank "drippings" off their tents.[109]

Wretched food and sanitation caused the death of Lt. W. P. Calahan of the 25th Missouri and 2nd Lt. J. C. C. Cooper of the 35th North Carolina. Seven men too weak to walk were removed from the stockade to hospitals. When their names were added to those of officers taken from the *Crescent* at Hilton Head, the number over whose heads an estimated 4,000 Confederate shells flew was reduced

Capt. Leon Jestremeska of the 10th Louisiana found Morris Island to be "the most dangerous spot in the northern hemisphere."—CHARLESTON COUNTY LIBRARY

to about 550. Yet when the emaciated survivors were hailed as "immortal," Southern military mythology was enriched by the term "The Immortal 600." Once bestowed, it stuck so firmly that it made all other labels for these men obsolete.[110]

Several lists of "The Immortal 600" are available, but no two are exactly alike.[111] When liberated from their Morris Island stockade, most of the "immortals" were imprisoned at Fort Pulaski, Georgia, where many died of disease and malnutrition. Nearly all of those who survived were eventually sent back to Fort Delaware, where they took the oath of allegiance to the United States in June 1865 and were released from custody.

"Victory Is the Name of the Game"

Oral tradition has it that Ulysses S. Grant, who was unheralded when he arrived in Washington to accept his commission as lieutenant general, stood around awkwardly after arriving at the Executive Mansion. After having shaken hands with Abraham Lincoln and having thanked him for his confidence, Grant reputedly summed up his military philosophy in a single short sentence: "Mr. President, victory is the name of the game!"

Regardless of whether or not that encounter took place as described, Grant had only one goal in mind when he took command of Union forces. He planned and expected to crush Rebels and bring them to their knees. Nothing else counted. When he suffered horrendous losses, he regretted them—but knew that a virtually bottomless pool of manpower was at his disposal. When the flow of Union prisoners produced horrendous conditions in Confederate stockades, Grant chewed on his cigar only briefly before commenting that most of these fellows were in no condition to fight, so it would not be profitable to agree to their exchange.

With victory considered to be the only thing that mattered, many commanders were careless about what to them seemed to be minor details. Frequently they instructed their gunners to shoot just a trifle over the heads of their own advancing comrades. Many times, they ordered the use of naval guns or siege guns or field artillery with the knowledge that it would be difficult to get the exact range. Occasionally they deliberately ordered fire on mixed belligerents, believing it more important to kill the enemy than to spare the lives of men in their own command.

Very early, some leaders began taking basic precautions to prevent volleys of friendly fire. Little or nothing was done for months, however, to make sure that most or all Federals wore blue and that the bulk of

Rebels wore gray or chestnut-colored uniforms. Absolutely nothing could be done about tangled terrain, darkness, or smoke or fog so dense that battlefield visibility was reduced to a few feet.

Ammunition for guns, often believed or known to be defective, was likely to be the only ammo at hand. As a result, it was issued to batteries with the knowledge that some projectiles were likely to trace faulty trajectories that could lead to casualties among comrades of the gunners who used it. Men who manned batteries were almost always under fearful pressure; no matter how skilled they might be in handling their pieces, it was a virtual certainty that an occasional fuse would be cut too short or too long. Some shells that were rated as good or better, notably the Hotchkiss, had components that were prone to fall off in flight and land on whatever body of troops happened to be beneath at the moment.

All of these factors plus numerous others contributed to the fact that on average a known instance of friendly fire occurred about every ten days during the entire war. Overriding all other contributing causes, however, was the expressed view by commanders on both sides that the ultimate goal was victory at any cost.

Viewed from the perspective of hindsight, it seems strange that no one followed Benjamin Butler's action in coining the label *contrabands* in order to give a name to fire that was directed upon comrades. Perhaps the omission was deliberate; after all, this was a matter that men preferred to think took place only in the ranks of the enemy or other commanders. Whatever the case, there is no cause for wonder that friendly fire erupted at least 150 times. In the utter confusion and madness that marked many a battle in which opposing leaders considered victory to be the only thing that ultimately mattered, the real wonder is that there were so few instances of friendly fire during about 1,400 days of conflict.

NOTES

PART I

1 *Journal of the Southern Historical Society*, 10, 368; *War of the Rebellion, Official Records of Union and Confederate Armies*, 2, 891

2 *War of the Rebellion, Official Records of Union and Confederate Armies*, 2, 894; *Journal of the Southern Historical Society*, 10, 369

3 *War of the Rebellion, Official Records of Union and Confederate Armies*, 2, 272; *Battles and Leaders*, 1, 487–88; *Journal of the Southern Historical Society*, 10, 370–71; Norman Shavin, *The Atlanta Century*, #67

4 *Journal of the Southern Historical Society*, 10, 372–73

5 *Journal of the Southern Historical Society*, 10, 373

6 *The Rebellion Record*, diary, 1, 19

7 Benson J. Lossing, *Pictorial Field Book of the Civil War*, I, 510; *Journal of the Southern Historical Society*, 29, 198

8 *War of the Rebellion, Official Records of Union and Confederate Armies*, 2, 77–104; *Supplement to the Official Records*, 1, 115–24

9 *Supplement to the Official Records*, 1, 121

10 *War of the Rebellion, Official Records of Union and Confederate Armies*, 2, 77, 84, 87; Benson J. Lossing, *Pictorial Field Book of the Civil War*, 1, 503

11 *War of the Rebellion, Official Records of Union and Confederate Armies*, 2, 83, 85

12 *War of the Rebellion, Official Records of Union and Confederate Armies*, 2, 87; *Supplement to the Official Records*, 2, 115–16; Benson J. Lossing, *Pictorial Field Book of the Civil War*, 1, 507; *Confederate Military History*, 4, 135–41

13 *Supplement to the Official Records*, 1, 123

14 *War of the Rebellion, Official Records of Union and Confederate Armies*, 2, 77–88; *The Confederate Veteran*, 1, 205; *The Confederate Veteran*, 31, 296; *The Confederate Veteran*, 34, 26; *Civil War Times*, 6/67, 82

15 *Battles and Leaders*, 1, 148f; *War of the Rebellion, Official Records of Union and Confederate Armies*, 2, 78; Clint Johnson, *Civil War Blunders*

16 *Confederate Military History*, 4, 135; *War of the Rebellion, Official Records of Union and Confederate Armies*, 2, 77–88; Benson J. Lossing, *Pictorial Field Book of the Civil War*, 1, 505; William C. Davis, *First Blood*

17 *War of the Rebellion, Official Records of Union and Confederate Armies*, 2, 86; *The Rebellion Record*, diary, 2, 164

18 *The Rebellion Record*, diary, 2, 164, 165; *War of the Rebellion, Official Records of Union and Confederate Armies*, 2, 87

19 *Confederate Military History*, 4, 137; *Battles and Leaders*, 1, 148; *War of the Rebellion, Official Records of Union and Confederate Armies*, 2, 88–105

20 *War of the Rebellion, Official Records of Union and Confederate Armies*, 1, 79–90; Benson J. Lossing, *Pictorial Field Book of the Civil War*, 1, 510; *Journal of the Southern Historical Society*, 21, 12f

21 *Battles and Leaders*, 1, 241; Benson J. Lossing, *Pictorial Field Book of the Civil War*, 1, 588

22 Stewart Sifakis, *Who Was Who in the Civil War*, 394; Jeffrey D. Wert, *General James Longstreet*, 62

23 Stewart Sifakis, *Who Was Who in the Civil War*, 394; Wert, op. cit., 65; James Longstreet, *From Manassas to Appomatox*, 36ff

24 *Battles and Leaders*, 1, 178f

25 *The Confederate Veteran*, 2, 291

26 Longstreet, op. cit., 39f

27 William G. Piston, *Lee's Tarnished Lieutenant*, 13

28 *War of the Rebellion, Official Records of Union and Confederate Armies*, 2, 242; W. H. Morgan, *Personal Reminiscences*, 60

29 *The Confederate Veteran*, 2, 291–92

30 Longstreet, op. cit., 39f; *Battles and Leaders*, 1, 175; Benson J. Lossing, *Pictorial Field Book of the Civil War*, 1, 589

31 Benson J. Lossing, *Pictorial Field Book of the Civil War*, 1, 589

32 *Official Records*, 2, 402–3

33 *Official Records*, 2, 406–7

34 Richard Wheeler, *Voices*, 34; *Official Records*, 2, 418–19

35 Evans, *Confederate Military History*, 118

36 *Official Records, Supplement*, 1, 194–95

37 *Civil War Times*, 5/63, 12
38 Wert, *General James Longstreet*, 68
39 *Official Records*, 2, 369–70; Lossing, *Pictorial Field Book*, 1, 600; William C. Davis, et al., eds., *Civil War Journal*, 2, 81–82
40 Henderson, *Stonewall Jackson*, 113
41 *Pictorial History*, 8, 39
42 *Pictorial History*, 8, 95
43 *Official Records*, 4, 580
44 *Official Records*, 6, 122–26
45 *Official Records*, 4, 582, 589; Evans, *Confederate Military History*, 5, 27; *Official Records of the Union and Confederate Navies*, 6, 135
46 *Official Records*, 4, 581, 584, 588, 591; *The Rebellion Record*, documents, 3, 24; Evans, op. cit.; *Confederate Military History*, 5, 26
47 *Official Records of the Union and Confederate Navies*, 4, 583; *Journal of the Southern Historical Society*, 37, 48; *Official Records of the Union and Confederate Navies*, 6, 137
48 *Official Records*, 4, 589
49 *Official Records of the Union and Confederate Navies*, 6, 124
50 *Official Records of the Union and Confederate Navies*, 6, 126, 136
51 *The Rebellion Record*, documents, 3, 24
52 Evans, op. cit., 5, 26; *The Rebellion Record*, documents, 3, 25
53 *Official Records of the Union and Confederate Navies*, 6, 137
54 *Official Records*, 4, 580, 585
55 Ronald Mosocco, *Chronological Tracking*, 27
56 *The Confederate Veteran*, 26, 392; *War of the Rebellion, Official Records of Union and Confederate Armies*, 3, 170
57 *The Rebellion Record,* poetry and incidents, 33
58 *St. Louis Evening News*, dispatch of September 21
59 *War of the Rebellion, Official Records of Union and Confederate Armies*, 3, 182
60 Military Order of the Loyal Legion , 15, 353; *The Confederate Veteran*, 35, 460; Military Order of the Loyal Legion, 50, 126; Evans, *Confederate Military History*, 1, 421
61 *The Confederate Veteran* , 4, 460; *Journal of the Southern Historical Society*, 9, 485
62 Evans, op. cit., 2, 61–62
63 *Official Records, 5*, 218
64 *Official Records, 5*, 219–20
65 *Official Records, 5*, 217
66 *National Intelligencer*, September 30, 1861
67 Sifikas, *Who Was Who*, 68; *Official Records,* 6, 460
68 *The Confederate Veteran*, 19, 337
69 *Journal of the Southern Historical Society*, 21, 220; *The Rebellion Record*, documents, 3, 86
70 *The Rebellion Record*, documents, 3, 83; *Official Records,* 6, 444–46
71 *The Rebellion Record*, documents, 3, 84–85; *Official Records,* 6, 439–56
72 *The Rebellion Record*, documents, 3, 85–88; Evans, op. cit., 16, 33
73 *Atlanta Intelligencer*, October 12
74 *Official Records,* 6, 444, 448, 451, 454
75 *Official Records,* 6, 458; 53, 200
76 *Official Records,* 6, 440–41, 444
77 *The Confederate Veteran*, 11, 20–21
78 Sifikas, *Who Was Who*, 430; Faust, *Historical Times Illustrated Encyclopedia,* 787
79 *Official Records of the Union and Confederate Navies*, 7, 41; Shavin, *The Atlanta Century*, no. 107; *The Rebellion Record,* documents, 4, 54–55, 266–80
80 *The Rebellion Record*, documents, 4, 272; Wheeler, *Voices,* 66
81 *Official Records of the Union and Confederate Navies*, 7, 3–8, 20–24, 29–32, 330–38; *The Rebellion Record,* documents, 4, 270
82 *Official Records of the Union and Confederate Navies*, 7, 70–71
83 Arthur Mokin, *Ironclad*, 245; Wheeler, *Voices,* 69; *Official Records of the Union and Confederate Navies*, 7, 4; *The Confederate Veteran*, 39, 456; Boatner, *The Civil War Dictionary*, 592; *The Rebellion Record,* documents, 4, 276
84 Boatner, op. cit., 592
85 *Official Records*, 8, 228, 282

86 Military Order of the Loyal Legion, 12, 227–31; *The Rebellion Record*, documents, 4, 244–47; *New York Herald*, March 16, 1862

87 Military Order of the Loyal Legion, 12, 220–22; *The Rebellion Record*, documents, 4, 248

88 *Official Records*, 8, 224; Dee Brown, "Pea Ridge," *Civil War Times*, 10/67; Michael A. Hughes, "Pea Ridge." *Blue & Gray*, 1/88

89 *The Rebellion Record*, documents, 4, 263–64

90 *Official Records*, 10, 323–24; Nevin, *The Road to Shiloh*, 140

91 *War of the Rebellion, Official Records of Union and Confederate Armies*, 10, 324

92 Ward, *The Civil War*, 113–14; Leckie, *None Died in Vain*, 284

93 *Blue & Gray*, 4/97, 10; *Official Records of the Union and Confederate Navies*, 22, 643–48; McDonough, op. cit., 128; *Official Records*, 10, 582–89

94 Daniel, *Shiloh*, 226; Ward, op. cit., 116; McDonough, op. cit., 128ff

95 Sword, "Shiloh," *Civil War Times*, 5/787, 38; Davis, op. cit., 43, 61; Foote, *The Civil War*, 1, 337; Ward, op. cit., 114; Leckie, op. cit., 284

96 Miers, *Lincoln Day by Day*, 3, 93–96; E. Neely, Jr., *The Abraham Lincoln Encyclopedia*, 188–89

97 Miers, op. cit., 109; Sandburg, *Abraham Lincoln, the War Years*, 4, 486–87

98 Sifikas, *Who Was Who*, 731; Miers, op. cit., 109–10; Shavin, *The Atlanta Century*, no. 116; *Official Records*, 14, 153

99 *Official Records of the Union and Confederate Navies*, 7, 336–40; *Official Records*, 14, 153–55

100 *Official Records of the Union and Confederate Navies*, 7, 332–39; *Official Records*, 14, 338

101 Joynt, "Commander Lincoln at Norfolk," *Civil War Times*, 2/83, 27

102 Shavin, op. cit., no. 116; *Official Records of the Union and Confederate Navies*, 7, 335; Sifikas, op. cit., 441

103 Peter M. Chattin, *TheCoastal War*, 110

104 *War of the Rebellion, Official Records of Union and Confederate Armies*, 20, 984–86

105 Ibid., 286, 41–42, 44

106 *Official Records of the Union and Confederate Navies*, 13, 104; *Confederate Military History*, 7, 82; *Official Records of the Union and Confederate Navies*, 28, 78, 76

107 *War of the Rebellion, Official Records of Union and Confederate Armies*, 20, 48–49, Chaitin, op. cit., 111; *War of the Rebellion, Official Records of Union and Confederate Armies*, 20, 53–64

108 Chaitin, Ibid.; *Official Records of the Union and Confederate Navies*, 13, 104, 108, 170

109 Stewart Sifakis, *Who Was Who in the Civil War*, 50; *Official Records of the Union and Confederate Navies*, 13, 166

110 Ezra J. Warner, *Generals in Blue*, 30; *War of the Rebellion, Official Records of Union and Confederate Armies*, 20, 979–1008

111 *Official Records of the Union and Confederate Navies*, 30, 161

112 Fox, *Regimental Losses*; Livermore, *Numbers and Losses*

113 *The Rebellion Record*, documents, 5, 266; *Journal of the Southern Historical Society*, 18, 57

114 Cullen, "Malvern Hill," 6/66, 4–14

115 *Official Records of the Union and Confederate Navies*, 8, 26; *Official Records*, 13, 530–31; *Official Records of the Union and Confederate Navies*, 28, 39, 90, 132; *Official Records*, 12, 224

116 *Official Records*, 12, 256–58; *Lee Takes Command*, 70

117 *Official Records*, 12, 259; emphasis added

118 Reprinted, *Century War Book*, 122, and later in *Battles & Leaders*; emphasis added; cf. *Lee Takes Command*, 72; Mississippi's *Grenada Appeal,* dispatch of July 7

119 *Century War Book,* 122

120 *Official Records*, 13, 815, emphasis added; Bernard, "Malvern Hill," *Journal of the Southern Historical Society*, 115, 56–71

121 *Official Records*, 13, 724–25

122 Evans, *Confederate Military History*, 13, 66; *Official Records of the Union and Confederate Navies*, 19, 130; Shavin, *The Atlanta Century*, no. 129

123 Dispatch of August 7 to Mississippi's *Grenada Appeal*; Evans, op. cit., 13, 67, 70

124 *Official Records*, 21, 92–93, 104; Mississippi's *Grenada Appeal*, dispatch of August 7

125 *Official Records*, 21, 94, 104; *The Rebellion Record*, documents, 5, 311

126 *Rebellion Record*, documents, 5, 308

127 Ibid., 74–75

128 Delaney, "General Thomas Williams," *Civil War Times*, 7/75, 36

129 *Official Records*, 21, 25–27, 39, 42–43, 46–53, 59–60, 64, 66, 69–70, 74, 490, 628, 714

130 *Official Records of the Union and Confederate Navies,* 19, 117, 120–138; Evans. op. cit.,13, 67; *The Rebellion Record*, documents, 5, 308–9

131 *New York Times*, September 17, 1862

132 *Journal of the Southern Historical Society*, 39, 43; Military Order of the Loyal Legion, 41, 362; Shavin, *The Atlanta Century*, no. 134; Faust, *Historical Times Illustrated Encyclopedia*, 432, 706; Evans, *Confederate Military History*, 5, 108–9; *Official Records*, 128, 283

133 Evans, op. cit., 5, 110–11; Military Order of the Loyal Legion, 30, 344; 36, 230; *Journal of the Southern Historical Society*, 39, 40–41

134 Priest, *Before Antietam*, 81–82; Sifikas, *Who Was Who*, 297, 419; Evans, op. cit., 5, 111–12

135 *Journal of the Southern Historical Society*, 13, 25–27; Evans, op. cit., 5, 185

136 Priest, *Before Antietam*; Priest, "The Death of Jesse Reno," *Civil War* magazine, May–June 1992

137 Military Order of the Loyal Legion, 58, 484; *Official Records*, 27, 63–64, 178, 186–87, 197, 419, 442, 425–27, 441–42; 444, 446–48, 457; 28, 197, Priest, *Before Antietam*, 338; Priest, "Death," 45, 47

138 Warner, *Generals in Blue*, 394–95; Military Order of the Loyal Legion, 52, 148

139 Ibid., 41, 380–82

140 Priest, *Before Antietam*, 215–18

141 Priest, *"Death,"* 45–47

142 Boatner, *Dictionary*; Military Order of the Loyal Legion, 5, 216; 41, 364; Warner, op. cit., 395

143 Commager, *The Blue and the Gray*, 213–15; *Official Records*, 27, 246, 254

144 John M. Priest, *Antietam*, 85, citing *Report of the Ohio Antietam Battlefield Commission*

145 Priest, op. cit., 63, 115; James M. McPherson, ed., *Battle Chronicles of the Civil War*, 1862, 228

146 James M. McPherson, ed., *Battle Chronicles of the Civil War*, 1862, 236–37

147 Ronald H. Bailey, *The Bloodiest Day*, 90; *Official Records*, 27, 319–20; James M. McPherson, ed., *Battle Chronicles of the Civil War*, 1862, 237

148 Schell, "A Great Raging Battlefield in Hell," *Civil War Times*, 6/69, 14–22; Priest, op. cit., 138

149 McPherson, op. cit., 1862, 240; Bailey, *op cit.*, 137; Priest, op. cit., 144

150 Hildebrand, *Antietam Remembered*, 53

151 Priest, op. cit., 280

152 *Battles & Leaders*, 655; McPherson, op. cit., 1862, 231, 239, 242, 250; *Official Records*, 27, 323–24; *Civil War Times*, 4/87, 21–22

153 McPherson, op. cit., 1862, 250–51, 253; Bailey, op. cit., 136

154 Lincoln, *Collected Works*, 5, 336–38, 433–36

155 Current, *Encyclopedia of the Confederacy*, 1, 396–97; *Civil War*, 5, 341, 359n; Faust, *Historical Times Illustrated Encyclopedia*, 160–61

PART II

1 Dyer, *A Compendium of the War of the Rebellion*, 3, 1418; Lord, "Killed, Not in Action,"*Civil War Times*, 10/69, 32–33

2 *War of the Rebellion, Official Records of Union and Confederate Armies*, 4, 196–98

3 *Official Records*, 4, 198; *Boston Transcript*, October 11, 1861

4 Dyer, op. cit., 3, 1559; Longacre, "The Most Inept Regiment of the Civil War," *Civil War Times*, 11/69

5 *Official Records of the Union and Confederate Navies*, 22, 363; *War of the Rebellion, Official Records of Union and Confederate Armies*, 3, 270–71

6 *Official Records*, 5, 474–76, 491–94; *Journal of the Southern Historical Society*, 35, 69–78

7 Harrison, "Mill Springs," *Civil War Times*, 1/72, 4–9, 44–47; Boatner, *Dictionary*, 954; Sifikas, *Who Was Who*, 231f., 740

8 Chattin, *The Coastal War*, 35

9 *Official Records of the Union and Confederate Navies*, 7, 108–10

10 *Official Records of the Union and Cnfederate Navies*, 117–18; Chattin, op. cit., 34

11 *Official Records of the Union and Confederate Navies*, 7, 118

12 *Official Records*, 9, 96–97, 102–4; *The Rebellion Record*, documents, 3, 89–93; Evans, *Confederate Military History*, 11, 36–38

13 Sauers, "Laurels for Burnside," *Blue & Gray*, 5/88, 8–20; *Official Records*, 9, 77–79, 85– 88, 223–29, 305–8; Commager, *The Blue and the Gray*, 798–802

14 *Official Records*, 7, 166–67

15 *Official Records of the Union and Confederate Navies*, 22, 590–91

16 *Official Records*, 9, 487–93, 504–5

17 *Official Records*, 18, 705; see vols. 5, 12, 19, 21, 25, 27, 29, 37, 42, 43, 61; *Spies, Scouts, and Raiders*, 108–9

18 *Official Records*, 15, 14; Freeman, *Lee's Lieutenants*, 1, 420–21

19 *Official Records*, 11, 210–20; Jones, "Personal Recollections and Experiences," Military Order of the Loyal Legion, 6, 113– 23

20 *Official Records*, 15, 72, 713, 739–40, 773; Freeman, op. cit., 1, 438–43

21 Carmichael, "The Battle of Savage's Station," *Civil War*, 51; *Official Records, 12*, 62–65; 13, 659–60, 679–81

22 *Official Records of the Union and Confederate Navies*, 13, 178–81

23 *Official Records* 32, 67–156; 111, 458–61; Neul, "Slugfest in the Ozarks," *America's Civil War*, 5/94, 27–32

24 Quoted by Josephy, *War on the Frontier*, 151

25 Strother, "Personal Recollections of the War," *Harper's New Monthly Magazine*, 1868, 275–78

26 *Official Records*, 27, 344–56; Bailey, *The Bloodiest Day*, 153–55

27 *Official Records, 27*, 204, 348; 352–54

28 Boatner, *Dictionary*, 644; *Century War Book*, 159–60; Shelby Foote, *The Civil War*, 1, 736

29 *Official Records*, 22, 1079–81; *The Rebellion Record*, documents, 5, 511; *Journal of the Southern Historical Society*, 30, 246; Foote, *The Civil War*, 1, 736

30 Faust, op. cit., 1; Foote, op. cit.; *Journal of the Southern Historical Society*, 11, 466–70; *American Cyclopedia*, 1862, 797

31 *Great Battles of the Civil War*, 241; *Official Records*, 31, 481–84

32 Commager, op. cit., 240; Davis, *They Called Him Stonewall*, 359

33 *Official Records*, 31, 542, 554, 560

34 Royster, *The Destructive War*, 77

35 McWhiney and Jenkins, "The Union's Worst General," *Civil War Times*, 6/75, 30–39; Sifikas, op. cit., 232–33

36 Freeman, "The Battle of Stone's River," Military Order of the Loyal Legion, 12, 242–44

37 *Official Records*, 26, 129; Stewart Sifakis, *Who Was Who in the Civil War*, 143–44

38 *Official Records*, 26, 132–45; *The Rebellion Record*, documents, 6, 75

39 Boatner, *Dictionary*, 451, 475; Sword, "Cavalry on Trial," *Civil War Times*, 4/74, 32– 40; *Official Records*, 51–63

40 Quoted, from Commager, *The Blue and the Gray*, 854–55

41 *Official Records*, 21, 371–74

42 Warner, *Generals in Blue*, 193–94; *Official Records*, 21, 373

43 *Official Records*, 21, 374–79

44 Shelby Foote, *The Civil War*, 2, 298–300; *Official Records*, 39, 384–96, 669–72, 676–84

45 *Official Records*, 76, 82, indices; *Official Records, Atlas*, 18; Goodman, "Decision in the West," 74

46 *Official Records*, 36, 24, 151, 158, 160, 267, 320

47 Ezra J. Warner, *Generals in Blue*, 341–43

48 Warner, op. cit., 353, 359; *Official Records of the Union and Confederate Navies*, 25, 45–47, 56–57, 94–100, 111–14, Martin, *The Vicksburg Campaign*, 182–85

49 *Official Records of the Union and Confederate Navies*, 21, 337, 355–67; 25, 20–21, 353–57, 356–58; *Official Records*, 21, 563

50 Jeane Heimberger Candido, "Sisters and Nuns Who Were Nurses," Commager, op. cit., 353–57, 356–58; *Official Records, 41*, 229, 601, 605, 650, 656

51 *Official Records*, 21, 563

52 Alexander," Gettysburg Cavalry Operations," *Blue & Gray*, 10/88, 9

53 Coco, *War Stories*, 39

54 Ibid.

55 Ibid.

56 Cook, "Personal Reminiscences of Gettysburg," Military Order of the Loyal Legion, 15, 222–36; emphasis added

57 *Journal of the Southern Historical Society*, 17, 184– 85

58 Rollins, *Pickett's Charge*, 394; Pfanz, *Gettysburg: The Second Day*, 388, 417, 429

59 Ibid., 38, citing the *History of the 20th Connecticut Infantry*

60 Faust, *Historical Times Illustrated Encyclopedia*, 480; Garth W. James, "The Assault on Fort Wagner," Military Order of the Loyal Legion, 46, 9–30; *The Rebellion Record*, documents, 7, 211– 14

61 James, op. cit., 28

62 Sutherland, "The Negro in the Late War," Military Order of the Loyal Legion, 46, 164–83; Robertson, *Soldiers Blue and Gray*, 33; *The Rebellion Record*, documents, 7, 215–16

63 *Official Records of the Union and Confederate Navies*, 25, 243–45, 254–59

64 Weaver, "Morgan's Raid," Military Order of the Loyal Legion, 4, 302–5; *Official Records of the Union and Confederate Navies*, 25, 257–59

65 Evans, *Confederate Military History*, 6, 222–23; Boatner, op. cit., 418

66 Evans, *Confederate Military History*, 6, 223–47

67 *Official Records of the Union and Confederate Navies*, 14, 368–69; *Official Records*, 47, 195–96

68 *Official Records of the Union and Confederate Navies*, 14, 368–72; *Confederate Military History*, 6, 235–37

69 Faust, op. cit., 145

70 Korn, *The Fight for Chattanooga*, 68–70; Davis, *Battlefields of the Civil War*, 185–88; Bowers, *Chickamauga and Chattanooga*, 163

71 Trimble, "Rosecrans," *Civil War*, 18, 38–39

72 Sifikas, *Who Was Who*, 728–29

73 Royce Shingleton, "Confederate Commando," *Civil War*, 26, 74

74 Boyd, *Civil War Diary*; *Battles & Leaders*, 4, 418; *Official Records*, 32, 82; 96, 1249; *The Confederate Veteran*, 20, 379

75 *Official Records*, 57, 165, 252, 254, 356; *Journal of the Southern Historical Society*, 55, 8–9; Lossing, *Pictorial Field Book*, 3, 238–40; Rani-Villem, "Forrest's Okolona Victory," *Civil War Times*, 4/85, 37

76 *Official Records*, 61, 1152; 111, 477–78; Josephy, *War on the Frontier*, 61–62

77 Fitz-Simons, "Sigel's Fight at New Market," Military Order of the Loyal Legion, 12, 62

78 *Official Records*, 73, 378–81, 434; Sifikas, op. cit., 60; *Civil War Times*, 11/82, 78; *Blue & Gray*, 10/89, 49

79 Miller, "Strike Them a Blow," *Blue & Gray*, 4/93, 44–45

80 *Official Records*, 75, 592–93

81 *Official Records*, 78, 695–96, 727; Stinson, "Hot Work in Mississippi," *Civil War Times*, 7/72, 9–10

82 *Official Records*, 76, 188

83 Davis, *Death in the Trenches*, 103

84 Ibid., 149

85 *Official Records*, 77-3; 120, 926–27; 121–88; Evans, *Confederate Military History*, 11, 409–11; Faust, 395; Michael B. Ballard, "'Stovepipe' Johnson Raids Indiana," *Civil War Times*, 11/82, 22–26

86 Sifikas, op. cit., 424, citing Jones, *Gray Ghosts and Rebel Raiders*

87 Ladd, "From Atlanta to the Sea," quoted in *Civil War Chronicles*, winter 1993, 7

88 *Official Records*, 41, 948; Sifikas, op. cit., 120–21, citing Craig, *The Fighting Parson*

89 Boatner, *Dictionary*, 304–5; Sexton, "The Battle of Franklin," Military Order of the Loyal Legion, 13, 478–79

90 Gordon, "Gen. Patrick Cleburne," *Journal of the Southern Historical Society*, 18, 267–69

91 Faust, op. cit., 273, 574; Commager, op. cit., 843–45

92 Korn, *Pursuit to Appomattox*, 34–38

93 *Official Records*, 103, 444, 1188; *The Confederate Veteran*, 9, 209

94 Korn, op. cit., 115–17

95 *Official Records*, 96, 1389; Lawton, "The Sharpshooters of Mahone's Brigade," *Journal of the Southern Historical Society*, 22, 105

96 Ibid., 121

97 Boatner, op. cit., 428; *Civil War*, no. 62, *Civil War Times*, 7/90, 57; Greeno, "The Capture of Jefferson Davis," Military Order of the Loyal Legion, 7, 414–17; Current, *Encyclopedia of the Confederacy*, 2, 453

98 Evans, *Confederate Military History*, 15, 124–29; Faust, op. cit., 556

PART III

1 *Official Records*, 21, 272–73

2 *Official Records of the Union and Confederate Navies*, 19, 668–69; Foote, *The Civil War*, 2, 212–14

3 *Official Records of the Union and Confederate Navies*, 19, 680

4 Parker, "A Night with Farragut," Military Order of the Loyal Legion, 14, 141–44; *The Rebellion Record*, documents, 6, 451–54; *Official Records of the Union and Confederate Navies*, 19, 778

5 *Official Records of the Union and Confederate Navies*, 19, 683–84

6 Henderson, *Stonewall Jackson*, 665–68; Douglas, *I Rode with Stonewall*, 205; Davis, *Battlefields of the Civil War*, 129–32; Freeman, *Lee's Lieutenants*, 2, 545–56; Bowers, *Stonewall Jackson*, 313

7 Freeman, op. cit., 2, 563–65; Farwell, *Stonewall*, 505–7

8 Ibid., 566–68; Foote, *The Civil War*, 2, 301; Olson, "A Fatal Full Moon," *Blue & Gray*, Spring 1996, 24–26

9 Ibid., 569–71; Davis, op. cit., 133–34; Henderson, op. cit., 677–79; Farwell, *Stonewall*, 511–14; Freeman, op. cit., 222; Davis, *They Called Him Stonewall*, 420–29

10 Ibid., 572–73; Farwell, op. cit., 510

11 Henderson, op. cit., 680; Freeman, op. cit., 547–77

12 Henderson, op. cit., 670–81; Farwell, op. cit., 516–17

13 Davis, op. cit., 136; Henderson, op. cit.; Sifikas, *Who Was Who*, 317–18; Farwell, op. cit., 516–17

14 Freeman, op. cit., 2, 567; Douglas S. Freeman, *R. E. Lee*, 2, 533n; Lane, op. cit., 495; Warner, *Generals in Gray*, 17–18; Davis, op. cit., 134

15 *Battles & Leaders*, 3, 551–71; Hankinson, *Vicksburg 1863*, 64; Miers, *The Web of Victory*, 205; Sifikas, *Who Was Who*, 515; *Official Records*, 37, 130, 159, 167

16 Miers, op. cit., 210

17 *Official Records*, 37, 160–63, 245

18 Quoted in Hoehling, *Vicksburg*, 35

19 *Official Records*, 37, 169; *Battles and Leaders*, 3, 495–97; Miers, op. cit. 201f

20 Henry Seaman's Vicksburg Diary, *Civil War Times*, 9/83, 124–25

21 Hoehling, op. cit., 35, 37–38

22 *Official Records*, 37, 162; Martin, *The Vicksburg Campaign*, 118

23 *Official Records*, 37, 264; Miers, op. cit. 211–12

24 Drury, *The Civil War Military Machine*, 117

25 *Official Records*, 37, 167; Miers, op. cit., 308; Martin, op. cit., 126

26 Rhea, *The Battle of the Wilderness*, 54–58; Cullen, "Battle of the Wilderness," *Civil War Times*, 4/71, 3

27 Sifikas, *Who Was Who*, 681–82; *Official Records*, 67, 539–41

28 *Official Records*, 67, 1069–71

29 Jaynes, *The Killing Ground*, 60–65; *Official Records*, 67, 123

30 Longstreet, *From Manassas to Appomattox*, 18; Evans, *Confederate Military History*, 1, 660–64; Wert, *General James Longstreet*, 50–53

31 Priest, *Antietam*, 206–8

32 Rhea, op. cit., 345; Gallagher, *The Wilderness Campaign*, 162–69; Longstreet, op. cit., 556–60

33 *Journal of the Southern Historical Society*, 20, 90; Commager, *The Blue and the Gray*, 981; *Blue & Gray*, 6/95, 58; *Official Records*, 67, 540; 68, 561, 792; Boatner, *Dictionary*, 882–83

34 "The Battle of the Wilderness," *Journal of the Southern Historical Society*, 20, 71, 91

35 Rhea, op. cit., 370–71, 450–51; Longstreet, op. cit., 564–66; Wert, op. cit., 387–88; Commager, op. cit., 6, 95, 58; *Journal of the Southern Historical Society*, 20, 95; d, 491; Piston, *Lee's Tarnished Lieutenant*, 26; *Civil War Times*, 2/70, 38; 4/63, 24

36 Wert, op. cit., 387–88; *Blue & Gray*, 9/81, 21–25

37 Wert, op. cit., 388; Canaan, *The Wilderness Campaign*, 212; *Official Records*, 68, 517, 522

38 *America's Civil War*, 5/93, 33; Wheeler, *Voices of the Civil War*, 386; Gallagher, op. cit., 164

39 *Journal of the Southern Historical Society*, 20, 98; *Official Records*, 67, 1090–91

40 Burton, *The Siege of Charleston*, 16–19; Faust, *Historical Times Illustrated Encyclopedia*, 713–14

41 Ibid., 527–28, 789

42 Longstreet, *From Manassas to Appomattox*, 95, 100, 135; Piston, *Lee's Tarnished Lieutenant*, 69

43 Evans, *Confederate Military History*, 6, 404–6; Gallagher, *The Wilderness Campaign*, 248; Longstreet, op. cit., 437, 462, 467, 475–77, 495

44 Gallagher, op. cit., 251; *Blue & Gray*, 6/95, 58

45 *Official Records*, 67, 324; Rhea, *The Battle of the Wilderness*, 368–69; *Civil War Times*, 4/71, 18; Commager, *The Blue and the Gray*, 981

46 Longstreet, op. cit., 564; quoted by Robert L. Krick in Gallagher, op. cit., 252

47 *Official Records*, 67, 1061–63;*Journal of the Southern Historical Society*, 20, 73, 82, 86, 94

48 Ibid., 89; *Official Records*, 67, 1062; Rhea, op. cit., 369–71; Wert, *General James Longstreet*, 387; Sifikas, *Who Was Who*, 360–61

49 *Journal of the Southern Historical Society*, 20, 86, 89

50 Longstreet, op. cit., 566; Evans, op. cit., 6, 406

51 Ibid., 6, 404; Warner, *Generals in Gray*, 155

52 *Charleston Mercury*, June 14, 1864; cf. *Charleston Daily Courier*, June 14, 1864

53 *Charleston Daily Courier*, June 14, 1864

54 Sifikas, *Who Was Who*, 571

55 Boatner, *Dictionary*, 392, 733, 734, 902

56 *Charleston Daily Courier* and *Mercury*, June 10–16, 1864

57 *Official Records*, 66, 132; *Official Records of the Union and Confederate Navies*, 15, 528

58 *Official Records*, 66, 144–45

59 *Journal of the Southern Historical Society,* 35, 277; Joslyn, *Immortal Captives,* 287

60 Faust, *Historical Times Illustated Encyclopedia,* 23

61 Ibid., 298, 397

62 Ibid., 717; 755

63 *Official Records,* 120, 709–10

64 *Official Records,* 66, 161–63, 170; 120, 378; *Journal of the Southern Historical Society,* 3, 77–81

65 Faust, op. cit., 558

66 *Journal of the Southern Historical Society,* 11, 86; 30, 77–104; 40, 279–81; 46, 147–48; 50, 249–50, 277–78, 365–66; 51, 350–51; *Official Records,* 120, 874–75, 1129–30; *Charleston Mercury,* June 18, 1864

67 *Official Records of the Union and Confederate Navies,*15, 614

68 *Official Records,* 66, 213–14; 120, 805–6. A formal list of Federals involved in this special exchange appears in the *Official Records,* with the unit to which each man belonged identified. A list of the Confederate captives, compiled much later, appears in Joslyn, op. cit., 287–88

69 Murray, *The Immortal Six Hundred,* 36–42

70 W. Gordon McCabe,"Defense of Petersburg," *Journal of the Southern Historical Society,* 2, 283

71 Trudeau, *The Last Citadel,* 106; for other accounts, see Davis, *Death in the Trenches,* 75; Wilkinson, "Bury Them If They Won't Move," *Civil War Times,* 3/90, 29

72 *Official Records,* 80, 545; Trudeau, op. cit., 100; Boatner, *Dictionary,* 647–48

73 *Official Records,* 82, 660; Horn, *The Petersburg Campaign,* 97–98, 102–7

74 *Official Records,* 80, 527; Horn, op. cit., 102; Trudeau, op. cit. 103, 107

75 *Official Records,* 80, 758–59; Trudeau, op. cit., 99– 100; Horn, op. cit., 101; *Journal of the Southern Historical Society,* 33, 359

76 Horn, op. cit., 104; Wilkinson, op. cit., 25; Davis, op. cit., 75

77 McCabe, op. cit., 283; Wilkinson, op. cit., 27; Horn, op. cit., 109; Davis, op. cit., 65; Trudeau, op. cit., 107

78 *Official Records,* 80, 549; *Journal of the Southern Historical Society,* 2, 283; 18, 3; 25, 80; Davis, op. cit., 75; Wilkinson, op. cit., 31; Trudeau, op. cit., 110; Horn, *op. cit.,* 109;*The Confederate Veteran,* 27, 455

79 Davis, op. cit., 75; Horn, op. cit., 110–11; *The Confederate Veteran,* 31, 176; *Journal of the Southern Historical Society,* 18, 31

80 Trudeau, op. cit., 113, 121, 123; *Journal of the Southern Historical Society,* 33, 363; *Official Records,* 82, 663, 676

81 *Journal of the Southern Historical Society,* 18, 18; 33, 361; 36, 166; Trudeau, op. cit., 117, 119

82 *Journal of the Southern Historical Society,* 33, 360; *Official Records,* 82, 648–90

83 *Official Records,* 11, 167; *Journal of the Southern Historical Society,* 25, 81; 33, 360, 365, 367, 370; 36, 172; Trudeau, op. cit., 127; *Journal of the Southern Historical Society,* 33, 370

84 *Journal of the Southern Historical Society,* 25, 85; 33, 355, 365; Trudeau, op. cit., 124; *Official Records,* 82, 640, 667; Warner, *Generals in Blue,* 24–25

85 *The Confederate Veteran,* 27, 455; McCabe, op. cit., 294; Trudeau, op. cit., 125; McPherson, *Battle Chronicles of the Civil War, 1864, 1867*

86 Horn, op. cit., 118; Boatner, op. cit., 107, 277, 474

87 *The Confederate Veteran,* 2, 153

88 *Journal of the Southern Historical Society,* 2, 292; 18, 18; 33, 364; Davis, op. cit., 74; Trudeau, op. cit., 115; Horn, op. cit., 101

89 *Official Records,* 42–125; Wilkinson, op. cit., 43

90 "Graphic Account of Battle of Crater," *Journal of the Southern Historical Society,* 33, 364

91 Trudeau, op. cit., 109;*The Confederate Veteran,* 31, 174; *Journal of the Southern Historical Society,* 2, 292; 18, 17; 33, 363; 36, 165; *The Confederate Veteran,* 31, 174; 33, 177

92 George Clark, "Alabamans in the Crater Battle," *The Confederate Veteran,* 3, 68–69

93 Cook, "The Story of the Six Hundred," *The Confederate Veteran,* 5, 119

94 Faust, *Historical Times Illustrated Encyclopedia,* 332; *Official Records,* 65, 21

95 *Official Records,* 120, 608

96 *Official Records,* 120, 625

97 *Official Records,* 60, 254

98 Fulkerson, "The Prison Experience of a Confederate Soldier," *Journal of the Southern Historical Society,* 22, 130; Sifikas, *Who Was Who,* 572

99 *The Confederate Veteran,* 29, 178; *Official Records of the Union and Confederate Navies,* 15, 637; Evans, "Southern Boys in Southern Armies," *The Confederate Veteran,* 2, 6

100 McRae, "Confederate Prisoners at Morris Island,"*The Confederate Veteran,* 29, 178

101 *The Confederate Veteran,* 7, 323, 415; 24, 80; 27, 348; 28, 386; 36, 425, 468

102 Cook, op. cit., 117; *Official Records of the Union and Confederate Navies*, 15, 655

103 *The Confederate Veteran*, 9, 391; 29, 178; Cook, op. cit., 117; Fulkerson, op. cit., 138

104 Quisenberry, "The Eleventh Kentucky Cavalry, C.S.A.," *Journal of the Southern Historical Society*, 35, 275

105 Fulkerson, op. cit., 139

106 Goldy, "The Swamp Angel," *Civil War Times*, 4/89, 23–25; *Blue & Gray*, 5/84, 21ff.; Faust, op. cit., 738

107 Cook, op. cit., 118; *The Confederate Veteran*, 7, 415; 24, 80; 27, 348; 28, 386; 36, 425, 468; 9, 391; 29, 178–79

108 Ibid., 9, 391; Fulkerson, op. cit., 132, 139

109 *The Confederate Veteran*, 7, 323, 425; 9, 391; 28, 386; 29, 179; 36, 425; *Journal of the Southern Historical Society*, 35, 274

110 "A List of Confederate Officers, Prisoners, Who Were Held on Morris Island, S.C., Under Confederate Fire from September 7th to October 21st, 1864," *Journal of the Southern Historical Society*, 17, 34–46

111 See the *Journal of the Southern Historical Society*, 17, 34–46; *Confederate Veteran*, 7, 313–23; and Mauriel P. Jones, *Immortal Captives*, 294–306

BIBLIOGRAPHY

Alexander, Ted, "Gettysburg Cavalry Operations," B/G 10/88, 8–32.

The Annals of the Civil War. New York: DaCapo reprint, 1994.

"Another Story of the Crater Battle, *Journal of the Southern Historical Society*, 28: 204–21.

Atlanta Intelligencer, October 1861.

Augusta (Georgia) *Chronicle*, November 1861.

Bailey, Ronald H., *The Bloodiest Day*. Alexandria: Time-Life, 1984.

Ballard, Michael B., "Deceived in Newburgh," *Civil War Times*, 11/82, 22–26.

Baltimore American, March 1862.

Basler, Roy P., *The Collected Works of Abraham Lincoln*. 8 vols., index. New Brunswick, N.J.: Rutgers Univ. Press, 1953–55.

Battles and Leaders of the Civil War. 4 vols. Edison, N.J.: Castle reprint, 1984.

Benson, P. H., "Severe Prison Experiences," *The Confederate Veteran*, 9, 12–16.

Bernard, George S., "The Battle of the Crater," *Journal of the Southern Historical Society*, 18, 3–38.

Blue & Gray magazine, 1980–98.

Boatner, Mark M., *The Civil War Dictionary*. Rev. ed. New York: McKay, 1988.

Bowers, John, *Chickamauga and Chattanooga*. New York: Avon, 1994.

———, *Stonewall Jackson*. New York: Morrow, 1989.

Brown, Dee, "Pea Ridge," *Civil War Times Illustrated*, 10/67.

Brown, J. R., "Captured with the Flags," *The Confederate Veteran*, 22, 217–18.

Brown County (Indiana) Union, September 1861.

"Capt. C. C. Grace," *The Confederate Veteran*, 27, 348.

"Capt. William D. Ivey," *The Confederate Veteran*, 27, 186.

Carmichael, Peter S., "The Battle of Savage's Station," *Civil War*, 51, 65–69.

The Century War Book. New York: Arno reprint, 1978.

Chaitin, Peter M., *The Coastal War*. Alexandria: Time-Life, 1984.

Chambers, H. A., "The Bloody Crater," *The Confederate Veteran*, 31, 174–77.

Charleston Daily Courier, June–October 1864.

Charleston Mercury, June–October 1864.

Civil War Times and *Civil War Times Illustrated*, 1960–98.

Coco, Gregory A., *War Stories*. Gettysburg: Thomas, 1992.

Commager, Henry S., *The Blue and the Gray*. 2 vols. Indianapolis: Bobbs-Merrill, 1950.

"Comrades at Wichita, Kans.," *The Confederate Veteran*, 28, 190.

The Confederate Veteran. 40 vols., 3-vol. index. Wilmington: Broadfoot reprint, 1986–88.

Cook, Henry H., "The Story of the Six Hundred," *The Confederate Veteran*, 5, 116–18, 148–50, 219–20; 6, 118–20.

Cook, John S., "War Talks in Kansas," Military Order of the Loyal Legion of the United States, 15, 320–41.

Crozier, Emmet, *Yankee Reporters*. New York: Oxford, 1956.

Cullen, Joseph P., "Battle of the Wilderness," *Civil War Times*, 4/71.

Current, Richard N., ed., *Encyclopedia of the Confederacy*. 4 vols. New York: Simon & Schuster, 1993.

Daniels, Larry J., *Shiloh*. New York: Simon & Schuster, 1997.

"Darden's Mississippi Battery," *The Confederate Veteran*, 9, 209.

Davis, Burke, *They Called Him Stonewall*. New York: Wings reprint, 1988.

Davis, William C., *Battle at Bull Run*. Baton Rouge: LSU Press, 1977.

——, *Battlefields of the Civil War*. London: Salamander, 1991.

——, ed., *Civil War Journal*. 3 vols. Nashville: Rutledge Hill Press, 1997–99.

——, *Death in the Trenches*. Alexandria: Time-Life, 1986.

——, *Duel Between the First Ironclads*. New York: Barnes & Noble, 1975.

——, *First Blood*. Alexandria: Time-Life, 1983.

Delaney, Norman C., "General Thomas Williams," *Civil War Times*, 7/75, 5–9, 36–47.

Douglas, Henry K., *I Rode with Stonewall*. Chapel Hill: Univ. of North Carolina Press, 1940.

Drury, Ian, and Tony Gibbons, *The Civil War Military Machine*. London: Dragon's World, 1993.

Dyer, Frederick H., *A Compendium of the War of the Rebellion*. 3 vols. New York: Yoseloff reprint, 1959.

"Edward Bagby, of Virginia," *The Confederate Veteran*, 28, 453–58.

"Edward Carter, One of The Immortal Six Hundred," *The Confederate Veteran*, 36, 468.

Evans, Clement A., ed., *Confederate Military History*. 19 vols., 2-vol. index. Wilmington: Broadfoot reprint, 1987.

——, "Northern Boys in Southern Armies," *The Confederate Veteran*, 2, 5–9.

Farwell, Byron, *Stonewall*. New York: Norton, 1992.

Faust, Patricia L., ed., *Historical Times Illustrated Encyclopedia of the Civil War*. New York: Harper, 1986.

Featherstone, John C., "The Battle of the Crater as I Saw It," *The Confederate Veteran*, 14, 23–26.

——, "Brilliant Page in History of War," *Journal of the Southern Historical Society*, 36, 161–73.

"Field of Blood Was the Crater," *Journal of the Southern Historical Society*, 33, 351–57.

Fitz-simons, Charles, "Sigel's Fight at New Market," Military Order of the Loyal Legion of the United States, 12, 61–67.

Foote, Shelby, *The Civil War*. 3 vols. New York: Random House, 1958–74.

Freeman, Douglas Southall, *Lee's Lieutenants*. 3 vols. New York: Scribner's, 1942–44.

——, *R. E. Lee*. 4 vols. New York: Scribner's, 1934–51.

Fulkerson, Abram, "The Prison Experience of a Confederate Soldier," *Journal of the Southern Historical Society*, 22, 127–46.

Godman, Al W., Jr., "Decision in the West—Part IV," *North & South*, 5/95, 74–80.

Goldy, James, "The Swamp Angel," *Civil War Times*, 4/89, 22–27.

"Graphic Account of Battle of Crater," *Journal of the Southern Historical Society*, 23, 358–74.

"Great Battle of the Crater," *Journal of the Southern Historical Society*, 23, 204–21.

Great Battles of the Civil War. New York: Gallery, 1989.

Greeno, Charles L., "The Capture of Jefferson Davis," Military Order of the Loyal Legion of the United States, 7, 411–21.

Grenada Appeal (Mississippi), July–August, 1862.

Hankinson, Alan, *Vicksburg 1863*. London: Osprey, 1993.

Harrison, Lowell, "Mill Springs," *Civil War Times*, 1/72, 19–28.

Hempstead, Junius L., "How Long Will This Misery Continue?" *Civil War Times*, 2/81, 20–23.

Henderson, G. E. R., *Stonewall Jackson*. New York: Grossett & Dunlap, 1943.

Higginson, Thomas W., *Massachusetts in the Army and Navy, 1861–65*. Boston: n.p., 1896.

Hildebrand, Virginia M., *Antietam Remembered*. New York: Book Craftsmen, 1959.

Hoehling, A. A., *Vicksburg*. New York: Fairfax, 1969.

Horn, John, *The Petersburg Campaign*. Conshohocken, Pa.: Combined, 1993.

Hughes, Michael A., "Pea Ridge," *Blue & Gray*, 1/88, 12–38.

"The Immortal Six Hundred," *The Confederate Veteran*, 13, 519.

"The Immortal Six Hundred May Have a Monument," *The Confederate Veteran*, 16, 423.

"Incidents of the Battle of the Crater," *The Confederate Veteran*, 14, 107–8.

Johnson, Clint, *Civil War Blunders*. Winston-Salem, N.C.: Blair, 1997.

Johnson, Swofford, *Great Battles of the Confederacy*. New York: W. H. Smith, 1985.

Jones, Frank J., "Personal Recollections and Experiences," Military Order of the Loyal Legion of the United States, 6, 113–23.

Jones, Garth W., "The Assault on Fort Wagner," Military Order of the Loyal Legion of the United States, 46, 1–54.

Jones, Virgil C., *First Manassas*. Conshohocken, Pa.: Eastern Acorn, n.d.

———, *Gray Ghosts and Rebel Raiders*. New York: n.p. reprint, 1959.

Josephy, Alvin M., Jr., *War on the Frontier*. Alexandria: Time-Life, 1986.

Joslyn, Mauriel P., *Immortal Captives*. Shippensburg, Pa.: White Mane, 1996.

Journal of the Southern Historical Society. 52 vols., 3-vol. index. Wilmington: Broadfoot reprint, 1990–92.

Joynt, Robert H., "Commander Lincoln at Norfolk," *Civil War Times*, 2/83, 26–35.

Korn, Jerry, *The Fight for Chattanoga*. Alexandria: Time-Life, 1985.

———, *Pursuit to Appomattox*. Alexandria: Time-Life, 1987.

Ladd, James R., "From Atlanta to the Sea," *Civil War Chronicles*, Winter 1993, 4–7.

Leckie, Robert, *None Died in Vain*. New York: HarperCollins, 1990.

Lee Takes Command [by the editors]. Alexandria: Time-Life, 1984.

Leech, Margaret, *Reveille in Washington*. New York: Harper, 1941.

"Lieut. Benjamin H. Hutchinson," *The Confederate Veteran*, 24, 80.

"Lieut. E. Lee Bell," *The Confederate Veteran*, 38, 386.

"Lieut. Hopkins Hardin," *The Confederate Veteran*, 34, 149.

"A List of Confederate Officers, Prisoners, Who Were Held by Federal Authorities on Morris Island, S.C., under Confederate Fire from September 7 to October 21, 1864," *Journal of the Southern Historical Society*, 17, 34–46.

Livermore, Thomas L., *Numbers & Losses in the Civil War*. Boston: n.p., 1901.

Longacre, Edward J., "The Most Inept Regiment," *Civil War Times*, 11/69, 4–7.

Longstreet, James, *From Manassas to Appomattox*. New York: Mallard reprint, 1991.

Lossing, Benson J., *Pictorial Field Book of the Civil War*. 3 vols. Baltimore: Johns Hopkins Univ. Press reprint, 1997.

McCabe, W. Gordon, "Defense of Petersburg," *Journal of the Southern Historical Society*, 2, 257–306.

McDonough, James L., *Shiloh*. Knoxville: Univ. of Tennessee Press, 1977.

McMaster, F. W., "The Battle of the Crater," *Journal of the Southern Historical Society* 31, 119–30.

McPherson, James, ed., *Battle Chronicles of the Civil War*. 6 vols. Lakeville, Conn.: Grey Castle, 1989.

McRae, Walter G., "Confederate Prisoners at Morris Island," *The Confederate Veteran*, 29, 178–81.

"Maj. Hugh Dunlap," *The Confederate Veteran*, 27, 106.

Martin, David G., *The Vicksburg Campaign*. New York: Gallery, 1990.

Miers, Earl Schenck, ed., *Lincoln Day by Day*. Vol. 3. Washington, D.C.: Sesquicentennial Commission, 1960.

———, *The Web of Victory*. Baton Rouge: LSU Press, 1955.

Military Order of the Loyal Legion of the United States. 67 vols., 4 vol. index. Wilmington: Broadfoot reprint, 1991–98.

Miller, Francis T., ed., *Photographic History of the Civil War*. 10 vols. New York: Review of Reviews, 1910.

Miller, J. Michael, "Strike Them a Blow," *Blue & Gray*, 4/93, 12–22, 44–55.

Mobile Advertiser, October 1861.

Mokin, Arthur, *Ironclad*. Novato, Calif.: Presidio, 1991.

Morgan, W. H., *Personal Reminiscences of the War of 1861–65*. Lynchburg: J. P. Bell, 1911.

Moore, Frank, ed., *The Rebellion Record* [diary]. New York: Arno reprint, 1977.

———, *The Rebellion Record* [documents]. New York: Arno reprint, 1977.

———, *The Rebellion Record* [poetry and incidents]. New York: Arno reprint, 1977.

Mososcco, Ronald A., *The Chronological Tracking of the American Civil War*. Williamsburg: James River Publications, 1993.

The National Intelligencer, September–October 1861.

Neul, Robert C., "Slugfest in the Ozarks," *America's Civil War*, 5/94, 27–32.

Nevin, David, *The Road to Shiloh*. Alexandria: Time-Life, 1983.

New York Herald, March 1862.

Official Records of the Union and Confederate Navies in the War of the Rebellion. 30 vols; cited by serial numbers. Washington, D.C.: U.S. Govt. Printing Office, 1892–1930.

Olson, Donald W., "A Fatal Full Moon," B/G, 4/96, 24–26.

Parker, J. C., "A Night with Farragut," Military Order of the Loyal Legion of the United States 14, 132–45.

Pfanz, Harry W., *Gettysburg: The Second Day*. Chapel Hill: Univ. of North Carolina Press, 1987.

Piston, William G., *Lee's Tarnished Lieutenant*. Athens: Univ. of Georgia Press, 1987.

Priest, John M., *Antietam*. Shippensburg, Pa.: White Mane, 1989.

———, *Before Antietam: The Battle for South Mountain*. Shippensburg, Pa.: White Mane, 1992.

———, "The Death of Jesse Reno," *Civil War*, May–June 1992.

"Prisoners of War." *Encyclopedia of the Confederacy*, 1256–64.

Quisenberry, Anderson C., "The Eleventh Kentucky Cavalry, C.S.A.," *Journal of the Southern Historical Society*, 35, 259–89.

Raleigh Standard, March 1862.

Rani-Villem, "Okolona Victory," *Civil War Times*, 4/85, 33–39.

"Remnant of Immortal 600 at Richmond," *The Confederate Veteran*, 15, 375.

Ripley, Warren, ed., *Siege Train*. Columbia: Univ. of South Carolina Press, 1983.

Robertson, James I., *Soldiers Blue and Gray*. Columbia: Univ. of South Carolina Press, 1988.

Rollins, Richard, ed., *Pickett's Charge*. n.p.: Rank and File, 1994.

St. Louis Evening News, September 1861.

Sandburg, Carl, *Abraham Lincoln—The War Years*. 4 vols. New York: Harcourt, Brace, 1939.

Sauers, Richard A., "Laurels for Burnside," *Blue & Gray*, 5/88, 8–20, 44–62.

Schell, Frank H., "A Great Raging Battlefield in Hell," *Civil War Times*, 6/69, 14–22.

Seamans, Henry, "Vicksburg Diary," ed. Miriam Poole, *Civil War Times*, 9/83, 18–31.

Sears, Stephen W., "America's Bloodiest Day," *Civil War Times*, 4/87, entire issue.

Shavin, Norman, *The Atlanta Century*. Atlanta: Capricorn, 1965.

Shingleton, Royce, "Confederate Commando," *Civil War*, 26, 12–17, 74–76.

Sifakis, Stewart, *Who Was Who in the Civil War*. New York: Facts on File, 1988.

"The Six Hundred Confederate Officers," *The Confederate Veteran*, 7, 313–23.

"The Six Hundred to Meet in Louisville," *The Confederate Veteran*, 8, 116.

Spies, Scouts and Raiders. Alexandria: Time-Life, 1985.

Stewart, William H., "The Charge of the Crater," *Journal of the Southern Historical Society*, 25, 77–90.

Supplement to the Official Records of the Union and Confederate Armies. 12 vols. Wilmington: Broadfoot, 1995–98.

Sutherland, George E., "The Negro in the Late War," Military Order of the Loyal Legion of the United States, 46, 164–83.

Swinton, William, *Decisive Battles of the Civil War*. New York: Promontory reprint, 1992.

Sword, Wiley, *The Battle of Shiloh*. N.p.: Eastern Acorn, 1982.

Trimble, Tony L., "Rosecrans," *Civil War*, 18, 20–39.

Trudeau, Noah A., *The Last Citadel*. Baton Rouge: LSU Press, 1991.

"True to Their Colors," *The Confederate Veteran*, 5, 119.

"Two of the Six Hundred," *The Confederate Veteran*, 7, 415.

"A View on the Crater Battle," *The Confederate Veteran*, 33, 176–78.

The War of the Rebellion: Official Records of the Union and Confederate Armies. 128 vols.; cited by serial numbers. Harrisburg: National Historical Society reprint, 1971.

Ward, Geoffrey C., *The Civil War*. New York: Knopf, 1990.

Wert, Jeffrey D., *General James Longstreet*. New York: Simon & Schuster, 1993.

INDEX

abolitionist, 10
acoustic shadow, 117, 156
Adelaide, 27
Adkins, James S., 125
Admiral, USS, 196
Albatross, 152
Albuquerque, New Mexico, 168
Alexander, E. Porter, 186
Alexandria line, 5, 9
Alexandria, Virginia, 5, 67
Allegheny Belle, 131
Allen, W. B., 197
Allen's Farm, Virginia, 76
Amelia Station, Virginia, 144
Anaconda Plan, 27
Anderson, Robert, 3, 44
Anderson, Richard H., 42, 168
Andersonville Prison, Georgia, 183, 193, 199
Andrew, John, 130
Antietam Creek, Maryland, 94, **95**
Antietam, Maryland, 10, 90, 93–98, 168
Archer, James J., 181
Aristook, USS, 80
Arkansas, 83, 87
Arlington, Virginia, 36
Armistead, Lewis, 77, 78
Army of Northern Virginia, 88, 97, 126, 166, 174, 181
Army of the Potomac, C.S., 37
Army of the Potomac, U.S., 38, 76, 79, 80, 102, 104, 112, 166, 186
Army of Tennessee, 59
Arnold, Lewis G., 42
Arrow Rock, Missouri, 33
Atlanta, Georgia, 138
Atlanta Intelligencer, 43
Averill, W. W., 121

Back River, Virginia, 11
Bailey, William, 122
Bailey, Major, 104
Baker, Edward D., **39**

Ballentine, W. D., **199**
Balls Bluff, Virginia, 110
Baltimore, Maryland, 179, 181
Baltimore & Ohio Railroad, 140
Banks, Nathaniel P., 37, 122, 135, 150, 181
Barbour, George W., 127
Barksdale, Randolph, 170
Barlow, Francis C., 144
Barnes, James, 116
Barry, John D., 157, 160
Bartlett, William F., 189
Baton Rouge, Louisiana, 83–87, **84, 86**
Battery Wagner, South Carolina, 130
Baylor, George W., 135
bayonet, 11, 154, 155, 164, 188, 191
Bean's Station, Tennessee, 133
Beaufort, South Carolina, 130
Beaufort, 48
Beauregard, P. G. T., 3, **6**, 8, 17, 21–25, 62, 63, 132, 174
Belmont, Missouri, 103, 104
Bendix, John E., 13–14
Benham, Henry W., 72, 74
Benjamin, Judah P., 74
Berdan, Hiram, 144
Bernard, George S., 175
Bethel, Big, 9–16, **10, 12**, 24, 45
Bethel, Little, **10**, 13–15, 45
Big Black River Bridge, Mississippi, 125, 161
Black Kettle, 141
Blackburn's Ford, Virginia, 17–20, 24
Blair, Frank, 138
Blakeman, Noel, 122
Blocher, William D., 114
Blodgett, Wells H., 55
Blue Mills Landing, Missouri, 32
Blunt, James, 114
Blunt, USS, 114
Bobyshell, Oliver, 186
Boteler's Ford, Virginia, 115
bounty, 22
Boyd, Belle, 197

Boldface page numbers indicate photographs and illustrations.

Bradford, Richard, 44
Bragg, Braxton, 41, 44, 116, 130
Bragg, Edward S., 94
Branch, Lawrence O., 106
Brandywine, 48
Brazilia, 48
Breckinridge, John C., 83, **84**
Brooklyn, New York, 47
Brown, Dee, 57
Brown, Harvey, 42, 44–45
Brown County, Indiana, 35
Brown County Union, 33
Buchanan, Franklin, 47–48, 51
Buchanan, James, 75
Buchanan, McKean, 49
Buckley, John, 127
Buell, Augustus, 142
Buell, Don Carlos, 111, 116
Buffington Island, Ohio River, 130–31
Buford, Napoleon, 103
Bull Run, First battle of, 21–26, **24**, 168
Bull Run, Second, 174
Bull Run, Virginia, 17–18, 20, 22, 36
Bull's Bay, South Carolina, 113
Burnside, Ambrose, 88, 106, 107, 131,
    185–87, 190, **190**
Butler, Benjamin F., 9, 10, 12–15, 27–28,
    30, 126, 188, 202
Butterfield, Daniel, 136

Cadwallader, Sylvanus, 162, 164, 165
Cairo, Ilinois, 102
Calahan, W. P., 200
Cambridge, 48
Cameron, Simon, **36**, 37
Camp Chase, Ohio, 196
Camp Cowskin, Missouri, 32
Camp DuPont, Missouri, 36
Camp Hamilton, Virginia, 12
Camp Lawton, Georgia, 193
Canby, E. R. S., 110
Capitol, U.S., 36, **37**
Carondelet, USS, **108**, 109
Carr, Eugene A., 162
Carrington, E. C., 112
Carrion Crow Bayou, Louisiana, 122
Carson, J. Charles, 196

Carter, Edward, 196
Catherine Furnace, Virginia, 124
Catskill, USS, 129
Cayuga, USS, 83, 87
Centreville, Virginia, 17–18, 23, 104
Century magazine, 81
Cerro Gordo, Mexico, battle of, 91, 168
Chain Bridge, District of Columbia, 126
Chamberlain, A. P., 14
Chambers, H. A., 188, 192
Champion's Hill, Mississippi, 125
Chancellorsville, Virginia, 124, 154–60, 181
Chapultepec, Mexico, battle of, 17, 91
Charleston, South Carolina, 3, 41, 75,
    129, 131, 177–84, 193–200
Charleston Daily Courier, 177
Charleston Mercury, 177, 180
Chase, Salmon P., 67
Chattanooga, Georgia, 138
Cherokees, Confederate, 53, 55
Chester, Virginia, 144
Chicago Board of Trade, 119
Chicago Times, 164
Chickahominy River, Virginia, 139
Chickamauga, Tennessee, **129**, 133, 174
Chippewa, USS, 129
Chivington, John M., 141
Churchill, C. C., 27
Churubusco, Mexico, battle of, 168
Cincinnati, Ohio, 130
Cincinnati Commercial, 117
Citadel, The, 71, 172, 173
City Point, Virginia, 79
Clark, George, 192
Cleburne, Patrick R., 63
Clem, Johnny, 61, **132**, 133
Clinton, Louisiana, 84
Cobb, Howell, 30
Coburn, John, 136
Coco, Gregory A., 127
Coffin, W. A., 33
Cold Harbor, Virginia, 165
colors, 30
Colquitt, Alfred H., 94, 96
Columbus, Kentucky, 103
Comstock, Cyrus B., 162
Congress, C.S., 30, 46

Congress, U.S., 61
Congress, USS, 49–50, **50,** 51–52, 53
conscription, 22, 61, 98
Cook, Asa M., 97
Cook, Henry Howe, 193
Cook, John S., 127
Cooper, J. C. C., 200
Cooper, Samuel, 44
Copeland, R. Morris, 37
Corcoran, Michael, 120–21, **121**
Corinth, Mississippi, 59, 111
Cornfield, The, 94, 96, 97
Cosmopolitan, USS, 184
Covington, C. D., 196
Covington, Georgia, 141
Cox, Jacob D., 89, **131**
Crater, The, 165, 185–192, **187**
Crawford, Samuel, 138, 139
Crescent, 196, 197, 200
Crew's Farm, Virginia, 9
Crittenden, Thomas L., 117
Cross Keys, Virginia, 182
Cullen, Dorsey, 170
Culpeper, Virginia, 121
Culp's Hill, Viginia, 127
Cumberland River, Tennessee, 109
Cumberland, USS, 27, 48–49
Curtis, Samuel R., 53–58, **55**

Dacotah, 48, 68
Dahlgren, John A., 180, 183, 197
Dana, Napoleon, 95
Davis, Jefferson C., 32, **34,** 35, 55
Davis, Jefferson Finis, 17, 30, 46, 65, 98,
    134, **145,** 174
Davis, William C., 64
Delaware, 106
Delaware River, 196
Deming, Henry C., 87
Dent, Julia, 168
Department #1, Confederate, 32
Deserted House, Virginia, 121
Desmoines, 33, 35
Dewey, George, 152
Doby, Alfred E., 176
Doles, George P., 127
Donaldsville, Louisiana, 126

Douty, Jacob, 187
Dragoon, 182
Dranesville, Virginia, 104
Drayton, Percival, 73, **74**
Drayton, Thomas, 73, 90
Drewry's Bluff, Virginia, 178
Duffie, Alfred Napoleon Alexander, 121, **124**
Dunn, Andrew, 170
DuPont, Samuel F., 72, 74, 122, **123,** 127
Duryée, Abram, 11, 14
Dutch, J. C., 122
Dwight, William, 123, 125

E. A. Stevens, 68–70
E. B. Hale, USS, 73, 74
Eads, James D., 32
Early, Jubal, 19–20, 69, 141
East Woods, The, 94
Edisto Island, South Crolina, 122
Elk Horn Tavern, Arkansas, 53
Ellen, USS, 73–75
Emancipation Proclamation, **98**
Ericsson, John, 47, **51**
Essex, USS, 83, 85, 87
Etheridge, William H., 192
Ewell, Benjamin S., 5
Ewell, Richard S., 111, 167
Ewing, Hugh, 97
Ewing, 450
Executive Mansion, 66

Fairfax County, Virginia, 104
Fairfax Court House, Viginia, 3–8, **7, 8,** 9,
    12, 16, 23, 36
Falls Church Road, 6
Fanny, 27
Farmville, Virginia, 144
Farnham, N. L., 22, **23**
Farragut, David G., 87, 126, 149–53
Featherston, John C., 189, 191
Feild, Everard M., 175
Ferrero, Edward, 91, 109, 186, **189,** 190, 191
Ficken, Martin, 91
Field, Charles W., 171, 175
Fire Eater (horse), 63, 64
First Manassas, 21–26
Fitch, LeRoy, 1–31

Fitz-Simons, Charles, 136
Flag, USS, 113
Florence, South Carolina, 193
Foote, Andrew H., 109
Foote, Shelby, 116
Forrest, Nathan B., 135, 138
Fort Baker, District of Columbia, 38
Fort Bartow, North Carolina, 108
Fort Beauregard, South Carolina, 198
Fort Clark, North Carolina, 27–31
Fort Delaware, Delaware, 180, 196, 200
Fort Donelson, Tennessee, **108**
Fort Fisher, North Carolina, 142
Fort Haskell, Virginia, 143
Fort Hatteras, North Carolina, 28
Fort Johnson, South Carolina, 198
Fort McHenry, Maryland, 196
Fort Monroe, Viginia, 9, 10, 27, 50, 67, 190
Fort Moultrie, South Carolina, 198
Fort Pickens, Florida, 41–45, **43**
Fort Pulaski, Georgia, 193, 200
Fort Stedman, Virginia, 143
Fort Stevens, District of Columbia, 6, 70, 75
Fort Sumter, South Carolina, 3, 41, 46,
    101, 131, 168, 172, 184, 194, 198
Fort Wagner, South Carolina, 127–30,
    132, 182, 197–98
Fort Thompson, North Carolina, 106
Foster, John G., 106, 108, **109**, 118, 180,
    182, **183**, 184, 193–95, 199
Fox, Gustavus V., 47, **49**
Fox's Gap, Maryland, 88, **89**, 90, 92
Franklin, James, Jr., 20
Franklin, William B., 23
Franklin, Tennessee, 141, 202
Frayser's Farm, Virginia, 174
Frederick, Maryland, 37, 88, 115
Fredericksburg, Virginia, 117, 154, 165,
    168, 174, 181
Freeman, Douglas Southall, 154
Freeman, Henry R., 119
Fremont, John Charles, 35, 102, 179
French, William H., 97
Fry, Speed S., 105
Fuilam, Lt. Col., 87
Fuller, Charles, 168
Fulton, 184

Gaines' Farm, Virginia, 179
Gaines's Mill, Virginia, 76, 174
Galena, USS, 79, 80
Gardner, Franklin, 181
Gardner, W. W., 164
Garland, Samuel, 89, 96
Garnett's and Golding's Farms, Virginia, 76
Gates, Theodore B., 94
general, political, 10, 28
general, Democratic, 10, 28
George Peabody, 27
Georgetown, South Carolina, 197
Gerhardt, Joseph, 91
Gettysburg, Pennsylvania, 10, 59, 127–28,
    181, 196
Gibbon, John, 94, 117
Gillan, Sgt., 38
Gillis, James H., 74
Gillis, John P., 30
Gillmore, Quincy, 132
Glasgow, Missouri, 32–35
Goldsborough, Louis M., 52, 67, 68, **69**, 106
Gooding, Michael, 116
Gordon, George B., 142
Gordon, John B., 79, 143
Gosport Navy Yard, 46
Grace, C. C., 196
Grant, U. S., 101–02, 103, 109, 125, 142,
    149–50, 161, **162**, 165–67, **168**, 168,
    171, 179, 183, 185, 186, 190, 194, 201
Greble, John T., 11, **14**, **15**
Greek Fire, 198
Greeley, Horace, 16
green troops, 12, 19, 24, 84, 91, 95, 115,
    131, 191
Greeno, Charles L., 146
Gregg, David M., 169
Gregg, Maxcy, 118
Gresham, Walter Q., 138
Grimsley, James, 85
Grover, Cuvier, 122
Grubb's Crossroads, Kentucky, 139, 140
Gurley, Phineas T., 67
Gwyn, James, 115

habeas corpus, 98
Hall, Edward D., 117

Halleck, Henry W., 109, 111, 180, 182, 193, **194**, 195, 199
Hampton, Virginia, 10, 68
Hampton Roads, Virginia, **10**, 46–52, 53
Hancock, Winfield Scott, 167, 174
Hannibal & St. Joseph Railroad, 32
Harpers Ferry, Virginia (now West Virginia), 5, 111
Harriet Lane, USS, 27–28, **30**
Harris, Isham G., 61, 63
Harrison, Benjamin, 136
Hartford, USS, 151–52
Hatteras Inlet, North Carolina, 27
Hatteras Island, North Carolina, 30
Hayes, Rutherford B., 89
Haynesworth, George E., 172
Hazel Grove, Virginia, 23
Heckman, Charles A., 118, 178
Heintzelman, Samuel P., 22, 126
Helm, Ben Hardin, 83
Hempstead, Junius L., 199
Henderson County, Kentucky, 140
Hendricks, Lt. Col., 33
Henry Brinker, 106
Herron, Francis J., 114
Hetzel, 106
Higginson, Thomas W., 10
Hill, Ambrose P., 77, 79, 115, 157, 169
Hill, Daniel H., 11, 16, 88
Hilton Head, South Carolina, 71, 113, 130, 179, 182–84, 193, 197, 200
Hindman, Thomas C., 114
Hines, John, 146
Hobson, Edward H., 131
Holcomb, Richard E., 123
Holmes, Oliver Wendell, Jr., 70
Holt, Joseph, 74
Hood, John B., 89
Hooker, Joseph, 89, 93, 154, 156, **157**, 159
Hornet's Nest, The, 59
Howard, Oliver O., 23, 101, 138, 156
Howe, Orion H., 164
Huger, Benjamin, 81
Hunt, Henry J., 77
Hunter, David, 72, 132
Hutchinson, Benjamin H., 196
Hutchinson, James, 122

Iberville, Louisiana, **86**
Immortal 600, The, 193–200
Indian Village, Louisiana, 123
Intan, 33
Ironsides, USS, 129
Irwinville, Georgia, 145
Island No. 10, Mississippi River, 104

Jackson, Clairborne F., 33, 182
Jackson, Thomas J. ("Stonewall"), 77, 78, 93, 111, 112, 118, 124, 154–60, **155**, **159**, 170–71, 173, 181, 182
Jacobs, George, 168
James River, Virginia, 76, 79, 81
James River Squadron, 47
James, Garth W., 130
Jamestown, 48
Jefferson City, Missouri, 35
Jenkins, Micah, **173**, 173, 176
Jennifer, W. H., 110
Jestremeska, Leon, **200**
Johnson, Adam R., 139
Johnson, Charles F., 109
Johnson, Edward ("Allegheny Ed"), 127, 181
Johnson, John H., 158
Johnson's Island, Ohio, 180, 181
Johnston, Albert S., 32, 59–65, **64**, 92
Johnston, Joseph E., 104, 138
Jones, Catesby, 51
Jones, David R., 89, 173
Jones, Frank J., 112
Jones, Samuel, 182, 183, 190, 193–95
Jones, William E. ("Grumble"), 133

Katahdin, USS, 83, 87
Kautz, August V., 139
Keane, John R., 196
Kellogg, J. J., 164
Kelly's Ford, Virginia, **120**, 121
Kelly's Store, Virginia, 120–21
Kennesaw Mountain, Georgia, 138
Kershaw, Joseph B., 95, 112, 174, **175**
Kiawah Island, South Carolina, 71, 82
Kilpatrick, Hugh J., 11
Kineo, USS, 83, 87
King, Charles, 25
King's Mountain military school, 173

King's School House, Virginia, 76
Kirk, Jonathan C., 137
Knock Knee, 141
Knoxville, Tennessee, 133, 174

Ladd, James R.,141
Lake, George B.,191
Lamar, T. G., 73, 75
Lane, James H.,159, 160
Laughton, John E., 44
Lawler, Michael, 162
Lay, J. F., 183
Leavenworth, Kansas, 91
Lebanon, Tennessee, 196
Ledlie, James H., 118, 186, 188, 190
Lee, C. N., 162
Lee, Fitzhugh, 121, 144, 155
Lee, H. C., 109
Lee, Robert E., 5, 76, 88, 93, 112, 118, 134,
    144, 154, **155, 156**, 166, 168, 170, **171**
Lexington, Missouri, 32
Lexington, USS, 63, 104
Lincoln, Abraham, 3, 15, 27, 67, **68**, 71,
    74, 97, 98, 101, 171, 179, 183, 195, 201
Lincoln, Mary Todd, 66, **86**
Lincoln, Thomas ("Tad"), 66
Lincoln, William Wallace ("Willie"), 66, **67**
Little Raven, 141
Little Sorrel (horse), 157
Livingstone, David, 61
Lockwood, 106
Logan, John A., 103
London Times, 9
Long Bridge, District of Columbia, 36, **37**
Longstreet, James, 17–20, 77, 133, 144,
    154, 167–171, **171**, 173–76
Lord, S. C., 110
Lossing, Benson, 9
Loudon County, Virginia, 110
Louisiana, 106
Louisville, Kentucky, 116, 130, 196
Ludlow, Benjamin C., 188
Lynchburg, Virginia, 144

Maccoun, Robert T., 153
Magruder, John B., 10–11, 14, 16, 77–79, 112
Mahaska, USS, 80

Mahone, William, 77, 139, 144, 169, 189,
    190, **192**
Mallory, Stephen R., 46, 48
Malvern Hill, Virginia, 76–82, **77, 78, 82**
Manassas Junction, Virginia, 5, 17, 27
Mansfield, Joseph K. F., 51, 97
Marr, John Quincy, 5
Martin, W. T., 133
Martinsburg, Virginia (now West Virginia),
    115
Marye's Heights, Virginia, 168
Massanutten Ridge, Virginia, 110
McCall, George A., 105
McClellan, George B., 37, **38**, 66–67, 76,
    79, 88, 93
McClernand, John A., 102, 125, 162
McCulloch, Ben., 55
McDowell, Irvin, 17–18, 20–23, 101, 111
McGuire, Hunter, 158
McKinley, William, 89
McMillan, James, 136
McNeill, John H., 140
McRae, Alexander, 110
McRae, Walter G., 196
Meade, George G., 144, 167, 185, 190
Meagher, Thomas F., 97
Mechanicsville, Virginia, 76
Medal of Honor, 37, 94, 144, 164
Memphis Appeal, 104
Merrimack (or *Merrimac*), USS, **47, 48**
Mexican War, 17, 21, 67, 91, 93, 168,
    173, 181
Miami, 67–68
Military Division of the Mississppi, 162
militia, 90-day, 12
Mill Springs, Kentucky, **100**, 105
Milner, W. J, 45
Milton, John, 44
Minnesota, USS, 27, 48, 50
Mississippi River, 103–04, 125, 149–50
Mississippi Squadron, 161
Mississippi, USS, 151–53, 154
Missouri River, 33
Mobile, Alabama, 104
Molino del Rey, Mexico, 168
Monitor, USS, 47–48, 52, 68, 69
Monongahela, 126, 151

Montauk, USS, 129
Monterrey, Mexico, 168
Monticello, USS, 27–28, 30
Moose, USS, 131
Morgan, John H., 130, 131, 139, 180
Morris Island, South Carolina, 128,
   131–33, 172, 177, 182, 193–200, **195**
Morrison, Joseph G., 157
Morristown, Missouri, 32
Mosman, D. F., 113
Mount Carmel, Virginia, 111, 112
Mount Jackson, Virginia, 140
Mount Vernon, Virginia, 67
Mount Vernon, 48
Munson's Hill, Virginia, 36–40
Myer, Albert J., 80

Nantucket, USS, 129
National Road, 88
Naugatuck, USS, 68
Neafie, 42
Nelson, William ("Bull"), 32, **33**, **34**, 61
Neuse River, North Carolina, 134, 137
New Berne, North Carolina, 106, 109, 134
Newburg, Indiana, 139
New Iberia, Louisiana, 122
New Market, Virginia, 173
New Orleans, Louisiana, 71, 126, 149
Newport News, Virginia, 10, 13, 79, 104
New York, New York, 3
New York Evening Post, 7
New York Herald, 29, 51, 55, 164
New York Tribune, 16, 130
New York World, 151
Nodine, Frederic, 57
Norfolk, Virginia, 5, 68, 70
North Anna River, Virginia, 137
North Atlantic Blockading Squadron, 48,
   52, 67, 79
North Carolina Military Institute, 12, 173
North Star, 86
North Woods, The, 96

Oak Grove, Virginia, 76
Occaquan River, Virginia, 6
officer, general, 14, 19
Ohio State Penitentiary, 180

Ohio River, 131
Okalona, Mississippi, 135
Old Capitol Prison, District of Columbia, 197
Olustee, Florida, 134
Oneida, 68
Opelousas, Louisiana, 123
Orange & Alexandria Railroad, 17, **18**
Orange Plank Road, 167, 169, 171, 175
Orchard, The, 76
Ord, Edward O., 104, 188
Osterhaus, Peter J., 125, 162
Ottawa, USS, 129, 197
overcoats, 108
O'Doud, Michael, 44
O'Kane, Dennis, 37–38

Paducah, Kentucky, 102
Paine, E. A., 102
Paineville, Virginia, 144
Palmito Ranch, Texas, 146
Palo Alto, California, 168
Parke, John G., 106
Parsonage, William, 44
Patapsco, USS, 129
Patrick Henry, 48
Patterson, John R., 175
Pattison, Thomas, 56
Paul Jones, USS, 129
Pawnee, USS, **29**, 73
Pea Ridge, Arkansas, 53–58, **54, 55**
Peach Orchard, The, 63, 64
Peachtree Creek, Georgia, 138
Peck, John J., 120
Pemberton, John C., 125, 161, **164**
Pender W. Dorsey, 158
Pendergrast, Austin, 50–51
Pendleton, A. S., 159
Peninsula Campaign, 76
Pennypacker, Galusha, 142
Pensacola, Florida, 41
Pensacola, USS, 153
Perry, Matthew, 151
Perryville, Kentucky, 116, 117
Petersburg, Virginia, 139, 143, 185–192
Pettigrew, J. J., 134
Philadelphia, Pennsylvania, 102, 180, 196
Philadelphia, USS, 106

Pickett, George E., 134, 170
Pickett's Charge, 196
Pierce, Ebenezer, 11–12, 15–16, **16**
Pierce, Edward L., 130
Pike, Albert, 53
Pine Mountain, Georgia, 138
Pittsburg Landing, Tennessee, **60**, 61, **62**
Pleasant Hill, Louisiana, 135
Pleasants, Henry, 185, 187
Pleasaton, Alfred, 88
Plymouth, North Carolina, 178
Pocahontas, USS, 73
Pogue, W. T., 112
Point Lookout, Maryland, 196
Polk, Leonidas, 32, 103, 116
Poolesville, Virginia, 37
Pope, John, 111
Port Gibson, Mississippi, 161
Port Hudson, Louisiana, 149–53, **150,**
   152, 154, 181, 196
Port Republic, Virginia, 112
Port Royal, South Carolina, 71, 73
Port Royal, USS, 80
Porter, David D., 142, 161
Porter, Fitz-John, 77, 85
Porter, G. W., 85
Porter, Horace, 167
Porter, William D., 87
Potomac River, 66, 115
Potter, Robert, 186
Powhatan, USS, 3, 27
Prairie Grove, Arkansas, **113,** 114
Preliminary Emancipation Proclamation, 98
Prentiss, Benjamin M., 32, **35**
Preston, William, 133
Prevost, Charles E., 115
Price, Sterling, 32, 53–55, **57**
Priest, John M., 90
Prime, Frederick E., 162
Princess Royal, 126
Pryor, Roger A., 120

Quaker Guns, **140**
Queen of the West, 150

Raleigh, North Carolina, 51
Raleigh, 48

Raleigh Standard, 9
Rapidan River, 166
Rappahannock River, Virginia, **120,** 121, 155
Raymond, Mississippi, 161
Redwood, Allan C., 25
Rees, Henry, 187
Reno, Jesse L., 88, **91,** 106
Resaca de la Palma, Mexico, 168
Resaca, Georgia, 136
Restless, 113
Richardson, Israel, 18
Richmond Examiner, 194
Richmond Times-Dispatch, 9, 191
Richmond, 151–53
Richmond & York River Railroad, 112
Rio Grande, 10
Rion, James H., 132
Ripley, Roswell S., 89
Roanoke, 48
Roanoke Island, North Carolina, **107,** 108
Roberts, Willis S., 83
Robertson, James M., **44**
Robertson, J. W., 84
Rodes, Robert E., 89
Rodgers, John, 79
Roe, F. A., 153
Rowan, Stephen C., 106–7
Rumph, Major, 179
Rupert, John, 146

St. Helena Sound, South Carolina, 122
St. James Island, South Carolina, 72
St. John, Lidell, 116
St. Lawrence, USS, 48
St. Louis, Missouri, 35
Saline, Missouri, 33
Salisbury, North Carolina, 183
San Antonio, Texas, 168
San Jacinto, 68
Sand Creek, Colorado, 141
Santa Rosa Island, Florida, 41–45, **43**
Santa Maria Clara, Sister, 126
Savage's Station, Virginia, 76, 112
Savannah, Tennessee, 61
Sayler's Creek, Virginia, 144
Scammon, Eliakim P., 178
Schimmelfennig, Alexander, 180

Schofield, John M., 138
Schurz, Carl, 156
Scott, George, 10
Scott, William, 44
Scott, Winfield, 15, 23, 27
Secessionville, South Carolina, 71–75, **72**
Selma, Alabama, 143
Seminole, 68, 69
Semmes, Paul J., 82, 112
Senate, U.S., 15
Seven Days, The, 79
Seven Pines, 174
Seward, William H., 3
Sewell's Point, Virginia, 66–70
Sexton, James A., 141
Seymour, Truman, 178
Shackleford, James, 133
Shaler, Alexander, 178
Sharpsburg, Maryland, 93–98
Shaw, Robert Gould, 126, 127
Shelton, W. H., 167
Shenandoah Valley, The, 136, 181, 182
Sheperdstown, Virginia (now West Virginia), 115, 116
Sheridan, Philip H., 144
Sherman, William T., 111, 136, 138, 164
Shields, Thomas, 83, 84
Shiloh Methodist Church, 59, 61
Shiloh, Tennessee, 59–65, **60**
Ship Island, Mississippi, 130
Shipley, Alexander N., 44
Shipman, Seymour, 127
Sibley, Henry H., 110
Sickles, Daniel E., 124
Sigel, Franz, 55, 136
signal systems, 29
Signal Service, U.S., 80
Slocomb's Creek, 106
Slocum, Henry W., 124
Smith, Melancton, 151
Smith, A. B., 48
Smith, Andrew J., 125, 136, 162
Smith, E. Kirby, 117, 135
Smith, Thomas K., 163, 164
Smith, William ("Extra Billy"), 5–8, 38
Smith, William Sooy, 135, **139**
Sorrel, G. Moxley, 175

South Atlantic Blockading Squadron, 122, 184, 197
South Mountain, Maryland, 88–92, **89**, **90**
South River, Virginia, 112
Southfield, 106
Spaulding, 79
Special Orders #13, 27
Spotsylvania, Virginia, 181, 182, 196
Stanley, Henry M., 59
Stanton, Edwin M., 67
Star of the West, 172, 173
Stars and Stripes, 106
Stepping Stones, 79
Steuart, George H., 181
Stevens, Isaac I., 72
Stewart, Alexander P., 142
Stokes, James H., 119
Stone Bridge, 24
Stones River, Tennessee, 119–20
Stono River, South Carolina, 72, 73
Strasburg, Virginia, 111
Stringham, Silas H., 27
Strong, James H., 114
Strong, George C., 130
Stuart, J. E. B., 36, 104, 121, 154, 155
Suffolk, Virginia, 120
Sullivan's Island, South Carolina, 198
Sumner, Edwin V. ("Bull"), 95, **96**, 112
Sumter, USS, 83, 87
Sumter County, South Carolina, 172
Susquehanna, USS, 27, 68, 69
Swamp Angel, 198
Sword, Wiley, 64
Sykes, E. T., 117
Sykes, George, 115

Taggert, Charles A., 144
Taggert, William H., 34
Taliaferro, William B., 132
Tanner, George, 33–35
Tate, Thomas S., 138
Tattnall, Josiah, 69
Taylor, James E., 101
Taylor, Richard, 111, 135
Taylor, Zachary, 134
Teaser, 48
Tennessee, 126

Tennessee River, 59, 60
Terry, Alfred H., **142**
Thomas, George H., 143
Thomas, Lorenzo, 182
Thompson, Meriwether J., 182
Thornton, William W., 5
Tigress, 69
Tinkham, James, 23
Tompkins, Charles H., 6, 9
Totten, Joseph G., 44
Tower, Z. B., 44–45
Townsend, Frederick, 13–15
Treinner, W. H., 41
Tremain, Henry E., 137
troops, green; *see* green troops
Tucker, Joseph T., 180
Tuerk, Julius G., 143
Tupelo, Mississippi, **137**, 138
Turner's Gap, Maryland, 88, **89**, 90
Turpin, James A., 143
Tyler, Daniel, 17–19, **20**
Tyler, Robert O., 63, 81
Tyler, USS, 104, 110

Underwriter, USS, 106, 134
uniforms—color and style, 12, 13, 24–25,
    26, 96, 97, 112, 117, 185, 189, 202; *see
    also* Zouaves
Upton, Emory, 143

Valley City, 106
Valverde, New Mexico, 110
Van Dorn, Earl, 53–57, 83
Vanderbilt, 68
Venable, Charles S., 169
Veracruz, Mexico, 168
Vermillion Bayou, Louisiana, 123
Vermilion Bridge, Louisiana, 122
Vicksburg, Mississippi, 9, 125, 161–65,
    149–50, 152, 185, **163**
Vicksburg & Jackson Railroad, 125
Viele, Egbert, 70
Virginia Military Institute, 77, 173
Virginia, CSS, 47–52, **48**, **50**, 51, 68, 69, 70
Vodges, Israel, 42, 44
volunteers, 90-day, 21
Von Gilsa, Leopold, 156

Wadsworth, James, 167, 169
Wainwright, Charles S., 127
Walke, Henry, 104, 110
Walker, Leroy P., 32, **33**
Wallace, W. H. L., 65
Wangelin, Hugh, 55
War Eagle, 33
Ward, William T., 32
Warner, George W., 127
Warren, Gouverneur K., 139, 167, 169
Warrenton Turnpike, 17
Washington, Edward C., 164
watchword, 12, 13
Watie, Stand, 55
Weaver, H. C., 131
Weber, Max, 28, 96
Webster, Daniel, 167
Weehawken, USS, 129
Weldon Railroad, 139
Welles, Gideon, 30, 47, 109, 126, 131
Wells, George D., 19
Wessell, Henry W., 178
Western & Atlantic Railroad, 136
West Gulf Blockading Squadron, 126
West Point (U.S. Military Academy), 11,
    17, 19, 21, 91, 123, 168, 178, 181, 173,
    182
West Woods, The, 96
Wheat, C. R., 24
Wheatley, Col., 35
White, Benjamin B., 176
White, Elijah V. ("Lige"), 110, **111**
White Antelope, 141
White Cloud, 33, 35
Whitehall, North Carolina, 118
Whitney, Porter A., 168
Wiegel, William H., 28
Wilbourne, R. E., 157
Wilcox, Cadmus M., 138
Wilderness, The, 20, 154, **166**, 166–76, 189
Wilderness Tavern, 167, **174**
Wildy, M. W., 119
Willcox, Orlando, 186, 92
Williams, Alpheus S., 124
Williams, Seth, 105
Williams, Thomas, **85**, 86
Williamsburg, Virginia, 174

Willis, Edward, 127
Wills, Willam J., 101, **105**
Wilson, James H., 143, 145
Willson, T. Friend, 150
Wilson, William, 42, 44–45
Wilson's Creek, Missouri, 114
Winchester, Kentucky, 180
Winchester, Virginia, 136
Winder, John H., 111
Winona, 126
Winthrop, Theodore, 12
Wise, Henry A., 5
Wistar, Isaac J., 39
Withers, Jones M., 117
Woerner, Christian, 143
Wofford, William T., 169
Wood, Alexander, 92

Wood Charles R., 173
Wood, John Taylor, 51, 134, **135**
Wool, John E., 30, 51, 67
Woolsey, Melancthon B., 74
Worden, John L., 47
Wright, Ambrose R., 81, 82
Wright, Horatio G., 32
Wyatt, Henry L., 14
Wynne, Lt., 157

Yazoo Pass, 149
York County, South Carolina, 173

Zollicoffer, Felix, **100**, 106
Zouaves, 11–12, 45, 108, 109, 167
Zouave, 49